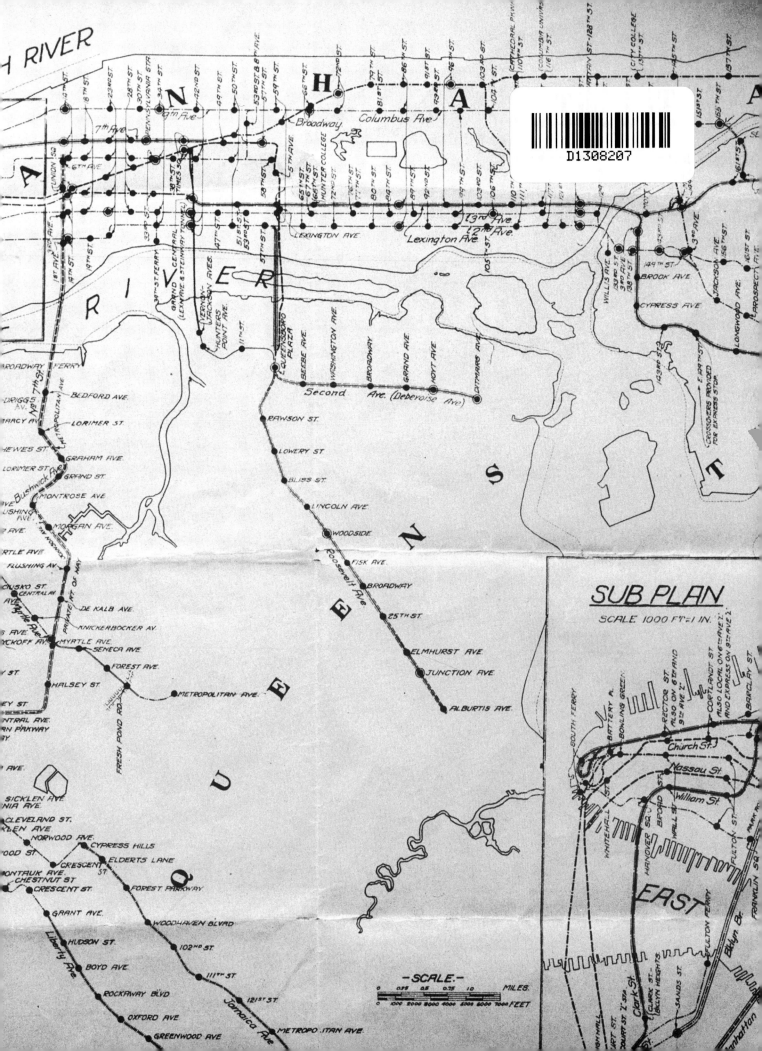

NOVEMBER 2004

THE SUBWAY

To John

Stay On The
Right Track.

Sincerely

THE
SUBWAY

A TRIP THROUGH TIME ON NEW YORK'S RAPID TRANSIT

STAN FISCHLER

RESEARCH EDITORS: Sean M. Spiller
Dan Saraceni

DRAWINGS: Ray Judd

H&M PRODUCTIONS II INC.
PUBLISHER/ NEW YORK

(rear end leaf)

WHAT MIGHT HAVE BEEN

This map depicts what the New York City subway system would have looked like as it approaches the 21st century. That is, if this were an ideal world, transit-wise.

Two months prior to the outbreak of World War II the Board of Transportation proposed an elaborate program for expanding the underground lines.

The result would have been Brooklyn extensions of the IRT to Sheepshead Bay and Floyd Bennett Field as well as Queens additions of the BMT Astoria Line along what is now the Long Island Expressway, as well as ambitious IND tracks all the way to the Nassau County line.

A tunnel connecting Brooklyn and Staten Island—proposed as far back as the early 1920s—also was blueprinted. This and still other links would have provided the Big Apple with enough rapid transit coverage to last for another hundred years.

By the time Uncle Sam entered the conflict in 1941 all plans were put on hold. Tiny bits and pieces are added in the post-war years but the basic dream of the perfect subway system remained unfulfilled.

If ever the lines of a poem befit this map they belong to John Greenleaf Whittier, author of Maud Miller:

For all sad words of tongue
or pen
The saddest are these: "It might
have been!"

H & M PRODUCTIONS II INC.
193-07 45 AVE.
FLUSHING, NY 11358

ISBN 1-882608-19-4

TABLE OF CONTENTS

DEDICATION

A man's passion for elevated and subway trains could get him in trouble.

Carried to an extreme it could lead to ostracism by one's wife and two sons.

A subway buff's constant yearning to stand at the front window of the first car of virtually every train he rides has been known to try the patience of family members beyond endurance.

The sometimes obtuse insistence on taking the subway even when a taxi ride would be more practical is the stuff that drives some folks to want to introduce the buff to a third rail.

Me. I've been lucky.

I am married to a woman, Shirley, who not only has tolerated and understood my passion but actually has shared much of it with me.

She has occasionally encouraged the obsession and—at times when it has reached dangerous extremes—managed to stifle her frustration well enough for me to hardly notice.

My sons, Ben and Simon, have been no less tolerant of this transit aberration in their father's make-up.

The two lads were broken in early in their lives—usually by sitting atop my shoulders—to enjoy the ride by peering through the front window with dad.

And we did this not only on virtually every subway-el line in the city but the PATH underground as well.

All of which is a roundabout way of saying that my family has always encouraged my love of subways and, as such, helped immeasurably in the creation of *Uptown, Downtown* and this, my newest tribute to the tubes.

This book, therefore, is dedicated to my three favorite people, Shirley, Ben and Simon as well as the memory of my parents, Molly and Ben, who never owned an auto and always rode the subways.

In addition I must credit my elementary school teacher, Mrs. Anne Yearwood, for the inspiration she provided at P.S. 54 in Brooklyn and has continued to offer to this day. Without her encouragement I would not have learned to write.

ACKNOWLEDGMENTS

Ever since I worked as a reporter covering transit for the *New York Journal-American* newspaper, I had an urge to write a book about the city's subway system.

I was fortunate.

In the early 1970s a literary agent named Chuck Neighbors hooked me up with Hawthorn Books which commissioned me to write a subway history.

The result was "Uptown, Downtown," which was published in 1976 and reprinted many times thereafter.

After the sixth printing Hawthorn disappeared in yet another publishing amalgamation. At the time interest in reprinting "Uptown, Downtown" waned.

In time the book became a collector's item and invariably I would receive calls and letters from folks interested in obtaining a copy. I would refer them to my friends Judith Stonehill and Barbara Cohen at, alas, now defunct, New York Bound book store in Rockefeller Center.

Eventually, New York Bound sold its last copy and signalled that it was time for a new edition.

It was my good fortune to have encountered train buff-hockey fan-publisher John Henderson at New York Bound one afternoon. John signed me on to write *Confessions of a Trolley Dodger From Brooklyn*.

I liked the man.

He had an instinctive feel for trolleys and trains. I could tell by his hands-on approach to the trolley book that Henderson was a publisher who treated each book with the love and meticulous care every author covets.

That's why I was so tickled when he agreed to publish "The Subway."

John knows the rails and reveres them. He has been a supportive mentor on this project as he was on *Confessions* and he ranks at the top of my list of acknowledgments. Without him, potential readers still would be vainly looking for *Uptown, Downtown*.

Many others contributed significantly to this project. Sean Spiller was an indefatigable and always gracious researcher whether he was prodding the Port Authority for photos or poring through back issues of the *New York Times* at the New York Public Library.

Our office staff—Jessica Cohen, Thomas Berk, Dan Saraceni, Christina Attardo—was always ready to find lost items, check facts and read manuscript. They did so with the enthusiasm that can only inspire an author.

Thanks also to the Metropolitan Transit Authority; in particular Termaine C. Garden of the Public Relations Department as well as Neil Neches of the TA. Albertein Anderson of the agency's Special Events Department helped immeasurably on the Movie section. Ditto for Angela Tarantino from Home Box Office as well as the Port Authority's Carolyne Bowers.

As always Bill Hirsch, Joe Cunningham, Allan Kreda, Ralph Hubbard, Nate Gerstein, John Landers, Bob Presbrey, Vincent Losino, Joe Vetere, Arthur Murphy, Don Harold, Bob Penisi, Joseph Frank, Joseph Calisi, Joe Spaulding, Tim Bond, John Tauranac, William J. Brennan, Irving (BMTussle) Sohn and Lawrence Stelter proved not merely good friends and dedicated transit buffs but either contributed valuable information and photographs at the drop of a phone call, or at the least directed us to useful leads.

When assistance was needed on the Hudson Tubes chapter, we turned to Alan Zelazo, his wife Delores and son Jonathan who opened their Hudson and Manhattan archives to us.

Many authors earlier works on transit provided research assistance in various ways. Their books and pamphlets merit kudos:

Joseph Brennan, author of *Abandoned Subway Stations*; Joseph Cunningham and Leonard DeHart, authors of *A History of the New York City Subway System, Rapid Transit in Brooklyn, The Independent System and City Ownership, The Manhattan Els and the IRT*; Brian J. Cudahy, author of *Under the Sidewalks of New York and Rails Under the Mighty Hudson*; Alan P. Kahn and Jack May, authors of *Tracks of New York*; Oscar Israelowitz, author of *New York City Subway Guide*; John A. Miller, author of *Fares, Please! From Horse-Cars to Streamliners*; Fred Westing, author of *Penn Station, It's Tunnels and Side Rodders*, and John Landers, author of *Twelve New York City Street and Transit Maps, From 1860-1967*.

To those and many others who helped in so many ways, I offer a smiling green light and hug-enfolding THANK YOU!

INTRODUCTION:
ABOUT LOVING THE SUBWAYS

I've never met a subway car I didn't like.

Whether in tunnels or on the els, I love our subway system.

How does one fall in love with a subway?

That question was repeatedly asked of me following publication of "Uptown, Downtown," my original paean of praise to our metropolitan railroad in 1976.

The question is still relevant more than two decades later because my romance with the rails—New York City-style—continues unabated despite years of graffiti, unintelligible public address announcements and breakdowns.

Why the affection?

Forgive me for answering a question with a question: why do kids—even adults—love toy electric trains?

To me the New York City subways are just like a set of Lionels, only bigger.

When the Broadway IRT express thunders past the 59th Street Station I look at it as I would have gaped at a set of Standard Gauge trains when I visited the Lionel showroom as a ten-year-old in 1942.

Everything about the subway remains an endless source of fascination from the blue telephone lights in tunnels to the rats stealthily—and with remarkable safety—crisscrossing the tracks outside the 157th Street IRT Station under Broadway.

Seemingly obscure items such as the safety "tripper" overhanging the tracks to the motorman's—or operator's, if you will—controller draw my attention the way amoeba do to a biologist.

Is there something in my past that has inspired this unabated affection for tracks, trains and rapid transit in general?

Of course there is!

I grew up on the right side of the tracks.

My definition of "right" is simplicity itself. A brand-new GG subway (the IND Brooklyn-Queens Crosstown Line) actually was built underneath our house in Brooklyn when I was only three-years-old and completed when I was five.

Meanwhile, the incredibly delightful Myrtle Avenue elevated line played its infectious *ta-dum-da-dum-ta-dum-da-dum* rhythm only a half-block away from my bedroom window on Marcy Avenue.

Sitting in the living room, I would simultaneously hear the whine of the GG's motor as it left Myrtle-Willoughby Station and the *click-clack* of the el's wheels dancing over the rail gaps.

In a way I'm surprised that the infatuation has lasted six decades. I say that because it no longer is as easy to be a train buff as it was when I was a nipper, pushing my head out of the Brighton Express train's open front window as it barreled around the curve at Beverley Road Station in Flatbush.

What could be a greater "rush" than having the wind blow through an eight-year-old's hair while a BMT Standard hit top speed careening down the hill from Avenue H Station to Newkirk Avenue below?

Those thrills of yesteryear have not abated with time. The front windows have long been sealed and the names have changed—can you imagine the IRT is now called the A-Division—but my love quotient remains the same.

I instinctively rush to the front window whenever the train arrives at the station and gaze at the track ahead as if I were riding the subway for the first time.

Everything, from the whine of the motors to the newly-installed speedometers in the cab, slakes my thirst for more and more subway kicks.

I am permanently hooked on the underground.

Which isn't such a bad state—or city—to be in since New York still has the greatest subway in the world.

Worth Street station the day before it closed on Labor Day 1962.
It was made superfluous by the Brooklyn Bridge station's extension.

10

EARLY FORMS OF TRANSIT

Origins

Although the first practical railroad in the world was George Stephenson's steam engine built in England in 1825, America's original railway was a horse-drawn contraption that, curiously, was a direct lineal descendant of the American Revolution. It was built to haul granite from the quarries of West Quincy, Massachusetts, to historic Bunker Hill, where a monument honoring the patriotic Colonials who fought on Bunker Hill would be erected. Even though a steam engine had just proven in Britain that it could haul large quantities of coal over wooden tracks, this first American railroad, which began operation on October 7, 1826, was nothing more than a horse-drawn tram whose roots could be traced back to the coal miners of England and Wales in the sixteenth and seventeenth centuries.

In that pre-railway era, coals were routinely carried by horseback in double panniers. It was a slow and costly operation but eventually coal-mine owners developed a method to avoid the expense of maintaining large numbers of horses, which then was a staggering financial imposition.

The brainstorm that changed the complexion of Great Britain's coal industry consisted of a pair of parallel wooden rails on which coal carts rolled. The carts were pulled, of course, by horses. Utilizing rails on which to pull their carts, coal barons discovered that the capacity of the horse was increased twenty to thirty times and that sixty, instead of two, coal bushels could be hauled. (Strangely, there is a direct kinship between the original horse-drawn coal train and the modern New York City subway. The coal-haulers built their rails just four feet eight-and-a-half inches apart for cart wheels. This happens to be the standard gauge of all New York subways and els as well as most rail lines worldwide.)

By 1800 horse-powered railways had become commonplace in England, and in 1803 an erratic genius named Richard Trevithick built a "portable fire-engine," otherwise known as a steam carriage. For reasons known only to Trevithick he chose not to run his steam engine on rails. By no small coincidence Trevithick, having a fortune in grasp, died a financial failure. There would, in time, be many like him involved in the development of New York's subways. Trevithick's major oversight was converted into a bonanza by George Stephenson, an unlettered engine-wright in a coal mine. He conceived the idea that the very coals themselves could be used to haul coal to the waterside, and in 1825 he built the first real steam railroad. What surprised Stephenson was that people wanted to ride his newfangled invention as much as they wanted to use it for coal-carrying. That being the case, Stephenson began experimentation in passenger railroading, which meant that rapid transit development could not be far behind.

And it wasn't. In 1863 London opened its first *Underground*. The world's first subway consisted of a steam railroad running through tubes far below London's streets. It was noisy and dirty, but it did reduce the unbearable surface traffic congestion and proved popular, despite its limitations.

Interestingly, the London *Underground* owed a debt of gratitude to America's very first railroad, the Granite Railway, and its creative builder, Gridley Bryant. It was Bryant who produced, among other inventions, the original track switch, the first swivel-trucked eight-wheel freight car, the turntable, and the portable derrick.

Not only did Bryant influence British railway and *Underground* construction but his success with the Granite Railway inaugurated in America the grand era of railroad building and westward settlement. Bryant, like Trevithick, died a poor man, but in 1826 he seemed to have the world on a string—or on rails, as it were.

On January 4, 1826 Bryant petitioned the Massachusetts state legislature for funds and land upon which to build his granite-carrying railroad. The request was granted two months later and ground for the line was broken on April 1 of the same year. In less than six months the Granite Railway was in business and on October 9, 1826 the first railroad in America, costing all of $50,000, took its first run. The *Boston Daily Advertiser* described it as follows:

"A quantity of stone, weighing sixteen tons, taken from the ledge belonging to the Bunker Hill Association, and loaded on three wagons which together weigh five tons, making a load of twenty-one tons, was moved with ease by a single horse from the quarry to the landing above Neponset Bridge, a distance of more than three miles.... After the starting of the load, which required some exertion, the horse moved at ease in a fast walk. It may, therefore, be easily conceived how greatly transportation of heavy loads is facilitated by means of this road."

As for the line itself, *The First Railroad in America*, a commemorative book, prepared by a Boston advertising company in 1926 on the railroad's 100th anniversary, tells us what it was like:

"The road-bed, deep enough to be beyond the reach of frost was built of crushed granite, and the sleepers were made of stone, placed eight feet apart, on which were rested wooden rails twelve inches high. On top of the rail was an iron plate three inches wide and one quarter-inch thick which was fastened with spikes; but at all places where the railroad crossed public highways stone rails were used with an iron plate four inches wide and one quarter-inch thick bolted firmly on the stone.... As the wooden rails began to decay, they were replaced with stone rails.... On account of its construction, the upkeep of the road for many years was less than ten dollars a year."

Bryant created every inch of the railroad; not only was the idea for the design of the roadbed and the track his, but he also designed the Granite Railway's rolling stock, which was described as follows:

"It had high wheels, six and one-half feet in diameter, the load being suspended on a platform under the axles by chains. This platform was let down at any convenient place and loaded; the car was then run over the load, the chains attached to the platform, and the loaded platform raised a little above the track by machinery on the top of the car. The loads averaged six tons each."

Considering the era, Bryant had accomplished a monumental engineering feat, for nowhere in the United States was there a rail system, or any comparable transit system for that matter, able to deliver tons of granite over hilly, irregular terrain. Bryant himself described in his notes how he was able to surmount the physical obstacles with an ingenious device:

". . . The foot of the tablelands that ran around the main quarry had an elevation of 84 feet vertical," which had to be overcome. How? This was done by an inclined plane, 315 feet long, at an angle of about 15 degrees.

"It had an endless chain, to which the cars were attached in ascending or descending. At the head of this inclined plane I constructed a swing platform to receive the loaded cars as they came from the quarry. This platform was balanced by weights, and had gearing attached to it in such a manner that it would always return (after having dumped) to a horizontal position, being firmly supported on the periphery of the elevated cam."

There were other problems, but Bryant conquered them as well. "When the cars were out on the platform," he noted, "there was danger of their running entirely over, and I constructed a self-acting guard that would rise above the surface of the rail upon the platform as it rose from its connection with the inclined plane, or receded out of the way when the loaded car passed on the track; the weight of the car depressing the platform as it was lowered down.

"I also constructed a turntable at the foot of the quarry. The railroad was continued in different grades around the quarry, the highest part of which was 93 feet above the general level; on the top of this was erected an obelisk or monument forty-five feet high."

When Gridley Bryant began operating his railroad in Massachusetts, the citizens of New York City were being transported about the southern tip of Manhattan Island by oxcart. At least one oxcart line was known to run from the Battery up Broadway, eventually being replaced in 1827 by lumbering, horse-drawn omnibuses. These, in turn, were succeeded by horsecars in the middle 1850s. Unlikely as it may seem today, horsecars remained in operation on New York City's streets until July 26, 1917 when both the Bleecker Street and Broadway horsecar lines made their last trips.

The Bleecker and Broadway horsecar photographed on its last day of operation, July 26, 1917.

In time steam came to American railroads and, more important, electricity made its debut in Richmond, Virginia in 1888 when the city's entire fleet of horse-drawn streetcars were equipped with electric motors. Once the Richmond electrified streetcars proved successful other metropoli turned away from steam to the new energy source. New York, Chicago, and Brooklyn abandoned their steam locomotives in favor of electricity on the elevated railroads.

Up until this time, however, nobody had installed electricity for underground transit purposes. In fact, politicians in Chicago and New York had successfully waged war against subways. Boston was the first to successfully put an electric railway underground in the United States. It happened because of Henry H. Whitney, boss of Boston's West End Street Railway and a man who was very impressed with—and yet concerned about—the Richmond trolley operation.

"Serious doubts plagued him at first," wrote rail historian Brian J. Cudahy in *Change at Park Street Under*. "In the peaceful, almost rural precincts of the quiet Southern city electric trolleys performed their routines with leisurely ease. Would such prove practical in brisk, congested Boston?"

Whitney was persuaded to take the big gamble and installed a fleet of electric trolleys in Boston. The streetcars were an immediate hit; even the poet Oliver Wendell Holmes penned a few verses in their honor, describing the characteristic pulley arm of the trolley:

> *Since then on many a car you'll see*
> *A broomstick plain as plain can be;*
> *On every stick there's a witch astride—*
> *The string you see to her leg is tied.*

The trolleys proved so popular they became unpopular because of their ubiquitousness. The bumper-to-bumper lineup along Tremont Street brought demands for some way of removing the streetcars from the street and putting them somewhere—anywhere!—even if it meant building an elevated railway or a subway. The Massachusetts Legislature approved the plans of a firm called the Boston Elevated Railway Company, which ultimately built the "elevated" railway underground!

Ground was broken for the monumental project on March 28, 1895, and two and one-half years and $5 million later the first leg of the subway was open for business. The *New York Times* observed: "That so conservative an American town should happen to be the pioneer in adopting this is viewed as remarkable."

If Boston could do it, why not New York? Boston's first four-wheel open-bench car rolled out of the Allston barns on September 1, 1897; it was only a matter of time before New York would build its own subway system. But it did not come easily.

Elevated Railroads— Phase I

In 1811 when City Hall was completed on Manhattan Island, New York planners estimated that the bulk of the city's population would reside in the area from the southern tip of the island (the Battery) to an area just south of City Hall. In fact, the builders of City Hall had used a cheaper, less cosmetic material on the northern facade of City Hall on the assumption that nobody would venture that far north and see the other side of the building.

Very quickly they were proven wrong. As immigrants poured into the United States from Europe, they were funneled through New York City and, naturally, many chose to live on Manhattan Island. The city grew so fast beyond City Hall that street congestion soon became a major problem for pedestrians

14

and drivers of wagons, horse-drawn omnibuses, and horse-drawn carriages.

Each year the city extended its limits farther north and, as a result, horsecar lines did a thriving business, but they were inadequate to haul the growing throngs. By mid-century the Hudson River Railroad station at 30th Street had become a major terminus, yet it took almost an hour to reach it by horsecar because of congestion along the route. "It was a slow, bumpy ride just to reach the railroad," according to the *Electric Railroaders Association* account. "Plans had been offered to let the railroad trains run all the way down (Manhattan Island) as a sort of transit facility, but they would have hindered rather than helped the situation."

Almost everyone in town agreed that some improvement was necessary to ease the flow of traffic; especially in view of the reckless competition between stagecoaches and horsecars. Robert Daley, writing in *The World Beneath the City*, described it as violent and cutthroat:

"No tracks hampered the operations of the stages, whose drivers ran over men, women and children in their haste to beat competitors to waiting passengers. Burly conductors shanghaied people into coaches and forced them to pay, so that heavy profits could be shown. Drivers were picked for heft not courtesy. Most swore at the passengers, and swindled them on tickets and on change. Axles broke, horses shied and policemen on boxes at intersections spent more time separating slugging rival drivers than directing snarled traffic."

Reflecting the public concern, the local press urged reform: "Modern martyrdom," asserted the *New York Herald* of October 2, 1862, "may be succinctly defined as riding in a New York omnibus." But the question remained: What

The New York Central and Hudson River Railroad's Ninth Avenue and 30th Street terminal, as photographed in 1914. This terminal, phased out after the opening of Grand Central Depot in 1871, remained standing until the 1930s. A popular woodcut shows the Lincoln funeral train departing from this station. Manhattan's first elevated cable railway had this depot as its targeted destination.

15

kind of transit reform?

Since 1825 various plans had been developed to transfer surface transit to elevated structures. Proposed propulsion systems ran the gamut from steam to cable to compressed air.

By the start of the 1860s more than 700,000 people filled the city from the Battery to the "suburbs" around 42nd Street and hundreds more were arriving by the week. The mostly undeveloped land north of 42nd Street was sprinkled with squatters' shanties and pasture. Farms still abounded north of Harlem, which was hardly populated, and deer could be seen grazing among the woodlands and meadow of what now is Central Park. This was unexploited land that soon would be developed if some convenient means could be devised to make it readily accessible.

The 10-cent stagecoach was not the answer, nor was the 6-cent horsecar. "The answer," said Hugh B. Willson, a Michigan railroad man, "is a subway line under Manhattan."

Willson promoted a Metropolitan Railway Company with $5 million of his own in working capital. A. P. Robinson, engineer for the project, conceived an elaborate right-of-way on his drawing board. It would be covered with glass sidewalks to allow light down into the tunnel while hollow lampposts on the street would transmit fresh air to the subway below.

"Our subway," boasted Robinson, "will signal the end of mud and dust, of delays due to snow and ice. The end of the hazardous walk into the middle of the street to board the car, the end of waiting for lazy or obstinate truckmen. Everything will be out of sight, out of hearing. Nothing will indicate the thoroughfare below."

But neither Willson nor Robinson bargained for the byzantine turns of New York politics. Opponents included such Gotham heavy-weights as Origen Vandenburgh and Jacob Sharpe, not to mention the powerful rail

SWETT'S PROPOSED ELEVATED RAILWAY—FOR BROADWAY.

baron, Cornelius Vanderbilt. When Commodore Vanderbilt learned of Willson's subway proposal he snapped, "I'll be underground a damned sight sooner than this thing!"

Most awesome of all the obstacles was William Marcy ("Boss") Tweed, kingpin of New York's Tammany Hall Democratic machine and the man who dominated, via the backrooms, the horsecar and stage companies. Clearly it was in Tweed's best interests to protect the horsecar and stage outfits from any competition, which is precisely what he did.

When the New York State Assembly approved the Willson subway proposal in the spring of 1865 by an unexpectedly large 89 votes, Tweed's puppet governor, Ruben E. Fenton, vetoed the bill. When Willson attempted to negotiate with the governor personally, he was shown the door. To be sure, there were those who truly believed that a subway would be a menace to Manhattan. A. W. Craven, chief engineer of the Croton Reservoir, feared that the underground railway would impinge on sewerage systems and contaminate the water supply. Others pointed out that the smoke pouring out of the subway's steam engines would damage the riders' throat and nasal passages. A second attempt by Willson to persuade the state legislature failed under Tweed's pressure.

Curiously, Tweed was indifferent to another transit proposal developed by inventor Charles Harvey. This was an elevated cable car to be built along the sidewalk line of Greenwich Street in downtown Manhattan. According to Harvey's plan, the cable pulling the train would be activated by stationary engines, anchored to bed rock every 1,500 feet.

Like Willson, Harvey went to Albany with his blueprints but, unlike Willson, he met no opposition. He called his company the West Side & Yonkers Patent (Elevated) Railway and went about the business of constructing an experimental track. On October 10, 1867 the first column of the line was erected on Greenwich Street. Preliminary field work had started on July 1 for construction of the first quarter mile of the line to Morris Street.

Relentlessly, Harvey pushed forward on his unique project and, on December 7, 1867, he demonstrated use of the line by riding a car truck instead of a car. This was a pivotal day for Harvey. If the ride failed in any way— many citizens were convinced that the el would collapse of its own weight—its inventor would lose the support of his financial backers. But the test ride worked, and directors of the West Side & Yonkers Patent Railway Company authorized expenditures to complete the remainder of the line to Cortlandt Street, which was approved by the State Legislature.

In 1868 the elevated project moved full speed ahead. On July 1 Harvey again successfully tested the device before a large and skeptical audience. Just two days later members of the Board of Railroad Commissioners made a test trip in a passenger car from Battery Place to Cortlandt Street. Pulled by a Roebling-made cable, powered by a stationary steam engine, the train worked well enough to win official approval.

In terms of its cable grip device Harvey's el was similar to the San Francisco cable-car system of the day. Harvey's track gauge was four feet ten and one-half inches with the rails on longitudinal girders without crossties so familiar on traditional railroads.

With offices at 48 Cortlandt Street, the West Side & Yonkers Patent Railway was ready for its great leap forward—uptown. All that was needed was money. But finding it proved to be difficult. Harvey had to go begging for lenders and eventually found enough to enable construction to continue toward the 30th Street railroad terminal.

Harvey knew that if his elevated railroad was to make money, it had to link with the Hudson River Railroad Terminal. On September 26, 1869 it was just a mile away, but on that same day the Great Depression of the sixties took place and Harvey was broke.

He looked everywhere for more backers and finally capitulated to a group of fast-buck operators who took over control of the el but temporarily retained its inventor as the titular boss. Construction moved forward to the target destination, and on February 14, 1870 regular operation for passenger service began from the Dey Street station in lower Manhattan to the line's new terminus at Ninth Avenue and 29th Street. The single-track structure followed the easterly curb line of Greenwich Street and the westerly curb line of Ninth Avenue. The line was powered by four new cable-operating plants. The railroad had three passenger cars in service.

To move the cars, the West Side & Yonkers Railway had its first cable-operating plant at Cortlandt and Greenwich Streets. This plant powered the line from Battery Place to Franklin Street. A plant at Franklin Street operated another cable from there to Houston Street, while another engine at Bank Street propelled the cable between Houston and Little West 12th Streets. From Little West 12th Street to the northern end at West 29th Street another cable ran to and from a plant at the northwest corner of West 22nd Street and Ninth Avenue. The original steam cable engine at 107 Greenwich Street, built for the first experiments, was closed down.

In its early months of operation the el

proved both a blessing and a curse. The idea of carrying passengers above the street was a good one, and planners soon realized that in theory Harvey had the ultimate cure for New York's transit problems. But mechanically the el left a lot to be desired. The cable frequently snapped, forcing the emergency crew to haul out a team of horses and pull the stranded car and passengers to the end of the line. Following this, the entire line had to be closed down for a considerable period while necessary repairs were made.

Despite the chronic disruption of service, it was apparent that the el was here to stay, and that is precisely what began to annoy Boss Tweed. At first he had treated it as just another crazy idea, but suddenly he realized it threatened his many surface transit interests. Tweed swiftly contacted his aides in Albany who pushed a bill through the New York State Senate branding the el a public nuisance. The bill authorized the commissioner of public works—one William Marcy Tweed—to raze it within three months. Since Tweed had the governor's vote in his pocket, he needed only the approval of the State Assembly to wipe out Harvey's el. But the desperate inventor was not about to throw in the towel. In fact, Harvey had a trump card sitting in Albany named Erastus Corning, an old friend. Corning was a major figure in New York State politics, having served as state senator, congressman, and vice chancellor of the University of New York. What's more, Corning was deeply indebted to Harvey dating back to the time when Corning was building a canal at the outlet of Lake Superior and was stymied by a major rock ledge. Corning's sandbar dredges could not break the ledge, and the promoter appeared doomed to a financial debacle.

It was then that Harvey invented a device for crumbling the ledge, and Corning was able to complete the canal. Now Harvey needed a favor from his friend. Corning, then seventy-eight years old, was not afraid to take on Boss Tweed. He went before the Assembly and filibustered in favor of the newfangled

elevated railroad. Corning had respect and he had clout. When the Assembly voted on the measure Tweed went down to defeat and the Ninth Avenue el lived.

On April 20, 1871 operation on the el resumed with one essential difference; instead of using cable cars the West Side & Yonkers Patent Railway had a small steam locomotive pulling the three former cable cars. The steam engine was boxed in to prevent it from frightening horses in the streets below. A 10-cent fare was charged and 237 passengers were carried on reopening day.

Despite optimism about the el, financial troubles continually intruded. In November 1870 the line had been auctioned off for $960 to bondholders, and now in 1871 it was auctioned off again for $5,000 to another group of bondholders who were organizing a new company, the New York Elevated Railroad Company.

The new company was chartered on October 27, 1871 with a capital stock of $10 million. By now Charles Harvey had been eased out of the el operation altogether, but the railroad prospered and many of his original ideas were soon realized. In the summer of 1872 the Little West 12th Street station opened with an innovation for the elevated. Instead of limiting the operation to a single track, which allowed just one train running back and forth, the directors built a passing track at the new station, thus enabling trains to roll in both directions, meeting at the double-track point. Shortly thereafter the Morris Street station was opened. On January 21, 1873 a station opened at Franklin Street, and running time over the entire route was twenty-eight minutes.

Having defeated Boss Tweed and a legion of skeptics, the elevated railroad proved—at least in the seventies—that it was the panacea for all Manhattan's street-level traffic problems. Year by year, the el grew like a horizontal beanstalk. In July 1873 it was extended to West 34th Street and Ninth Avenue. Later in the year an additional station was opened at West 21st Street. Some officials of the New York Elevated Railroad Company believed it should carry freight as well as passengers and voted to alter the superstructure.

In March 1875 the entire line was closed for major alterations. More than 200 men were hired to change the wheel widths on rolling stock to four feet eight and one-half inches. Rails were re-laid on crossties and the general superstructure was beefed up from start to finish. While they were at it, engineers installed a new siding at Franklin Street. By the end of 1875 trains were rolling as far north as 42nd Street, and sidings were installed at Bethune Street and 34th Street.

Business boomed up and down the line. In January 1876 the el was averaging 5,600 fares daily and was a full five miles long. Its bosses, Simeon E. Church and Cyrus Field, pushed it ever northward to 53rd Street. Because of the demand, double-tracking was begun in April 1877 and, during Christmas week that year, the directors celebrated their el with a dinner at posh Delmonico's Restaurant. "The el sold out to the sheriff in 1870," chortled Field, "but it seems to be doing all right now!" And so it was. In 1878 it was averaging 8,500 daily passengers, and work was progressing on a Sixth Avenue elevated line, under the direction of Dr. Rufus H. Gilbert, a former medical practitioner who

had become avidly interested in transit.

Dr. Gilbert's line suffered through much of the same financial affliction that befell Harvey. After a series of internal problems and legal complications, the company changed its name from the Gilbert Elevated Railway Co. to the Metropolitan Elevated Railway and erected an impressive line along Sixth Avenue.

Although the girder work on Gilbert's Sixth Avenue El differed from the style utilized by Harvey's railroad, it was constructed to conventional standards. The line began in downtown Manhattan at Morris Street on Trinity Place and proceeded north along Trinity Place and Church Street with stations at Rector Street, Cortlandt Street and Park Place. Then it moved up West Broadway with stops at Chambers Street, Franklin Street, Grand Street, Bleecker Street, and finally north on Sixth Avenue itself, stopping at 8th Street, 14th Street, 23rd Street, 33rd Street, 42nd Street, 50th Street, and 58th Street. At later dates stations at 18th Street, 28th Street, and 38th Street were opened.

To move rolling stock up to the elevated tracks an inclined plane was installed on Trinity Place behind Trinity Church, near Rector Street. Everything from the small steam locomotives to the passenger cars were hauled up the artificial train hill. The locomotives had a two-four-two wheel

The Sixth Avenue Elevated station at 14th Street on April 2, 1916.

This is a typical Forney steam locomotive used on the elevateds from their inception up until the introduction of electricity. This photo of engine #54 was taken in 1929 when only a very few steam locomotives were left and were used exclusively to haul work trains on the elevated lines. The footboard on the front of the locomotive was a later addition, probably after it left passenger service.

arrangement, weighed fifteen tons and were painted pea-green. The passenger cars were painted a light green, with pea-green and gold trim and had wheels of highly compressed paper with steel rims. The interiors had woodwork of oak and mahogany, Axminster carpeting, and kerosene chandeliers. The fare was 10 cents.

Like its predecessor on Ninth Avenue, the Sixth Avenue El did very well and eventually would link up with the Harvey road in 1879. The move northward in Manhattan continued through the end of the nineteenth century. Meanwhile, railroad planners were busily stretching their tracks through New York City's sister municipality across the river, Brooklyn. The growth of elevated railroads in Brooklyn was significantly different from that on Manhattan Island because of the then mostly rural nature of Kings County and the fact that it boasted several attractive seaside resorts.

Elevated Railroads— Phase II

A year before Charles Harvey made his initial test run on the Ninth Avenue El, Brooklyn's first major steam railroad line reached Coney Island. Like so many of that city's railroads, the Brooklyn, Bath & Coney Island Railroad was constructed to link the populous northern section of that city— Brooklyn remained an independent city until it incorporated as one of the five boroughs in 1898—with the popular seaside resorts at Coney Island, Manhattan Beach, Norton's Point and Sea Gate, all on the southern tip.

In time the Brooklyn, Bath & Coney Island would be known as the West End line of the Transit Authority's BMT system now called The B-Division, Group I. But in 1867 it was called the "Dummy Road," a euphemism for the steam dummies used for motive power.

The line had two starting points to provide linkage with Brooklyn horsecars as well as the ferry boats to Manhattan.

The ferry boat connection was located at 39th Street west of Second Avenue in Brooklyn. The ferry floated north across New York harbor to its Manhattan destination at South Ferry. The horsecar link was situated at 27th Street and Fifth Avenue, Brooklyn, from where the horsecars fanned out to various districts such as Park Slope, Borough Park, Bay Ridge and the downtown area in the north. After traversing the westerly portion of Brooklyn, the Brooklyn, Bath & Coney Island Railroad terminated at Tivoli's Hotel in Coney Island.

Swank came to Coney Island in 1875 when Cable's Hotel (later known as the Ocean View) opened and with it came another key rail link, the Prospect Park & Coney Island Railroad, founded by Andrew R. Culver.

Culver's first line started at a northern terminus near Prospect Park, 20th Street and Ninth Avenue and concluded its twenty-minute steam journey to Cable's Hotel in the West Brighton section of Coney Island. The Prospect Park & Coney Island Railroad charged 43 cents for a round-trip ticket and did a lively summer business.

There still were no elevated lines in Brooklyn when the Brooklyn, Flatbush & Coney Island Railroad opened in 1878 along much the same route now traversed by the Transit Authority's Brighton D and Q trains. One of the most successful operations, the Brooklyn, Flatbush & Coney Island operated between Atlantic Avenue, where it connected with the Long Island Rail Road, and the Hotel Brighton in Coney Island.

As more and more New Yorkers discovered the glories of Coney Island's clean sands and sparkling waters, there was increased demand for still another railroad to the Atlantic. Finally, in 1879 the New York & Sea Beach Railroad shot its line through the farms and small towns of Brooklyn from 65th Street in Bay Ridge (connecting with the steamboats to South Ferry) and the Sea Beach Palace Hotel in Coney Island.

The steamers cruised from Bay Ridge Landing to Whitehall Street, Leroy Street, and West 22nd Street in New York City. "Thus," wrote *Electric Railroaders Association* historian Bernard Linder, "Manhattanites discovered that a steamboat ride of an hour and 20 minutes, plus a half hour on the NYSB brought them to this lovely spot, where fresh-dug clams were available by the bushel. The flavor of Coney Island clams became quite as famous as the huge schooners of beer. Clams and beer were the universal food and drink of the early excursionists."

By 1880 Coney Island's beer, clams, and sea breezes assured an endless boom and, as a result, promoters erected the first authentic—albeit unconventional—elevated line in Kings County.

Steam locomotive "Coney Island" of the Prospect Park and Coney Island Railroad hauls a string of summer cars at Pabst loop, located at West 5th Street and Surf Avenue, in the late 1880s. Notice the Long Island Rail Road cars alongside.

The Culver Terminal at Coney Island, circa 1916. The rods visible in the foreground allow towermen to mechanically throw the switches in the yard. Notice the trolley loops visible on the far right and the trolley poles on the elevated cars. The line on MacDonald Avenue was still operated at grade.

Only a mile long, Brooklyn's pioneering el was built within view of the ocean to connect the Hotel Brighton with a terminal just west of the Culver Depot in Coney Island. It was completed in 1881 and called the Coney Island Elevated Railway. Purists hesitated to call it an authentic el since the line actually was more a long trestle than an elevated railway. Still, it was built above ground on wooden pilings and columns, utilizing iron bridges at road crossings. There were only two stations, at the start and finish of the route, and the Coney Island Elevated Railway ran only in the summer for the tourist trade. At first the wooden passenger cars were pulled by a steam engine but, years later, in 1898, after it was purchased by the huge Brooklyn Rapid Transit Company, the line was electrified with overhead wire.

Meanwhile the Brooklyn Bridge opened in May 24, 1883. Exactly four months later a cable-operated train service—with steam switching engines at the terminals—commenced across the span connecting Brooklyn and Manhattan. Bridge planners, anticipating a brisk business on the railway, hired six locomotive engineers, six locomotive firemen, one master of transportation, forty-five conductors, one trainmaster, four train dispatchers, four yardmen, and five switchmen, among other bridge railway employees. Train business was more than brisk. In the first year of operation the bridge cable line carried 9,234,690 passengers.

Still more business was guaranteed because construction had begun on Brooklyn's first conventional elevated railway from the

Fulton Street ferry, located on the East River, to Van Sicklen Avenue, near the city limits. The Brooklyn Elevated Railroad opened in 1885 and stimulated service on the bridge cable line. In 1885 the bridge trains, running twenty-four hours a day, handled nearly 20 million passengers. As a result its terminals were expanded and more cars were installed.

To New Yorkers the year 1888 is synonymous with the most awesome blizzard the city has known. To rail historians it is significant as the year of the great leap forward in Brooklyn's elevated railroad construction. From East River terminals no less than three major els fanned out across the city on Long Island. The Broadway (Brooklyn) El began at the ferry terminal at the East River and Broadway; the Myrtle

Avenue Line started at Sands Street near the Navy Yard and the Fulton Street Line left from the Fulton ferry. In less than six years five major elevated lines snaked eastward and southward to Brooklyn's city limits.

Coney Island's many steam lines were doing so well that rail promoters felt the need to exploit the shore resort with assorted attractions. Perhaps the most lavish of all Coney Island's extravaganzas was the Brighton Beach Hotel, built by the Brooklyn Rapid Transit Company (BRT). An enormous, *rococo* wooden structure, the hotel was among the first to have electric lights.

The BRT designers made one colossal mistake to go with their colossal hotel. They originally erected it at the very edge of the Atlantic Ocean. Once completed, the hotel

An el train heads on to the Brooklyn Bridge rolling toward Park Row in Manhattan. The line to the right curving under the bridge to Fulton Ferry was part of the original main line closed in 1904. According to previously published history this line was supposed to have disappeared early enough to have never been electrified, but that sure looks like third rail next to those tracks. Today, the southbound exit for the bridge off the Brooklyn-Queens Expressway follows the exact route of those tracks.

was assaulted by so high a tide that some guests were nearly drowned by the swirling waters. To prevent this happening in the future the BRT had to move the entire structure back from the edge of the beach, using Long Island Rail Road steam locomotives to accomplish the move.

Brooklyn's elevated lines continued proliferating through the turn of the century, and by 1900 every line in the borough but the Canarsie route was controlled by the Brooklyn Rapid Transit Company. In the year 1910 the borough of Brooklyn had a population of 1,634,000, and the 157-mile Brooklyn elevated network carried a total of 170,752,487 passengers in 928 cars.

The growth of elevated lines in Brooklyn was matched from the late seventies to the early 1900s only by the seemingly endless movement of the steel girders northward up Manhattan Island. The Ninth Avenue Line was a veteran of nine years when construction started on the Third Avenue El which, by 1891, marched all the way from South Ferry at the lower tip of Manhattan, across the Harlem River and up to 177th Street in the Bronx. In 1902 it reached Bronx Park and was electrified. Originally it was a two-track road but the heavy residential and business development that followed it overburdened the two-track capacity. A third, or express, track was installed from Chatham Square, Manhattan, to East 149th Street in the Bronx in 1916 and extended to 177th Street a year later, being used for southbound traffic in the morning and northbound in the evening. The golden era of elevated railroading was approaching its peak.

Coenties Slip's "S" curve on the 2nd and 3rd Avenue Els in 1895. Four cars was the maximum number that a platform could handle on the 3rd Avenue El prior to 1916. Even then the end doors overhung the platform ends.

This is the Chatham Square junction of the 2nd and 3rd Avenue Els circa 1904. The train on the left is a 2nd Avenue El consist bound for South Ferry and the train on the right is a north-bound 3rd Avenue El unit coming off the City Hall branch. Notice the fourth car on this train is an open trailer.

Beach's Bizarre Broadway Subway

Contrary to popular belief the Interborough Rapid Transit (IRT) subway line, which began operation in 1904, was not New York City's first public underground transportation system. The original Manhattan line actually ran under Broadway as early as 1870, following one of the most outlandish engineering operations any city has known.

The chief protagonist of what developed into an undercover underground operation was one Alfred Ely Beach, a gentleman of grand insight and dynamism. Beach had already invented the cable railway, the pneumatic tube, and a device that was to be pivotal in his subway production—the hydraulic tunneling bore. Journalists had revered Alfred Ely since he produced the world's first practical typewriter, which won him a gold medal at the Crystal Palace Exposition in 1853.

When he wasn't busy inventing something, Beach managed the affairs of the *New York Sun* (he and his brother were co-publishers), and founded several magazines while simultaneously working as a patent lawyer. Beach had been entertaining the idea of a subway since his early twenties. From his office overlooking City Hall in downtown Manhattan, Beach would regularly worry about the congestion that developed at the corner of Broadway and Chambers Street where neighing horses, screaming wagon drivers, and pedestrians vied for the limited space at the intersections.

Beach realized there were two possibilities for moving vehicular passenger traffic away from the streets—a road above ground or one below which would carry a railway train. The young inventor rejected the elevated idea, reasoning that it would be both unsightly and noisy. There was no question in Beach's mind that a subway was the answer. But first he had to find a means of moving rolling stock through a tunnel.

Horses were out of the question. A steam engine would produce too much soot. In 1866, when Beach was ready to put his ideas on the drawing board, practical gasoline and electric motors were not yet available. Pneumatic power seemed the only solution.

To say that Manhattan Island was suffering a transportation crisis by that time would be the understatement of the century. An area of approximately two square miles was jammed with nearly one million people. Their means of transportation—omnibus, street cars on rails and horse drawn stages—inevitably was overcrowded. Street jams were the order of the day making it even more difficult for public transit to work effectively. Beach's challenge was clear; develop a unique system for moving the hundreds of thousands of commuters.

To convince skeptics that it was possible to move a small railroad car through a tube by means of air power, Beach constructed a plywood tube, six feet in diameter. He then designed and built a small car, seating ten passengers, which would run inside the tube. For propulsion, Beach proposed to use a Helix fan, ten feet in diameter, which would funnel a blast of air into the tunnel. The air would move the train to the end of the tube and then, with fan reversed, pull it back to its point of origin.

Beach used the 1867 American Institute Fair held in the Fourteenth Street Armory to demonstrate the pneumatic-tube experiment. The armory was packed with spectators who gawked at and cheered the ten-car train as it moved through the tube that linked the 14th Street exit with the 15th Street doors.

The enthusiasm of the crowd during the weeks that the pneumatic train operated convinced Beach that he had himself a winner. But he was realist enough to know that it is one thing to construct a plywood tube and place it on the floor of an armory and quite another task to bore a tunnel under Broadway. Beach went right back to the drawing board to perfect such a tunnel driller. The result was a hydraulic shield which could tunnel seventeen inches with each press into the earth wall. Workers remained inside the shield, bricking the tunnel with comparative security from cave-in. Beach's earth-gouger was flexible enough to move left or right, up or down and, in experiments, proved that it could do the job on a genuine subway construction project. But hacking through political red tape was a project with which the hydraulic shield could not cope. New York City in 1868 was dominated by the Tammany Hall Democratic machine, the levers of which were controlled by William Marcy Tweed, the boss of all bosses.

Beach realized that, legally, he would require a franchise to build and operate a subway under Broadway. He also knew that Tweed would take as much money from him as could be extracted. During one three-month period following his appointment to the board of the Erie Railroad, Tweed pocketed Erie profits amounting to $650,000. Bribes to Tweed were written off as legal expenses. With this in mind, Beach decided to bypass the Boss. "I won't pay political blackmail," he told his brother. "I say, let's build the subway furtively."

That was extremely dangerous talk, considering Tweed's power and the near impossibility of constructing a full-scale subway in the middle of the metropolis without general public notice. (Some historians insist that many officials were aware of the project, but chose to ignore it.)

Beach dismissed the overwhelming obstacles from his mind. He would build the pneumatic tube. He would not inform the public officials about it. It would be warmly received and Tweed, in the end, would not be a problem. He concluded that the subway would be so beautiful, so efficient, indeed unique, so that when it opened public acclaim would erase any objections raised by Tweed or anyone else.

Having convinced his close associates that the subway would overwhelm all opponents, Beach took on the biggest challenge of his life. The first problem was gaining access to Broadway's subterranean depths. This was accomplished by renting the basement of Devlin's Clothing Store at Murray Street and Broadway; then Beach and his men began digging.

The ground under Broadway at that point was sandy and appeared amenable to Beach's hydraulic tunneling shield. In 1868 work commenced when a load of dirt was carried across the cellar of Devlin's Clothing Store and unloaded in a corner.

Beach put his twenty-one-year-old son, Fred, to work on the job as gang foreman. Fred and his crew hacked away at the underground wall of dirt, and gradually they could see that progress was being made, although many of the hired help were frightened off the job by the conditions confronting them under the clothing store.

Claustrophobia was a persistent problem. Fear that the horses galloping overhead, whose hoofbeats were acutely audible in the tunnel, would crash through and expose the

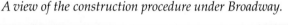

A view of the construction procedure under Broadway.

27

project constantly weighed on the workers. Many quit and never returned. Others worked apprehensively in the close tunnel air, guided by lantern light, pecking away at the dirt and sand.

For several nights the work proceeded without formidable obstacles. The sound of iron pick against an ever-expanding cave was a symphony to Beach's ear. But one night a dissonant noise was heard as a workman's spade struck a piece of stone. Then another and another. Suddenly all forward progress stopped. Instead of sand and dirt, easily penetrated, the laborers had run into a wall of stone.

Beach and his colleagues deduced that the stones were the foundation of an old fort. If a section of the foundation was removed the street might collapse around their heads. Beach had to make a choice; either abandon the project or conquer the obstacle. "Remove it," commanded Beach, "stone by stone!"

One by one, the stones were removed and boring continued while Beach watched the ceiling, hoping against hope that it would hold firm. After several days, during which there was no sign of sagging, Beach was convinced that he had made the right decision. The digging continued. Each night the workers would haul the bags of dirt out of the tunnel, dumping them on to wagons specially fitted with wheels muffled for silence. While these wagons hauled the dirt away, others arrived with tools and bricks for the tunnel walls. "Night after night," wrote Robert Daley in *The World beneath the City*, "gangs of men slipped in and out of the tunnel like thieves."

The project was costing Beach a fortune. By his own estimate some $350,000 of his own money would be needed to complete the subway by its target date of February 1870. A portion of the expense was for lavish fixtures that seemed more appropriate for the Metropolitan Opera House than for an experimental underground railway. But that was part of Beach's plan. A salesman at heart, he believed that an uncertain public had to be wooed with frills as well as efficiency.

To this end Beach designed a waiting room 120 feet long (the entire tunnel measured 312 feet) and embellished it with a grand piano, a fountain, ornate paintings and even a goldfish tank. Instead of entering a dank, dreary tunnel, the customers of the proposed Beach pneumatic subway would find themselves in an elegant, airy salon lighted with zircon lamps.

The digging went on without detection or further incident for fifty-eight nights. It was completed according to plan, whereupon Beach began installing the ostentatious trappings, which took longer than the boring and brick work. The walls of the waiting room were adorned with frescoes. Still, the *chef d'oeuvre* would be the subway itself.

Beach designed a single car which fitted snugly into the cylindrical tube nine feet in diameter. Propulsion would be supplied by a giant fan that the workers nicknamed "The Western Tornado." It was operated by a steam engine, drawing air in through a valve and blowing it forcefully into the tunnel. Thus the single car would be driven from Warren Street to Murray Street, the other end of the line, "like a boat before the wind."

Upon reaching the Murray Street terminus, the lone subway car would trip a wire that ran the length of the tunnel, ringing a bell back at Warren Street and alerting the engineer. The blower would then be reversed, and the train would be sucked right back to its starting point, "like soda through a straw." Air would be conveyed to the tunnel by means of an intake-exhaust grating installed on the surface of the street.

The giant fan, also known as the "Roots Patent Force Blast Blower," was designed to move the train at a top speed of ten miles an hour. The subway was completed five years after the end of the Civil War along with the frescoes, the fountain, and the fish tank, in February 1870 without the knowledge of Boss Tweed or, for that matter, nearly any other citizen of New York City.

Alfred Ely Beach, then forty-four years old,

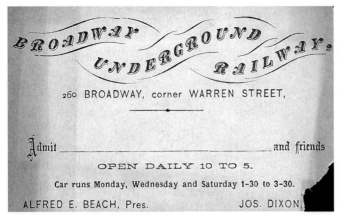

A ticket to ride the Beach Tube, fare 25 cents. A pretty expensive excursion to nowhere at 1870 prices.

was ready to reveal to an unsuspecting public the grand triumph of his life. The pneumatic subway would make its official debut on February 26, 1870. Beach invited the press and assorted dignitaries. His calculated gamble was that the subway would so impress them that potential foes would promptly muffle their opposition.

Beach was right—up to a point. Those who attended came away dazzled by the opulence and impressed by the subway's practicality. "This means the end of street dust of which uptown residents get not only their fill, but more than their fill, so that it runs over and collects on their hair, their beards, their eyebrows and floats in their dress like a vapor on a frosty morning," commented the *Scientific American* (also edited by Beach). "Such discomforts will never be found in the

tunnel!"

The twenty-two-seat subway car impressed observers with its rich upholstery and spaciousness, not to mention comfortable ride. Delighted with the initial response, Beach boasted that this subway was merely the forerunner of a line that would run for miles up and down Manhattan Island. "We propose to operate a subway all the way to Central Park," said Beach, "about five miles in all. When it's finished we should be able to carry 20,000 passengers a day at speeds up to a mile a minute." Press comments confirmed Beach's triumph.

The *New York Herald* proclaimed: "Fashionable Reception Held in the Bowels of the Earth!"

The reporter from the *New York Sun* marveled—as Beach had hoped—at the salon. "The waiting room is a large and elegantly furnished apartment, cheerful and attractive throughout."

Other journalists were no less enthused:

New York Mail, February 26, 1870. "The problem of tunneling Broadway has been solved. There is no mistake about it. Even as we write, a comfortable passenger car is running smoothly and safely between Warren and Murray Streets. This demonstrates, beyond contradiction, that it is only a question of time and money to give us rapid and comfortable transportation from the

An invitation to The opening of the Beach Pneumatic Tube.

The station on Warren St. as viewed from the tunnel.

Battery to Harlem and back again"

New York Times, February 27, 1870. "Every one of them came surprised and gratified. Those who expected to find a dismal and cavernous retreat under Broadway opened their eyes to the elegant reception-room, the light airy tunnel and the general appearance of taste and comfort in all the apartments; and those who entered to pick out some scientific flaw in the project, were silenced by the completeness of the machinery, the solidity of the track, and the safety of the running apparatus."

New York Sunday Mercury, February 27, 1870. "Thus far, then the work is a success. A

Inside the Beach Pneumatic car.

perfect tunnel, eight feet in diameter and nearly 300 feet long, has been made under Broadway, in its busiest portion, in fifty-eight days and ten hours working time, without disturbing travel or the street itself, and, in fact, without giving the public any idea of what was really in progress. But the Company's charter allows them only to use a tube of fifty-eight inches, and this for the transmission of packages. The success of the large tube has seemed to give an answer to the problem; How shall an Underground Railway be Constructed? And the Company will now go before the Legislature for permission to use their tunnel for the transfer of passengers, and to extend it from the Battery to the Central Park, on each side of the street. If this permission is obtained, over twenty openings will be made at once; and by working in each direction, the problem will be soon solved."

Nearly everyone of importance was heard from, except the man who counted most, William Marcy Tweed.

The flunkies at Tammany Hall were already hearing about Beach's subway from the Boss. He had read the papers and it was a toss-up, according to cronies, whether Tweed was more stunned or furious over the surprise subway. One thing was certain: he was not happy, nor was he impressed by the overwhelmingly favorable public opinion generated by Beach's underground.

Already wealthy and the most powerful man in the city, Tweed nevertheless feared Beach on two counts: the inventor had the courage to defy him and, further, his invention would cut into the Boss's profits. It was generally acknowledged that every trolley car company in the city paid tribute to Tweed. A subway of the magnitude proposed by Beach would cut heavily into those profits.

Tweed wasted no time deciding how to handle the upstart Beach; he would go after the fellow the way he'd stalk his most hated political enemy. Across City Hall Park, Beach sat in his office more valorous than discreet. "New York needs a subway," he countered when informed of Tweed's adamant and furious opposition. "I will go before the legislature at Albany."

Beach's single trump card was that his pneumatic tube under Broadway was open and operating; each day a horde of curiosity seekers poured into Devlin's basement to gawk at the grand piano, the fountain and frescoes, and to ride the wind-blown train. Months went by and more passengers paid their quarter-a-head for the ride, as well as the right to walk through the tunnel when the train was halted.

With public approval on his side, Beach went to the Legislature. The Beach Transit bill called for a $5-million expenditure, all to be privately raised. All work would be underground with little or no disruption at street level.

The New York State Senate passed the Beach Transit bill by a 22-5 landslide vote. The State Assembly gave it a 102-11 stamp of approval. There was only one catch: Boss Tweed, who came up with a transit idea to counter the Beach proposal. Dubbed Tweed's Viaduct Plan, the Tammany blueprint called for a series of elevated lines mounted on forty-foot-high stone arches. It would cost $80 million, the monies coming from public funds.

Not surprisingly, Tweed had clout in the State Legislature, which also approved his Viaduct Plan. One or the other plan—but not both—would be approved by Governor John T. Hoffman. Since Hoffman and Tweed were political brothers the Beach bill was doomed the moment it reached the governor's desk. Hoffman vetoed the plan and signed the Tweed Viaduct bill. Although the governor's action enraged editorialists who charged Tweed with hanky-panky, the fact remained that Beach was defeated. His only hope was that, somehow, he might marshal enough public support in the next year so that the Hoffman veto might be overcome.

Publicity was the key to Beach's campaign. If he could continue the momentum developed by public opinion in favor of his pneumatic tube the governor's veto would be overcome. Beach redoubled his efforts to lure dignitaries down to the tube. But Tweed's influence over politicians of every stripe was so complete that the only official of any stature to accept Beach's invitation was Secretary of the Navy Robeson (who rode it in December 1870). The cabinet member enjoyed the ride and said so to the press but the publicity was slight compared to what Beach required.

Still, the man-in-the-street liked it and when the Beach Transit bill came up for another vote it passed and then received Hoffman's expected veto. What mattered, of course, was the Legislature's attempt to override the veto. A two-thirds majority was needed. When the final tally was in, Beach had lost—by one vote.

A less determined battler would have despaired, but Beach insisted that he still had a chance. He needed a break or two in the political halls and in late 1872 he got it. Tweed's empire showed its first signs of crumbling as the *New York Times* began printing stories of corruption at Tammany Hall. The Boss was indicted and in November 1872 Governor Hoffman was voted out of office.

But Beach himself was showing signs of defeat. The pneumatic tube gradually lost its curiosity value and gate receipts dwindled to a point where Beach decided to close his subway as an economy measure. He hoped, however, to win the big battle in Albany and kept a collection of lobbyists on his payroll for just that purpose.

With Tweed down and Hoffman out, it appeared that Beach finally had the green light he needed for the subway bill. But now foes appeared from non-political quarters. Engineers argued that his hydraulic shield would be an ineffective tunneling device in rocky sections of Manhattan. Other scientists insisted that pneumatic power might be useful on a short subway such as the one Beach operated under Broadway, but certainly not on a five-mile run.

Deciding that if he couldn't beat his critics he'd join them, Beach rewrote the charter of his transit bill. If the pneumatic tube didn't work, he would provide for steam engines to pull the trains. And if his hydraulic shield failed to cut through Manhattan he would switch to the generally acceptable cut-and-fill technique.

Unfortunately, in his enthusiasm for the subway, Beach managed to alienate the millionaire John Jacob Astor, who had become one of New York City's major landlords. Astor and several of his colleagues feared that tunneling under Broadway might endanger the foundation of Trinity Church and its 280-foot tower, then Manhattan's tallest building. Other landlords were concerned about their buildings and the damaging effects the subway might have on them.

Despite the opposition the Beach Transit bill won approval from the State Legislature in 1873. It then went to the new governor, John A. Dix, who gave it his enthusiastic backing. At last Beach's perseverance and grim determination had paid off, on paper at least. Finding funds to build the subway was another story and a rather grim one. In fact, Beach's victory was a Pyrrhic one of the most traumatic variety. He was physically, monetarily and emotionally wasted. Inflation

had forced a revision in his cost estimate from $5 million to $10 million, all of which had to be raised from financiers such as Astor.

But John Jacob Astor wanted no part of Beach nor his subway. Other financiers refused him funds; one after another of Beach's attempts to raise cash failed and later in 1873 Governor Dix withdrew the charter for Beach's Pneumatic Subway.

Energetic efforts were made to provide new support for the inventor. One such movement included the distribution of handbills proclaiming, *"Un Fait Accompli."* The message on the handbill was clear:

"Is it not wasting time to discuss all sorts of plans 'how not to do it'—when it is already 'a fact accomplished? Should not every good citizen sustain and assist the men who have had the pluck and skill, under adverse circumstances, to solve, beyond a doubt, the problem stated by Mayor Hall? The Company applied to the Legislature last session for an amendment to its charter, backed by 30,000 petitions in its favor—not one against it — had the charter been given, the work would long ago have been in progress, in sections, all along the line from Harlem to City Hall. The Company is still prepared to carry forward the work with vigor and dispatch, as soon as the Legislature will give it such a charter as will warrant the necessary outlay. Agitate, petition, and give all the aid in your power to the Beach Pneumatic Transit Company, 260 Broadway, corner Warren Street. That which has already been done, without fuss or boasting, is sufficient evidence of what will be done when the Company gets Legislative authority."

Logical as the petition may have been, it failed to develop the necessary momentum and the proposal failed to generate a revival of the project. Beach, having spent his entire fortune, was forced to rent out the subway tube in order to make ends meet. It was first used as a shooting gallery and it later became a storage vault. Eventually, the tube was sealed.

New York's first subway remained forgotten

until February 1912 when a construction crew—digging for a new Broadway subway, the BRT—chopped through the wall of the Beach tunnel. Unaware of the pneumatic tube, the workers were flabbergasted at the ornate trappings before their eyes.

With the exception of some rotted wooden fixtures, the salon retained its original splendor. The magnificent station arrested the sandhogs' attention. Not only did they delight in the vision of an underground fountain but in the discovery that there had been a subway operating under Manhattan years before they had begun digging. Beach's tiny railroad car was still on its tracks.

Once the workers' discovery was reported, backers of the new subway decided that some form of acknowledgment should be made to the man who built New York's first underground railway. Their tribute was a plaque in honor of Alfred Ely Beach on a wall of the completed BRT City Hall station, which now includes part of the original pneumatic tube.

The Boynton Bicycle Railroad

In 1887, decades before the Brooklyn Rapid Transit and later the Brooklyn Manhattan Transit (BMT) crisscrossed the sands of Coney Island, an experimental railroad of unique proportions threatened to make the traditional rail-and-tie-type operation obsolete. The brains behind the project was an inventor named Eben Moody Boynton, an irascible, dogmatic individual. Boynton's theory was simplicity itself. The way to run a railroad was not to place two rails beneath a train, but to place one track overhead and one track underneath.

Dubbed "The Flying Billboard," Boynton's weird contraption actually was a century-ahead-of-time predecessor of the monorail, with appropriate variations. From the side view, the Boynton train appeared not greatly different from a traditional passenger railroad unit. The key difference, of course, was that the wheels on his train were placed in the middle of the top and bottom of the locomotive, tender, and passenger cars instead of on each side of the bottom of the vehicles.

Boynton's fascination with the bicycle's smoothness and ease of operation provided the inspiration for his train improvement. "A bicycle weighing 25 pounds," wrote Boynton, "can carry a rider weighing ten times as much."

If that was the case, why use a ton of steel and wood to carry a passenger, as was done on the railroads of the day? Boynton carried his research further. He discovered that a man had once pedaled 334 miles in twenty-four hours on a level track. Boynton figured up the number of ton-miles the man had transported simply by the strength of his two legs applied through the new spindle-type wheel.

Boynton was convinced beyond any doubt that the conventional railroad cars lost power through the sidesway of their four-wheeled design, not to mention the energy wasted through friction and air pressure. By applying bicycle principles to railroading, all of these "four-wheeled failures" would be rendered obsolete.

In its final blueprint form, Boynton's revolutionary bicycle train was, in the words of railroad historian Joseph Harrington, "the most fantastic-looking train ever built in America." Boynton had designed the passenger coach to be two stories high, and only four feet wide. It would seat 108 passengers and weigh but five tons. By contrast, railroad coaches of the day averaged in weight one ton to the passenger. "The lightness of Boynton's train," said Harrington, "was phenomenal."

So was the projected speed (100 mph cruising) and fuel savings. Boynton figured he could haul a payload from New York to Boston with a couple of scuttles of coal. After a decade of laborious development, Boynton was ready to lure investors to back his amazing invention. If there was one quality about him that could not be contained it was his enthusiasm. When it came to promoting the Boynton Bicycle Railroad, no press agent was necessary.

Boynton predicted that investors would come away with a company net profit of $80 million to $100 million annually at the start. He added that the railroads themselves would save $400 million a year, even after paying for Boynton's patents.

These projections were based on unusually low construction costs—$7,000 a mile for his heavier model and as little as $3,500 for the economy version. He told New Yorkers that their Sixth and Ninth Avenue elevated lines could be converted to his Boynton Bicycle system for $1 million and not a penny more.

"He said he would carry passengers to their destinations in New York at 100 miles an hour," said Harrington. "And he would go further. He would spin his lacy lines across the Hudson and the East River—for great iron bridges for support were unnecessary to the light Boynton Bicycles."

New York transit experts were fascinated by this inventor and his projections. What was especially appealing to economy-minded rail men was the idea that every single track line would become double track, and double-track lines would become four-track lines. "With the Boynton bicycle locomotives and passenger cars," he said, "the railroad trackage of the nation will be immediately doubled."

Skeptics warned that any vehicle that traveled more than 100 mph inevitably had to be a health hazard. But Boynton would have none of that. "My trains will be healthier than the conventional ones," he countered. "Ventilation will be considerably improved."

What's more, there would be less pollution. His lightweight cars could be pushed by the average human. A pair of strong men, he ventured, could push a Boynton "palace coach" as fast as they could walk. Imagine what could be done with a ton of coal. That is, in the countryside. For New York City use, Boynton promised—far ahead of his time—to design electric motors to move his bicycle coaches. For the moment, however, he would utilize steam to power his twenty-two ton locomotive.

A train designed to cruise at 100 mph was appealing but engineers questioned what would happen at a curve at such speeds. Boynton replied: "My train will be safer at 100 miles per hour than an ordinary train at 20 miles per hour." His hedge against tipping, of course, was the overhead rail, which would prove its worth during the premiere exhibition. The train won't tip, promised Boynton, and collisions are impossible because each train will operate on its own track.

Since Boynton had an interest in concessions in both the Coney Island and Sea Beach sections of Brooklyn, it was natural for him to gravitate toward that area when he searched for a testing ground. "His prospectus," said one near investor, "had the sound of a Coney Island barker." Those who knew Boynton well contend that his unbridled enthusiasm was his most persistent problem. Boynton thought too big. Instead of developing his Bicycle Railroad in New York City and then expanding, he thought on a worldwide basis from the very start and was convinced that he had conquered the world's railroading problems in one swoop.

His first report to his stockholders in 1887 reflected an *élan* shared by few others when it came to the future of the Bicycle Railroad:

"It will open up inaccessible continents like Africa....

"With its exceedingly narrow and light trains following a single thread of steel, bracketed to the cliffs and gorges of mountains, it will open up hitherto inaccessible regions, saving a million dollars per mile in the tunneling of mountains."

When Boynton went so far as to suggest

that passengers in his two-story coaches would be able to cross the continent from New York to San Francisco in twenty-four hours, investors thought that was a bit much! The time had come, they said, to see the Bicycle Railroad in action.

Boynton was ready. His locomotive and passenger car were built, and track was laid across a meadow in Coney Island. All he had to do was demonstrate that it worked.

He decided to use a half-mile testing ground for the big day at Coney. A crowd of more than 5,000, including 100 engineers, crossed Brooklyn for the event.

Boynton was ready, and so was his contraption. With a huff and a puff it was underway, moving smartly up to a speed of sixty mph. But that was as fast as it could go, not because it lacked the power, but because it had run out of track.

The reviews were immediately available and, at first, were glowing. "It ran," said one observer, "with incredible smoothness. It was extremely stable. The overhead rail seemed hardly necessary, even on banked turns."

More important, however, were the impressions—and, later, decisions—of professional engineers from New York City's rapid transit lines. One group of onlookers represented the Manhattan Elevated Railway (MER). They not only watched in awe, but later took a ride and commended Boynton for the silk-smooth ride.

Much as they applauded the project, however, the MER officials were not prepared to scrap their elevated lines for the Boynton Bicycle Railroad.

Typically, Boynton was looking ahead to still another project and virtually ignored the MER snub, since he was busy trying to persuade farmers that they should have a private railroad to bring their produce to market.

"Investors," said historian Harrington, "were repelled rather than attracted by Boynton's ballyhoo. They believed that his dream was impossible to realistically achieve." Those investors who did give

Boynton capital soon discovered that it was going no further than the half-mile strip of railroad in Coney Island. "But," said Harrington, "Boynton lost the most, and, in the end, there never was any question of his utter honesty."

Eventually the Boynton Bicycle Railroad crashed in the bankruptcy court. Boynton went to Boston, hopeful of persuading the Massachusetts Legislature to provide citizens with perfect, 100-mph train service at a low price. But Boynton kept running into resistance until his death in March 1927.

Monorails—using basic principles of the bicycle—are in use today in Germany, Japan, and even in America's Disneyland and Seattle, Washington. They all suggest that Boynton's ideas were sound.

"There are railroad historians," concluded Joe Harrington, "who have a suspicion that Boynton's chief trouble was that he was born a century too soon!"

(top) *Looking north from Rector St. station on the Ninth Avenue El. The tower in the distance controls the intricate trackwork used as a turnback for express trains not going to South Ferry. The interlocking is made more complex as a carry-over from the steam-hauled days when it was necessary for the engines to run around the train.*

(bottom) *The Ninth Avenue El station at 155th St. next to the Polo Grounds, baseball home of the National League's New York Giants, located at the far left. This 1935 view shows the bridge over the Harlem River, built in 1881, that carried the steam-hauled trains of the Putnam Division to connect with the El. After the Ninth Avenue El was torn down the bridge still carried subway trains from the Woodlawn-Jerome Avenue Line to the Polo Grounds. This lasted until 1958 when the Giants left Manhattan for San Francisco.*

The Ninth Avenue El hauled more than passengers. Here it is during the West Side subway construction north of Rector Street. The structure standing on the El was a hoist to bring dirt up from the subway and load it on dump cars to be carried away.

A Second or Third Avenue El train at the South Ferry Terminal in June 1914. The electric El cars made over from steam coaches had not yet had their ends enclosed and sliding doors affixed.

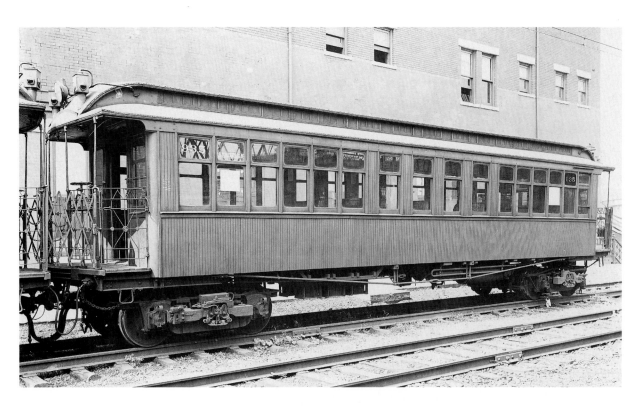

(previous page, top) *A typical steam era coach converted to electric operation.*

(previous page, bottom) *Sands Street Terminal in Brooklyn where the Fulton Street and Myrtle Avenue Lines converged to roll over the Brooklyn Bridge. Trolleys also used this station to gain bridge entrance. It was torn down during World War II.*

(this page, top) *The Fulton Ferry station nestled next to the Brooklyn anchorage of the Brooklyn Bridge. The picture was taken in 1940 shortly before its closure.*

The Tompkins Avenue station of the Fulton Street El in 1914 prior to its widening to three tracks.

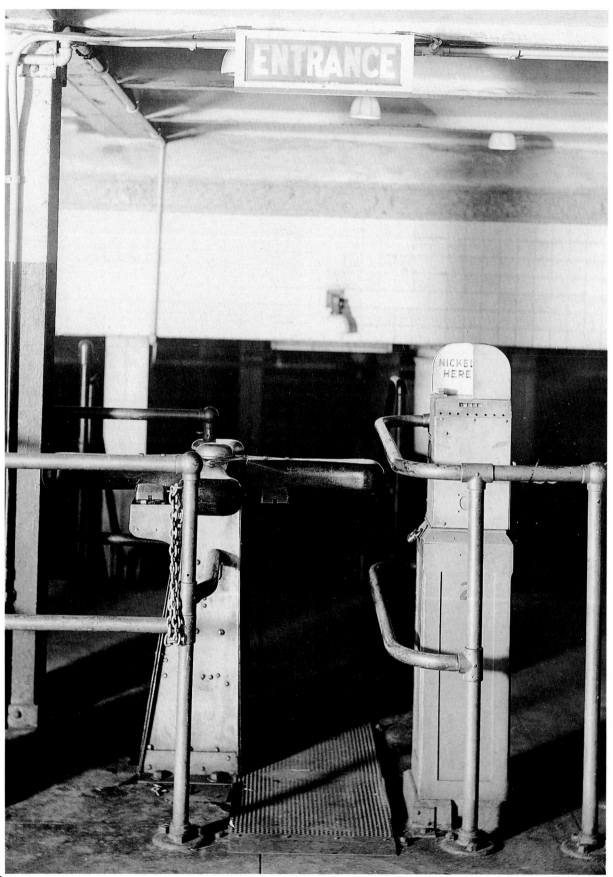

BUILDING THE GREATEST RAILROAD

Planning the First Subway

Without a doubt the elevated railroads were a smash hit in both Manhattan and Brooklyn late in the nineteenth century. With each year an older line was extended and a new route planned; there seemed to be no end in sight as long as there remained vast areas of undeveloped land in Brooklyn, Manhattan, the Bronx, and, eventually, parts of Queens. But there remained a vocal and significant bloc of el critics who carped about its obvious defects. It was loud, smelly and sometimes a detriment to the neighborhoods over which it thundered.

The earliest elevated lines employed four-wheel steam dummy locomotives to haul the passenger cars but the tiny engines were inadequate in terms of power and economy. An improved locomotive, designed by Pennsylvania inventor Matthias Forney, proved infinitely more effective. The Forney model had a small double-end tank engine with a swiveled truck under the tank. Unlike its predecessors, the Forney locomotive could haul seven cars and easily maintain a twelve-mph schedule, including stops.

All the el companies in Manhattan and Brooklyn bought Forney engines and by the early 1890s there were more than 500 in elevated railway service. But even the marvelous little Forney had its drawbacks. It relentlessly spewed smoke and cinders from its smokestack to the ground below, frightening horses, enraging merchants and inspiring city planners and inventors to come up with something better in the way of transit motive power.

The answer was supplied by two electrical inventors, Frank J. Sprague and Leo Daft, both of whom realized that the most practical method of moving the el cars was by electricity. Daft's offering was a nine-ton electric locomotive called *Benjamin Franklin*. In 1885 he ran it on the Ninth Avenue Line of the Manhattan Railway Company. The *Franklin* hauled four cars and accelerated to a speed of twenty five mph. That same year Sprague produced blueprints for the electric operation of the Manhattan El. Like Daft, Sprague developed an experimental car and won the attention of Jay Gould, one of the principal owners of the line.

Sprague persuaded Gould to allow him to run an electric car on the Manhattan Railway and even convinced the renowned financier to take a ride with him. That was Sprague's first mistake. His second was impetuosity. Having lured Gould into the experimental car, Sprague enthusiastically pulled hard on the controller to set the train in motion. But he yanked too abruptly and blew a fuse that sounded to Gould like a bomb exploding. "Gould was so startled by the report," wrote rail historian William D. Middleton, "that he had to be restrained from jumping off the car. After this unnerving experience the financier abandoned all interest in electric traction."

Rebuffed by el interests, Sprague turned his attention to street railways. He originally began with battery-operated cars, but then the Sprague Electric Railway & Motor Company reverted to pure electrification of surface transit. He obtained contracts to work on overhead power systems in Richmond, Virginia, and St. Joseph, Missouri. In 1888 he successfully electrified the Richmond trolleys, proving to the world that it was possible to electrify surface lines. Next in line were the els.

Early electrification experiments on the elevated trains concentrated on development of an electric locomotive which would be capable of pulling a string of as many as eight cars. This system had its drawbacks, especially since some highly successful lines considered use of as many as ten passenger cars on a single run and the electric locomotives of the time simply were not adequate for the job.

Sprague, who had since become involved with elevator experiments, was busy with an installation at the New York Postal Telegraph Building, where he invented a system by which a single master switch could regulate the movement of any elevator in the building or the movement of all of them at once. When the elevator experiment proved successful, Sprague decided to apply the same principles to elevated trains. His theory was that if an entire system of elevators could be operated by one master switch, then an entire train of electrified cars could be operated by a main controller. Each elevated car would have a controller and an electric motor but the "multiple-unit system" would be operated from the motorman's cabin in the first car.

By this time Sprague's transit firm had been bought out by burgeoning General Electric, but his ties to GE remained solid. On July 16, 1897 two of Sprague's experimental multiple-unit cars were tested by GE engineers at the company's Schenectady, New York, plant. Before the month was up an entire six-car train was successfully operated and by the end of the year a test train of five cars was running on the Chicago elevated system.

The multiple-unit train worked so well on Chicago's South Side Elevated that in 1898 Brooklyn's steam-operated els began converting to electricity and by 1903 all of New York City's els had disposed of their Forneys and re-equipped with Spragues. More important, those who had dismissed the idea of underground trains in Manhattan because of the hazards of smoke and steam now began a reappraisal, and by the turn of the century it had become apparent that New York not only needed but would build the greatest railroad in the world—most of it underground!

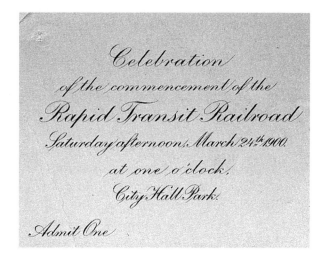

Celebration
of the commencement of the
Rapid Transit Railroad
Saturday afternoon, March 24th 1900,
at one o'clock,
City Hall Park.

Admit One

Constructing the IRT

While New York City's plans for underground rapid transit remained stalled throughout the latter half of the nineteenth century, other metropoli were developing subways with relative ease. London began the world's first subway in 1863. Another followed in Glasgow in 1886; Budapest, Hungary, unveiled a little underground railway system in 1896; and one year later North America's first subway, the West End Railway, began operating under Tremont Street in Boston, using trolley cars. The Paris *Métro* made its debut in 1900, whereupon Boston also displayed the first genuine—as opposed to trolley-operated—rapid transit subway in America when the Boston Elevated Railway began operation on el tracks and in subway tubes on June 10, 1901. Finally, the Berliners inaugurated their underground in 1902.

Meanwhile, New Yorkers had endured more than thirty years of subway talk, but no

action, when financier August Belmont and Mayor Robert A. Van Wyck broke ground in March 1900 at Borough Hall, Manhattan. New York's first subway would comprise nearly thirteen miles of underground line and more than three miles of el extensions between Manhattan and the Bronx.

The general plan called for the subway to tunnel northward from City Hall, then up the east side of the island to Grand Central Terminal. It would then turn left and proceed westerly under 42nd Street to Times Square, and then turn right and proceed north again under Broadway to a terminus at Bailey Avenue in the Bronx. The length of the route, of which about two miles would be outdoors on viaducts, was thirteen and one-half miles.

To build the subway, Belmont's planners had two options: they could copy the techniques used by London's *Underground* in which deep tubes were bored by shield method far below the streets, or they could try Budapest's trench method. Instead of sinking a pit and then driving a bore laterally, as did London and Glasgow engineers, the Hungarians simply cut a huge trench along

Looking south from 33rd. St. down Fourth Avenue (Park Avenue South) we see construction of the first subway proceeding on the right. The tracks in the center belong to the trolley line which negotiated the tunnel north to Grand Central Depot. The horsedrawn cars of the New York & Harlem once rode these rails. The building on the left is a carbarn, the site later of the 33rd St. Armory.

This is Broadway and 50th Street in December 1901. The cut and cover method is being used by builders of the first subway. The cut is wide here to accommodate the waiting area of the 50th Street station to be built at this location. The Sixth Avenue El station at 50th Street looms in the background.

the route of their subway, built their railroad at the bottom, roofed it with steel girders, and used a few feet of fill and paving on top of the roof. This "cut-and-cover" method was eventually to be universally employed in subway construction. It was infinitely cheaper, easier, and faster than driving a tunnel by the shield method.

While they were borrowing ideas from the Hungarians, American engineers also adopted the Budapest station plan. Unlike the English, the Hungarians did not build surface structures that resembled railroad terminals. Instead they borrowed a design from the gardens of ancient Persia and Turkey, where oddly shaped summerhouses called *kushks* abounded. New York subway engineers Americanized the *kushk* to kiosk, and thus it happened that the first subway under City Hall had strangely ornamental mosque-like roofs, although New Yorkers constructed the buildings of steel and glass instead of stone and tile. The kiosks also were believed to be functional. It was foreseen in 1900, when they were planned, that in a heavy rainstorm, without such protection, rain would pour in through an opening and platforms would become sloppy.

The Hungarian cut-and-cover method may have been cheap in dollars but New Yorkers quickly discovered that it was expensive in terms of public opinion. As hundreds of sandhogs ripped the guts out of Broadway, Fourth Avenue, and 42nd Street, business fell flat, storekeepers wailed, and the man-in-the-street wondered when the din would end.

Underground, the men with the digging machines wondered when the variation in earth formations would end. Between 14th and 18th Streets, for example, the underground rock protruded almost to the pavement. In other places, work gangs encountered water-bearing loam and sand. At Pearl and Grand streets, this problem was solved by employing a special supporting base for the subway. Confounding the engineers was the labyrinth of sewers, water and gas mains, steam pipes, pneumatic tubes, and electrical conduits. Then there were the elevated railway columns that had to be shored up while underground construction took place. At Columbus Circle, near the entrance to Central Park, great care had to be taken to prevent the undermining of the

(**previous page, bottom**) *This is the kiosk for the City Hall Station in 1949 several years after its closure. The building in the background is City Hall.*

(**above**) *Columbus Circle is being evacuated for subway construction in June 1901. Notice the temporary track on the right used to keep trolley service operating.*

Columbus Monument, which reached seventy five feet above street level and weighed 700 tons.

At 110th Street and Lenox Avenue, along the northern border of Central Park, engineers encountered a six-and-a-half-foot circular brick sewer. They had a choice of either removing the sewer completely or subdividing it. They opted for subdivision, and three 42-inch cast-iron pipes were passed under the subway.

In a number of sections of line the road was built in rock tunnel lined with concrete. All of this was executed by construction crews working an eight-hour night shift. Blasting took place early in the morning, with the day gang removing the rubble. All debris was dispatched to the surface in mule-driven cars.

Ironically, some of the most interesting construction took place above ground. Planners had decided that the subway would emerge from its tunnel at Broadway and 120th Street in Morningside Heights, adjoining Columbia University. It then would climb over Manhattan Valley (125th Street), and then reenter the tunnel under Broadway once more at 135th Street. To span Manhattan Valley, engineers blueprinted a 2,174-foot viaduct that, to this day, is one of the most impressive elevated structures on the system. The span features a two-hinged arch of 168.5 feet. The 125th Street stop is one of the more important stations on the IRT Broadway #1 and #9 lines.

For two years officials, sandhogs, and sidewalk superintendents managed to avoid what they feared most—an underground explosion. The potential for a sandpick ringing against a stone and igniting escaped gas from a leaky main remained a threat throughout the project.

On January 27, 1902 the threat became a

Contractor's bridges supporting the trolley line at 67th Street and Broadway in February 1902. The classic Ansonia Hotel is visible in the background, center.

New IRT subway cars (composites) line the southbound track at 123rd Street and Broadway. That's where the first subway emerged from the nether world to vault across Manhattan Valley. The rolling stock awaits the imminent opening of New York's first subway.

reality, but hardly because of the hazards most feared. Stupidity is the only explanation for powderman Moses Epps lighting a candle just a few feet from 548 pounds of dynamite, just so that he could warm his hands!

The incident took place in an IRT storage shed over the subway cut at 41st Street and Park Avenue, near Grand Central Terminal. After lighting the candle, Epps walked out of the shed for a breather. It was the worst move of his life. In the moments he was gone, Epps's candle had fallen to the floor and set his lunch wrapper ablaze. Thinking he had time to douse the fire, Epps grabbed a bucket of water and poured it on the flames. More water was needed, so the powderman dashed for a refill. Suddenly he wheeled in his tracks to be sure he had time for a second dousing.

He didn't. The fire had reached the dynamite and Epps ran from the shanty.

Epps screamed to passersby to run for their lives. In less than a minute, one of the loudest reports ever to be heard in New York City reverberated up and down 41st Street as if several bombs had been dropped in the Midtown area. Actually, the effect was as bad, if not worse, than a bombing, for in this case the pedestrians and guests at the nearby Murray Hill Hotel were taken completely unaware and had no opportunity to protect themselves. Those eating lunch in the hotel's restaurant were hurled about, crushed by debris and wounded by flying glass. When the dust had cleared, five people were dead and more than 180 injured.

The explosion shook down the plaster at the

The still incomplete Manhattan Valley Station (125th Street) in November 1903. The platforms have not yet been finished and the third rails yet to be installed. This view is directly opposite the one in the previous photo.

hotel and broke all windows in surrounding homes. Even the clocks in the Grand Central Station tower were blown in, while the Manhattan Eye and Ear Hospital had to close its doors to the wounded because of damage to its facility. Ironically, Epps suffered only bruises and the IRT-in-the making endured the blast with no serious damage at all. However, the blast propelled Mayor Seth Low into action and he immediately appointed a Municipal Explosives Commission, which revised the city regulations governing the storage and use of high explosives in the city limits.

Before the winter was over, the embryonic IRT had suffered another trauma just three blocks from the powderhouse disaster. This time a rock slide occurred in the deep tunnel under Park Avenue, between 37th and 38th Streets. Fortunately no lives were lost, but the

accident delayed construction, as did sporadic labor strikes throughout the contract.

No further mishaps marred work in the Midtown area, but a calamitous event took place in October 1903 at the northern sector. To complete tunneling at 195th Street and St. Nicholas Avenue, workmen had to drill through solid rock sixty feet below street level. The tunnel, which was 50 feet wide and 15 feet high, was pushed forward by workmen who planted sticks of dynamite, cleared the area for the blast, and then returned after the explosion was complete to remove debris and prepare for another move forward.

Dynamiting at 195th Street was under the direction of foreman Timothy Sullivan, who committed as monumental a mistake as Moses Epps had earlier. Sullivan planted the dynamite, cleared the tunnel, okayed the detonation, and then listened for the explosion. The foreman heard the same rumbling noise he had experienced so many times before: the sound of exploding dynamite. As if by reflex, he hustled his men back into the tunnel, all thirty of them, with Sullivan in the lead.

But the foreman had moved too fast. As soon as Sullivan and his sandhogs reached the dynamite site, they were greeted with three resounding reports as previously undetonated TNT went off in their faces. Before Sullivan could make a move, the tunnel roof caved in on him. The foreman and nine of his men died in the blasts, while many others were seriously injured. In *The World Beneath the City,*" Robert Daley detailed the horror of that moment:

"For some, pinned under a boulder estimated to weigh 200 tons, the agony was protracted. Three men hung head downward while rescuers attacked with drills the rock which crushed the lower part of their bodies. A fourth man was caught by the leg. Frantic efforts to pry up a corner of the boulder and free him failed. At last, a doctor amputated the leg. He was rushed to a hospital, but died en route."

Despite such disasters, the 10,000 men who excavated 3,508,000 cubic yards of earth had completed 90 percent of the work by the end of 1903. It was now clear that the subway would be open for business by the end of 1904, so the builders turned their attention to an area that had been considered vital from the start: attractive and practical rolling stock.

Safety was a persistent consideration, and because of this the IRT directors seriously considered all-steel cars, which then were a rarity. In fact, they placed an order for 500 all-steel cars, but were told that it would be impossible to produce so many of a new design in the time allowed. The compromise model was a car constructed of a wooden frame on a steel bottom, with sides sheathed with copper and the electric machinery encased in fireproof material. The car was fifty-one feet long, four feet longer than cars on the Manhattan Elevated Railroad, with a seating capacity for 52 passengers. When the first cars were completed in the winter of 1903-4, they were tested on the Second Avenue El and found to be satisfactory, but the IRT moguls continued to push plans for an all-steel car and eventually ordered 200 of the more-advanced design. Meanwhile, construction of the line from City Hall to 145th Street and Broadway was nearly finished.

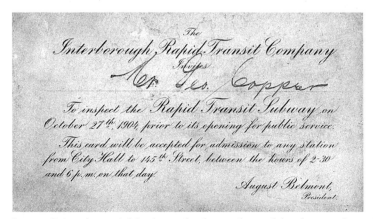

Mr. George Cooper's special invite to the dress rehearsal for the grand opening.

"Fifteen Minutes to Harlem"

The promise of IRT dreamers was unprecedented. They vowed that the new subway would whisk passengers from City Hall in the southern portion of Manhattan Island to 145th Street on the northern tier, in less than a half hour. Before the first flaming Tuscan red subway train rolled under Park Avenue, the slogan "Fifteen Minutes to Harlem" was heard throughout the city. Some thought it was the boast of overzealous subway promoters. To others, especially August Belmont, it was a feat that could be accomplished by his Interborough Rapid Transit Company. Belmont and his colleagues would get the answer on a snappy fall day in 1904 when the green light was flashed for New York's first major subway.

The date was October 27, 1904, a day that rarely has been equaled in the city's long history of major celebrations. Only Armistice Day, V-E Day, V-J Day, the Rangers' 1994 Stanley Cup victory celebration and the return of Charles Lindbergh after his solo flight across the Atlantic produced as enthusiastic an explosion of public joy. From the Atlantic Ocean, where foghorns sounded all day, to St. Patrick's Cathedral, which tolled its bells, the town roared its approval, even before the first train left City Hall station.

The official opening was actually launched in the Aldermanic Chamber at City Hall, where a series of speeches and benedictions was delivered by Mayor George McClellan, various politicians, and the city's highest churchmen. Financier Belmont and builder John B. McDonald looked on impatiently as the ceremony droned on. Finally, Archbishop Farley delivered a closing benediction, and

Mayor McClellan punctuated the fete with a simple declaration:

"Now I, as mayor, in the name of the people, declare the subway open." Belmont handed the mayor a mahogany case which held the crown jewel of the new IRT—an ornamented, silver controller. Belmont then intoned: "I give you this controller, Mr. Mayor, with the request that you put in operation this great road, and start it on its course of success and, I hope, of safety."

Mayor McClellan gave the officials some nervous moments, however. Instead of simply taking the controller and posing for a few dozen ceremonial photos, McClellan took Belmont literally and began operating the city's first eight-car train as if he intended to be a motorman instead of the mayor. He pulled the train out of City Hall station, while IRT general manager Frank Hedley nervously looked over his shoulder. The trains were built to run thirty miles an hour and McClellan seemed quite willing to make the most of the new motors. At Bleecker Street station, where there was already a "Subway Tavern," opened ten weeks earlier in anticipation of the great event, patrons were at the subway entrance, cheering lustily as the McClellan-operated train rolled by.

When Hedley suggested that perhaps the mayor was ready to allow an IRT professional to take over the controls, McClellan, son of a Civil War general, snapped: "I'm running this train!" And run it he did, to Broadway and 103rd Street where he finally surrendered the controller. The trailblazer continued on to its temporary terminus at 145th Street, making the run in twenty-six minutes; not quite as good as the slogan but nearly on time.

Once the mayoral special had run uptown and back to City Hall, the IRT offered free rides to several thousand invited guests until 6 P.M. when the line closed down for a special inspection of its 9.1 miles by Chief Engineer William Barclay Parsons. Exactly one hour

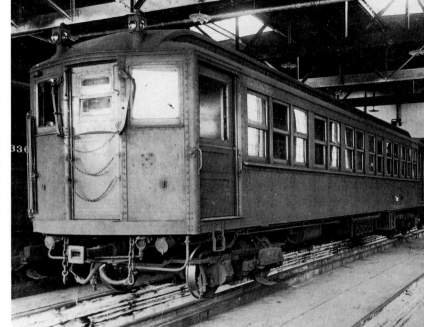

The First all-steel subway cars, Gibbs-style, were equipped with Van Dorn couplers. A center door eventually would be added and a fish-belly underframe installed to stiffen the body.

Three composite-type (steel-wood) cars with the center-door and fish-belly underframe added are operating on the Third Avenue El commemorating the first 25 years since the subway opened. These cars were the first to operate after power was turned on the subway's third rails. Frank Hedley operated the car in the foreground while August Belmont handled the one at the rear.

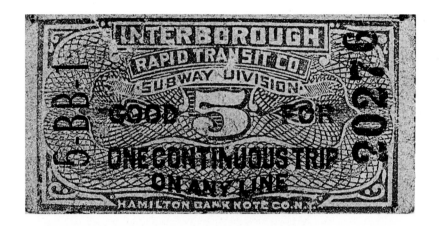

later, Parsons gave the signal and the IRT opened to revenue passengers at five cents a ride.

The response was overwhelming. On opening night, more than 150,000 people "tried" the subway. At the 145th Street terminal police used nightsticks to disperse the throng trying to enter. At times the crowds became threatening to life and limb. One young woman suffered a broken leg when she was pushed into the space between the subway car and the platform.

On Friday, October 29, the IRT opened for its first full day of operation and, once again, teeming hordes turned out for the new underground railway. Newspaper headlines told the story: RUSH-HOUR BLOCKADE JAMS SUBWAY.

Inspectors from the Board of Health who toured the first IRT tube in August Belmont's private car, *Mineola*, rated the underground air "excellent." However, their judgment may have been somewhat influenced by Belmont's

two stewards, who served them from a broiler and grill and popped bottles of champagne as the train click-clacked through the "excellent" subway ozone.

Belmont's instinctive knack for selecting the best, be it in wines, station ornamentation, or private rolling stock, also was reflected in his choice of high-level railroad men. For general manager Belmont hired Frank Hedley, whose great-granduncle had helped build the first steam locomotive in England near Newcastle-on-Tyne in 1813. Hedley's father was a master mechanic for the London and South-Western Railway during Queen Victoria's time, and Frank himself was a skilled machinist. "Any fool could be president of a railroad company," quipped Hedley, "but the general manager has to know something!"

Almost immediately after taking command of the IRT, Hedley launched a series of innovations on the city's underground railroad. One of these was a "recorder-coaster," which encouraged his motormen to coast when possible to cut costs. The dynamic general manager also introduced multiple doors in each car to alleviate crowding. A progressive Hedley safety advance was new coupling mechanisms to reduce the danger of telescoping trains in a collision. When it appeared that the IRT was being cheated by its own collectors, he introduced the nickel-in-the-slot turnstile.

The City Hall Station under construction.

The City Hall Station as it appeared in its first few years of service. Notice the antique vending machine and the liquor ad propped up against the wall, a practice abandoned early in IRT history.

The IRT directors acknowledged Hedley's genius by continually raising his salary until the late 1920s when he was earning $75,000 a year. Only the Transit Commission, which was controlled by the state, had jurisdiction over him. Yet, throughout his reign, Hedley cried poverty on behalf of his company and endlessly campaigned, with no luck at all, for a fare raise as the solution to the city's subway problems.

Once, when Hedley was assailed by city officials because his cars were so dirty, the general manager insisted that he could not afford to clean them as long as the fare held at five cents. "I saw a car with clean windows today," he said, "and when I got back to the office I raised hell to find out who spent all the money." Hedley was openly contemptuous of the politicians' practice of calling a conference or appointing commissions to get all the facts. "I will study the situation," the general manager was fond of saying, "and then do as I please."

But nobody seemed terribly concerned about Frank Hedley nor any of his fiscal idiosyncrasies in those first days of the IRT's operation. New Yorkers found the underground railway as thrilling as a Coney Island roller coaster.

The public enthusiasm seemed to take the IRT directors by surprise. "Nobody knows how many people are going to patronize the road," said Hedley. "But we shall be prepared to increase the number of trains to suit the demand. If it is necessary, we'll run them on a one-minute headway."

At the time, Hedley's eight-car express trains ran on five-minute headways from 6:30 to 7 A.M., four-minute headways from 7 to 9:30 A.M., and at five-to ten-minute intervals during midday. In the evening rush, it was four-minute headways again, with trains running five and six minutes apart until midnight. The five-car locals ran at three-minute headways the entire day, starting at 5:30 A.M. and at five- to ten-minute intervals after midnight.

The IRT's new construction kept pace with public demand for additional lines. Other parts of the first subway were opened for business as follows: Broadway, 145th to 157th Streets, November 5, 1904; Lenox Avenue branch in Manhattan, Broadway and 96th Street to 145th Street, November 20, 1904; and from 149th Street and Third Avenue along Westchester Avenue and Boston Road in the Bronx, to the terminus at 180th Street, November 26, 1904. The intervening link from 145th Street under the Harlem River to Westchester Avenue was opened later, and the remainder of the Broadway line, at 157th Street to Kingsbridge, in March 1906.

The IRT had earlier heeded the demand by Brooklynites to extend the subway under the East River and into Kings County, linking the Battery in Manhattan with Joralemon Street in Brooklyn Heights, overlooking New York Bay. In 1905, when the Interborough tunnel was being constructed, underwater tunneling lacked the sophistication of later years, and tragedy often lurked behind the next shield.

Serious underwater tunneling for passenger trains dates back to September 1879, when DeWitt Clinton Haskin's Hudson Tunnel Railroad Company began digging a hoped-for tube for trans-Hudson passenger service. The Haskin firm carved 1,200 feet under the huge river and lined the tunnel with brick at the New Jersey shore. But the caisson technique, then employed, caused a "blowout" on July 21, 1880, and twenty lives were lost.

"As with many tragedies," wrote rail historian Brian J. Cudahy in *Rails under the Mighty Hudson*, "this one produced heroism. When men in the airlock realized a blowout was imminent, they started for the pressurized door leading back to safety. Several were through when one Peter Woodland realized the loss of pressure in the tube was about to doom all, even those en route to safety. He closed the door, thereby sealing his own doom and that of the 19 others in the airlock with him, but insuring safety for the men already on the way out. His action is memorialized on his tombstone in New York Bay Cemetery in Jersey City, and the incident itself later formed the basis for a famous story by Theodore Dreiser entitled St. Columba and the River."

The Haskin tunnel soon was abandoned, but a British-backed firm resumed the project in 1888, and bored another 1,600 feet toward Manhattan. The new contractor, S. Pearson and Sons, used cast-iron rings instead of bricks and mortar to line the tunnel. In addition, Pearson brought along a major innovation, the Greathead shield, developed by a South African-born British engineer named Sir James Henry Greathead. The shield originally was invented for construction of London's 1880 Tower subway. Pearson erected Greathead shields at the forward positions of each tunnel to reduce the risk of pressure failure in the tubes and speed construction. But money problems applied the brakes until 1901 when William Gibbs McAdoo organized the Hudson and Manhattan (H & M) Railroad. McAdoo's engineer, Charles M. Jacobs, found that the Greathead shields were still in good shape and could be used for the new venture.

Interestingly, work on the H & M tunnel between Manhattan and Jersey City, and construction of the IRT tunnel between Manhattan and Brooklyn, proceeded simultaneously in a race to become the first to launch regular passenger service through a major underwater tunnel in the New York metropolitan area. Belmont's IRT won the race by a month in January 1908. But the IRT's victory was not achieved without mishap.

In 1905, when the Battery-Joralemon Street tunnel had reached the middle of the East River, a blowout developed in the tunnel roof. As the compressed air began escaping a well-disciplined sandhog named Dick Creedon did what he was supposed to do; he snatched one of many available sandbags and rushed to the weak spot, hoping to plug the leak with the sandbag. But Creedon lost his race against time: he was sucked up into the vortex— sandbag still in hand— through thirty feet of riverbed and, finally, up through the East River. The sandhog was alive and swimming when a tugboat arrived to haul him to safety. As for the hole in the IRT tunnel, it was plugged after scows delivered tons of sand to the leak location and then simply dumped them over the tunnel, where the break soon was repaired.

Another, and this time tragic, IRT accident occurred two years later when four workers were killed in a freak fire that caused a cave-in. The construction men were buried, but still alive and apparently capable of rescue, since their ventilating column had not been obstructed. Firemen arrived too late to douse the blaze before it spread to a load of rubber, and the men were asphyxiated by the poison fumes.

Several unsung heroes emerged from these underwater jobs. Once a fire broke out deep in the Joralemon Street tube. A one-armed foreman, "Wingy" Hawkins, hurried to the scene and carried out the dynamite, just seconds before it seemed likely to be set off by the heat or by the change in pressure.

IRT promoters were acutely aware that the public might fear suffocation in the depths of their tunnels. To allay these fears, the subway barons launched a propaganda campaign, distributing timetables which boasted in huge letters: SUBWAY AIR AS PURE AS YOUR OWN HOME. This was followed by more propaganda in the form of an impartial study conducted by Columbia University professor C. F. Chandler, supporting the theory that the air underground was as healthy as surface air.

In fact, the public would not be conned. IRT engineers, determined to waterproof the tunnels, had coated them with asphalt, which prevented any possibility of proper ventilation in hot summer months. Throughout the summer of 1905, complaints about excessive heat and poor air quality poured into the IRT offices. The city's Rapid Transit Commission retained Professor George A. Soper of Columbia University to study the air conditions. Soper reported that, while air in the subway was hotter than air in the streets in summer, it was not deleterious to health and would not have any bad effects if proper sanitary precautions were taken to keep the subway free of dust and odors.

Nevertheless, IRT engineers built fourteen ventilating chambers between Brooklyn Bridge and 59th Street to allow stale air to escape and fresh air to enter the tunnels. In addition, an experimental cooling plant was installed in the Brooklyn Bridge station. Two artesian wells were sunk, and the water from them pumped into a series of pipes installed on each side of the station. Air was pumped through the pipes in counter-current to the water becoming cooled in the passage and then delivered to the station via ducts.

The ventilating improvements all worked; and so did the IRT. Critics then and now agree that it was an engineering masterpiece. "There seems little doubt," said William H. Rudy of the *New York Post* in 1970, "that, for the times, the first IRT was well-built and well-equipped. Robert Ridgway, later chief engineer of the entire system, always thought this was due in great part to the terms: the contractor had to maintain and operate the subway for 50 years."

There were complaints about the original IRT, to be sure— inadequate service was a perennial beef—but, by and large, the city's new subway had scored a big hit on and off Broadway. Socialites thought nothing of donning their finest furs and taking the subway to the theater. When they entered a station, they discovered that colored tiles decorated the walls. Pottery, faience, and marble were used everywhere and, in some stations, glass roofs invited even more light.

But no one added more class and sophistication to the New York underground than the IRT's number one angel, August Belmont himself. One of the wealthiest New Yorkers of his time, Belmont was not the type of person to invest in the subway and then keep it at arm's length. Whenever possible, Belmont rode his rails and did it in a style that has never been equaled.

Belmont commissioned the Wason Manufacturing Company of Brightwood, Massachusetts, to build him a very special director's car. Wason obliged—at a cost of

The rather aged interior of Belmont's private car "Mineola" as it looked on arrival at the Branford Trolley Museum. This is the end facing the office and kitchen with the dining area in the foreground. A team led by Nate Gerstein is currently raising funds to restore this unique piece of rolling stock for the subway centennial in 1904.

(above left) *The parlor and observation end of the car.*

(Middle left) *For many years between its removal from subway property until its saving by the Shore Line Trolley Museum the "Mineola," sans trucks, resided on the farm of Joseph Gioscia in Flemington, New Jersey.*

(lower left) *The kitchen with coffee-maker and electric grill.*

$11,429.40—and in August 1904 the magnificent piece of rolling stock, dubbed the *Mineola*, made its debut.

The car's appointments included natural mahogany inlay, cut glass vases, individual pads on windowposts for smokers to scratch their matches, an arched Empire ceiling tinted pistachio green, brass trim, and its own motor and motorman. Belmont had special plate glass fitted to the front and rear ends for easier observation and had twelve special leather chairs built in.

Belmont built the Belmont Hotel at 42nd Street and Park Avenue and saw to it that he had easy access to the Grand Central IRT station below. In the basement of the hotel

The author at what I believe to be the covered-over entrance August Belmont used to access his private car "Mineola." The private car was stored on a siding just north of the southbound platform at what is now the 42nd Street Shuttle's Grand Central Station stop. Notice the remains of a period roll-up door hanging from the top of the opening.

was a circular bar at subway track level. It was specifically designed to fit inside the radius of the subway curve. When the spirit moved him, Belmont would hail his subway car, exit through his private passageway, and take his wife and friends for a joy ride. "A private railroad car," wrote Mrs. Belmont, "is not an acquired taste. One takes to it immediately."

In fact, the entire city had taken the IRT to its heart and when visitors came to Manhattan, a trip on the IRT was a must. Even Tin Pan Alley acknowledged its importance in 1912 with a popular song, "The Subway Glide."

By then the IRT had snaked its way to Brooklyn under the East River, and the subway had proven so popular an item in Gotham that there was a clamor from Queens to the Bronx to build more. The public's demand was translated into the most phenomenal growth of any underground railway anywhere. From the 9.1-mile section opened in 1904 at a cost of about $35 million, the system expanded to 239.87 route miles with 726.18 miles of track.

The second, and most energetic, spurt produced a unique bit of rivalry—and teamwork—between the IRT and the Brooklyn Rapid Transit (BRT) Company. The result was what became known as "The Dual System," or "Dual Contracts."

One of the finest examples of subway rolling stock, #2002 was part of the first set of BRT "Standard" cars. It was delivered in 1914 and is positioned, just north of the 8th Street Station on the Sea Beach Line.

Enter the BMT

If the Interborough Rapid Transit (IRT) was the patrician of the New York subway system, the Brooklyn Manhattan Transit (BMT)—originally Brooklyn Rapid Transit—emerged as the playboy of the underground. It boasted the flashiest rolling stock ever seen in New York, including experimental lightweight cars called Bluebird, Green Hornet, and Zephyr. The BMT (when it was still the Brooklyn Rapid Transit) produced the first sixty-seven-foot-long, ten-foot-wide "Standard" car in 1914, setting the criteria for subway cars for decades in the future.

The line was attractive right down to the smallest detail, including its kiosk lamps which, unlike the IRT's round blue-and-white globes, were ornate fifty-pound hexagons, alternately covered with green and white glass and extremely well constructed.

Although the BRT made its initial run from Coney Island to Chambers Street on June 22, 1915, its lineage can be traced to a much earlier date when the city of Brooklyn—later to become one of New York's five boroughs—developed southward to the Atlantic Ocean. The original ancestor of the BMT was a steam line known as the Bath and Coney Island Railroad, which opened in 1864 and reached Coney Island in 1867.

Developers envisioned Brooklyn's resort-by-the-sea in the most romantic terms. It was suggested that someday it might become another Riviera or, at the very least, America's answer to Brighton, England. Instead, Coney Island developed a razzle-dazzle character all its own, and by the turn of the century its image as an amusement paradise for the lower and middle classes was firmly established.

The turn of the century also signaled the consolidation of Brooklyn's elevated lines under the banner of the Brooklyn Rapid Transit Company. Technically, the BRT was not an operator but, rather, a holding company organized to acquire the security of such earlier corporate acquisitions as the Brooklyn Union Elevated Railroad Company (1899), the Transit Development Company (which ran the BRT's yards and shops and controlled its rolling stock) and the Brooklyn Union Elevated Railroad Company (which operated the elevated trains).

Already mighty but desiring still more power, the BRT watched the development of the IRT with great interest when the city's first subway opened in 1904. The instant success of August Belmont's underground immediately inspired city fathers to propose a web of new routes throughout New York and in 1905 plans were developed for no less than nineteen lines.

The Board of Rapid Transit Railroad Commissioners was largely responsible for the widely acclaimed IRT, but it had been so wonderful a system that New Yorkers demanded to know why the board had not done more, and done it much faster. "Instead of being commended," wrote James Blaine Walker in *Fifty Years of Rapid Transit*, "they [the board) were condemned, not because they had not done well with the first subway, but because it was such a great success that they had not multiplied it fast enough. Because the old board had not ended the crush at the Brooklyn Bridge, because it had not built subways into Brooklyn and Queens and in other parts of Manhattan, it was denounced by the press which clamored for its abolition."

The press got its wish and in 1907 the board was dissolved and replaced by the New York State Public Service Commission (PSC) for the First District, which laid out blueprints for a vast subway system that would make the original IRT look like a mere dot on a map.

The Public Service Commission inherited four different rapid transit projects from the old board. One was a Brooklyn extension of the IRT and another was a Van Cortlandt Park extension of the same line. The others, eventually to become part of the BMT system, included a Fourth Avenue Subway in Brooklyn and a Centre Street (Manhattan) line. The PSC decided to push these projects to completion and simultaneously produce still more lines.

On December 31, 1907 the PSC approved a Broadway-Lexington Avenue route and a few months later decided that trains should run over the Williamsburg and Manhattan Bridges, spanning the East River, to Brooklyn. In 1908 and 1909 the PSC engineers prepared detailed plans for this system, which would add forty-five miles of new road and cost about $147 million. And still more blueprints were on the way, including lines for Queens, the Bronx, Brooklyn, and, of course, Manhattan.

The IRT, the Long Island Rail Road, the New York Central Railroad, and the Hudson & Manhattan tubes all wanted a piece of the new subway pie, but by 1910 the field had been narrowed down to the IRT. Then the BRT suddenly made an eleventh-hour bid. In its proposal, dated March 2, 1911, the BRT suggested that a new subway be built from the Battery at the southern tip of Manhattan up Church Street northward to Broadway and up Broadway to 42nd Street and thence up Seventh Avenue to 59th Street, with an extension easterly to a connection with the Queensborough Bridge.

The BRT didn't stop there. It offered a number of other suggestions, including the unexpected idea that a tunnel be built under New York Bay to connect the Fourth Avenue subway in Brooklyn with Staten Island, linking with the already operating Staten Island Railway. Surprising as the BRT's last-minute offer may have been, the PSC greeted it with the most serious deliberations. "Probably nothing like the Dual System conferences ever had been held in New York City before," said James Blaine Walker.

In their efforts to expand the subway system and earn a hefty profit for themselves, the transit barons fought with each other as well as with the distinguished members of the PSC. Once Theodore P. Shonts, president of the IRT, was asked if his company had conceded certain points to the city's representative. "I was fairly well-dressed when I went into that room," replied Shonts, "but they've taken away everything but my shirt, and they would have had that if we hadn't adjourned."

By 1911, within six months after the conferences began, an agreement was hammered out among the PSC, the IRT, and the BRT: the companies would split the proposed routes, as spelled out in what became known as "the Dual (IRT-BRT) Contracts." The contracts themselves were officially signed on March 19, 1913 and Brooklyn, which eventually led the city in subway trackage (87.8 miles), benefited the most. BRT (later BMT) lines snaked over the Manhattan and Williamsburg bridges to such distant points as Jamaica, Flatbush, Bensonhurst, and Borough Park. A tunnel was opened to Astoria, Queens, as the subway sprawl continued.

The four contracts involved were approved by the Board of Estimate and Apportionment on July 21, 1911, and on July 31 ground was broken at 62nd Street and Lexington Avenue.

As fast as the PSC engineers turned out the plans the commission awarded construction contracts for other sections of the work, on the understanding that the Brooklyn company was to be the operator. The Dual Contracts ultimately produced much of what became the vast BMT—or Division B— system, including the Brighton Beach, West End, Sea Beach, and Astoria lines. On June 22, 1915, one of the biggest outgrowths of the Dual Contracts was unveiled when service was launched from Coney Island to Chambers Street via the Fourth Avenue subway and the Manhattan Bridge.

Like its older subway sister, the IRT, the baby BRT suffered severe growing pains. During construction of the Whitehall Street (Manhattan)-Montague Street (Brooklyn) Tunnel in 1916 compressed air escaped from the tube just as it had during work on the IRT's Battery-Joralemon Street tunnel in 1905.

This time three sandhogs were trapped under New York Bay when a fierce whistling, then a rush of air, was heard. Before they could make a move the men were sucked into the vortex.

One of them, Marshall Mabey, was lucky. After being vacuumed up through twelve feet of sand and then shot to the surface of the bay on top of a geyser that, onlookers said, appeared to rise forty feet above the water, he had the stamina and presence of mind to swim to a nearby boat. He was pulled safely from the water, but his two companions died in the accident. BRT engineers solved the leakage problem by depositing a large load of clay over the break.

The BRT was headed for completion without a serious accident in Manhattan until September 25, 1915, when a fault in the rock wall of the excavation at 38th Street set off a landslide that uprooted the supporting timbers. At that precise moment another loaded Broadway trolley approached the sagging street planking. But motorman Malachi Murphy anticipated the danger and, in a split second, threw his electric gears into reverse. Just when it appeared that another streetcar would plunge underground, the wheels stopped skidding and pulled the passengers and Murphy to safety. Less fortunate was a stout female pedestrian who fell to her death. Her male escort was merely bruised.

The only other victim was taxi driver George Sommerer who suffered a temporary case of shock. Sommerer had stopped his cab for a moment and walked to the corner for a few puffs on a cigarette while awaiting a fare. Sommerer did a double take as his cab moved down, down, down until it finally sank out of sight into the subway tunnel.

BRT engineers were bedeviled with another problem in building the 60th Street tunnel to Queens. This time the dilemma was posed by the great depth—107-feet below mean high water—and solved by constructing the tunnel with two-thirds of its diameter above the riverbed. In order to cover the tunnel,

A 1917 view from the Queens anchor of the Queensborough Bridge and construction of the BMT 60th Street tunnel to Manhattan.

contractors dropped a blanket of clay and riprap (large chunks of stone) from scows to the bottom of the river. "It was," said *New York Post* reporter William H. Rudy, "a case of: Don't lower the tunnel, raise the river."

In some cases the BRT found that it had to widen its tunnels to accommodate the new flagship of its fleet, the all-steel, sixty-seven-foot subway car, regarded by some as the single best piece of rapid transit rolling stock ever produced. The "sixty-seven-footers" made their passenger debut on the Sea Beach Line on June 22, 1915 and won instant critical acclaim for their design, power, and comfort.

One fatal flaw prevented the BRT from enjoying the full fruits of its new rolling stock. The company was too slow in replacing the rickety wooden cars with the sleek sixty-seven-footers, and even in 1918 the BRT was pockmarked with obsolete cars. One such train filled with wooden cars crashed at Malbone Street in Brooklyn, killing ninety-seven passengers and sending the BRT into receivership. In 1923 it was reorganized as the Brooklyn-Manhattan Transit or BMT.

In the years from the Malbone Street disaster (the worst subway disaster ever, causing the name of the street to be changed to Empire Boulevard) until the line's reorganization as the BMT, the New York City mayor, John Hylan, waged a self-declared war against the line, specifically because of his earlier experiences as an el employee (he was fired as a motorman in his younger days). Hylan constantly thwarted BRT attempts at expansion. When the line attempted to construct a massive repair shop and storage yard in Coney Island, Hylan blocked the project. Following the Malbone wreck, Hylan intensified his anti-BRT campaign.

Significantly, Hylan began losing public favor in 1923 and on April 23 of that year he was booed while delivering a speech at ground-breaking ceremonies for an IRT el extension into Flushing, Queens. Hylan, now in his second four-year term, was notorious for his irascible nature, but he had one policy that appealed to his constituents— save the five-cent fare. The mayor even had hundreds of thousands of silvery pins minted with the inscription in blue lettering: HYLAN FIVE CENT FARE CLUB.

Few of Mayor Hylan's "club members" were aware that he once worked as a motorman while going to law school at night. He was fired from the job when an inspector caught the law student-motorman rounding a curve too quickly. According to one report, he actually had been reading a law school book while operating the train. "To many people," wrote author George Walsh in *Gentleman Jimmy Walker*, "it seemed that he [Hylan] had devoted his entire stay in City Hall to fulminating against the traction interests."

Fortunately for the subway barons, Hylan's term came to a close in 1925 and he was succeeded by one of the most exciting, flamboyant, and lovable mayors in the city's history, James J. "Gentleman Jimmy" Walker. During Walker's administration the BMT filled in marshland near the Coney Island terminal and completed the Coney Island yards and repair shop, to this day the largest in the Transit Authority system. Most of the major work was concluded by November 9, 1927 when yard buildings were finished and put into use. In time the shops were capable of taking a worn-out car and turning it out completely rebuilt mechanically, repainted, and virtually as good as new in eight days. On some days the shops took in nearly 200 cars and turned out the same number.

Under the direction of Gerhard Dahl, chairman of the company, the line adopted a slogan: BMT FOR BETTER METROPOLITAN TRANSIT. Dahl promoted advanced engineering that enabled the BMT to operate a safe, efficient, and expanded subway system. The BMT even ran special trains between Brooklyn and Manhattan for playgoers traveling to the Broadway theater district to see such productions as *The Ziegfeld Follies* or John Barrymore in *Hamlet*.

The BMT also operated the Brooklyn and Queens Transit Corporation, which boasted an enormous fleet of streetcars. So many street cars rumbled across Brooklyn that the natives became known as "Trolley Dodgers" and the name of the borough's baseball team (once called the Superbas) was changed to Brooklyn Trolley Dodgers and, ultimately, Brooklyn Dodgers.

BMT became synonymous with advanced transit design. In February 1927 the system introduced D-type cars, articulated three-car units which enabled two cars to share one track. The D-type cars permitted passengers to walk freely from any one of the three cars to another without interference by a door.

Late in 1933 the BMT contracted with the Budd Company to build an experimental, lightweight, stainless steel car called the Zephyr or Train 7029. The car featured red leather upholstered seats, bull's-eye lighting, and a fancy braking system. Train 7029 lacked automatic couplers, however, and eventually was confined to the BMT's Franklin Avenue (Brooklyn) line until forced into premature retirement in 1956.

Of all the BMT's experimental trains, two of the most interesting were the Bluebird Special and a Pullman Company-built beauty named the Green Hornet. Pullman constructed the Green Hornet as an articulated lightweight train made up of five sections on six trucks. It also was known as the Blimp because of its

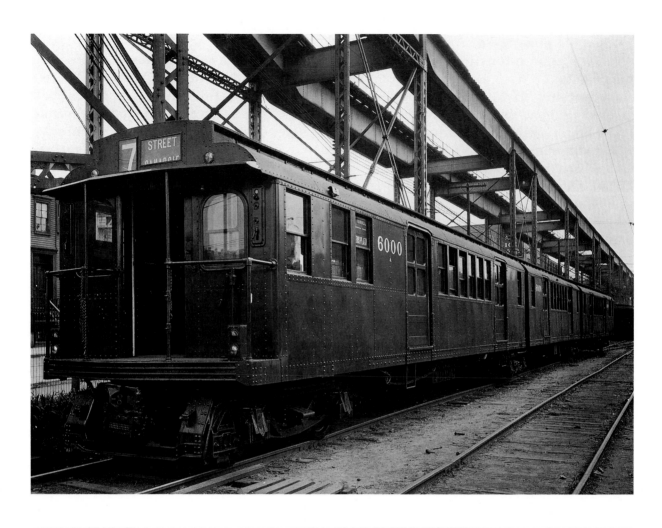

rounded look.

The Green Hornet-Blimp was a remarkable hunk of machinery. It was the city's first lightweight, all-aluminum train and featured a number of extras. Whenever the Green Hornet-Blimp entered a tunnel, its lights automatically flashed on and, of course, when it climbed out into daylight the interior lights turned off. Dulcet-toned chimes signaled the closing doors and indirect incandescent lighting made reading easier and more pleasant. Even more enjoyable was the Hornet-Blimp's rapid acceleration and braking powers, not to mention its ability to run both in subways and—because of its light weight—on elevated structures.

The Hornet-Blimp's medium green hue further appealed to straphangers who were fortunate enough to ride it on the Fulton Street (Brooklyn) El or the Franklin Avenue Shuttle to Prospect Park Station. Like the other BMT experimental trains, the Hornet-Blimp suffered from a paucity of parts. When a malfunction developed, or a part was needed, the BMT maintenance men had to wait for delivery from the Pullman plant.

(previous page, top) *The first Type D #6000 upon delivery in 1925. It is perched on the South Brooklyn Railway right-of-way. The porch railings were later removed.*

(previous page, bottom) *The "Bluebirds" at Brooklyn's Broadway Junction in 1947.*

(above) *The Budd Company's stainless-steel "Zephyr," the only one of its kind.*

(below) *The Green Hornet-Blimp upon delivery at Coney Island shops of the BMT.*

In 1941 the Hornet-Blimp was sitting in the 36th Street BMT (Brooklyn) yard waiting for a part to be delivered when scrap birddogs from the federal government heard about it. At the time all available aluminum was being collected to help the defense effort prior to America's entry into World War II. While the Hornet-Blimp was sidetracked, the Feds told the BMT to make

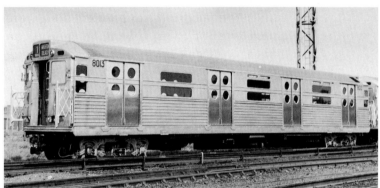

(above) *These multi-section trains were the production version of the Zephyr. They were built two years later, in 1936. They spent most of their service life on the Canarsie Line.*

(left) *The first silver streamliner, the R-11. Destination: Brighton Beach.*

(below) *The interior of the R-11.*

do with its standard sixty-seven-footers and other pieces of regular rolling stock.

The Pullman part never arrived and in 1942 the Hornet-Blimp was tossed on the scrap heap.

Resplendent in several shades of blue, with white stripes, the Bluebird Special was odd in every way. It was built by a relative novice in the subway-car field, the Clark Equipment Company of Battle Creek, Michigan. The Bluebird consisted of a single, articulated unit in which three sections were linked together. Instead of traditional subway-el trucks, the Bluebird was fitted with trolley-type wheels and brakes similar to those which had made such a hit on Brooklyn's streamlined PCC streetcars. These were extremely lightweight, streamlined trolley cars designed in the early thirties and called "PCC" (Presidents' Conference Committee) in honor of the streetcar presidents' conference which had been convened to produce an efficient trolley to compete with motor buses. The PCC car featured spring-suspended motors, eddy-current brakes, magnetic track brakes, not to mention improved heating, lighting and ventilation systems.

Bluebird went into service on March 30, 1939 and immediately captured the hearts and eyes of straphangers. In March 1941 five more units were added to the Bluebird and it appeared that it could, in time, become the standard of BMT esthetic excellence. The cars featured mohair seats, bull's-eye lighting, and even mirrored walls at the end of each car. August Belmont would have been proud. But the advent of World War II and the eventual standardization of rolling stock (based on the IND's R-1) rendered the articulated-car concept obsolete. "It was a magnificent-looking hunk of subway train," a Transit Authority official conceded, "but it was too hard to maintain." In 1958, the Bluebird died on the scrap heap.

On June 2, 1940 the BMT's era as the most romantic of the city's two privately-owned lines ended when the BMT was placed under the control of the New York City Board of Transportation. The IRT joined the BMT as a city-operated line nine days later. Nevertheless, even as a municipally-run system, the BMT retained much of its unique, flashy flavor.

In 1949 the BMT Division unveiled a silver streamliner called the R-11. It ran on the Brighton Line to Coney Island and included ten cars, a mechanical dust separator, sterile lamps to kill germs, crank-operated windows, and a special braking system. Unfortunately, the braking system proved to be too special and in 1957 the R-11 was taken out of service and placed alongside the Zephyr in the Coney Island yard. Thus, two of the prettiest subway trains ever to grace a railroad were left rusting on the BMT tracks.

The first Presidents Conference Committee or PCC Car making its Brooklyn debut.

The IND 53rd Street tunnel, just east of the Lexington Avenue Station, prior to its opening.

The Last Big Line— The IND

The third and final golden era of subway construction in New York City spanned the mid-twenties and thirties when more than fifty additional miles of underground railroad were opened in Manhattan, Brooklyn, Queens, and the Bronx. Unlike its predecessors, the newer Independent Subway (IND) was city-owned and city-operated from the start.

Like the IRT and the BMT, the Independent, for years known simply as the Eighth Avenue Subway, was built to satisfy the commuting needs of a still-growing city. Ground-breaking took place on March 14, 1925. "It is," said the *New York Times*, "Father Knickerbocker's latest and most gigantic effort to improve his sluggish circulation. It promises the subway rider more room to breathe and more safety for his corns."

Safety was a major concern in construction of the IND and such catastrophes as befell the IRT during earlier projects were avoided. One pedestrian was killed when he fell into an excavation and the death of one workman on the job was reported to have been due to heart disease. In addition two men were killed by a cave-in at 53rd Street and two others were fatally hurt when struck by cranes, but these tragedies were few in number compared with the serious accidents that occurred during construction of the IRT and the BMT.

While safety was a high-priority item in the construction of the IND Subway, frugality was not. Development of the Eighth Avenue subway was the Walker administration's single important improvement, but New York paid dearly for its third major line. The cost of building the IND was $800 million— approximately twice what many transit experts believed should have been the true cost. "The city did not get what it paid for," quipped Fusion Party financial expert Joseph D. McGoldrick, "although it certainly paid for what it got!"

Despite his questionable behavior, Walker was a popular official. New Yorkers loved their smiling, goodhearted mayor and didn't seem to mind the fact that he was two-timing his wife or that he was dipping into the public treasury. "One thing about Jimmy," his cronies would say, "he may steal a dime, but he'll always let you take a penny!" A few of those dimes apparently were taken from the new Eighth Avenue Line.

Nevertheless, New Yorkers were appropriately proud of their new subway, which encompassed six basic units with a seventh added to service the World's Fair at Flushing Meadow in 1939. The units were: (1) Washington Heights to East New York; (2) Bronx-Grand Concourse; (3) Coney Island; (4) Queens-Manhattan; (5) Sixth Avenue Houston Street; (6) Brooklyn-Queens Crosstown. Construction was, of course, more advanced in concept than methods used in building the IRT and BMT, although many of the earlier features were included in the IND's development.

Wherever possible the cut-and-cover system was used rather than the shield method of boring laterally underground. While this minimized the problems in a great congested city like New York no construction project is simple. The contractors had to cut through the underground ganglia that supply Manhattan with water, steam, electricity, gas, and telephone lines without interrupting these necessary services. They also had to see to it that no buildings fell into their big holes.

In places the line ran too deep for open cutting and hard-rock experts had to be brought in to tunnel. At 191st Street and Fort Washington Avenue, they cut through the rock 165 feet below the surface. The job throughout, as in other parts of the new system, was marked by increased use of machinery wherever it could be substituted for hand work, and by short cuts to reduce unnecessary operations. In former days, dirt and rock were usually lifted out by the bucket method.

Most observers probably thought that steam shovels were being used. As a matter of fact, they were gasoline-operated shovels, introduced because steam engines made too much smoke. In the deep rock work the older type of drilling machinery was largely replaced by the so-called "jack" hammers. In general, however, this was just one more job of boring, blasting, and digging, heroic in its magnitude, calling for daily risk of life and

A westbound IND World's Fair Special as viewed from the 69th Road overpass in 1940. The Fair's Trylon and Perisphere are in the distance with the Parachute Jump on the far right.

These R-1 to R-9s are in the IND's new Euclid Ave. Station, five days before its opening on November 28, 1948.

limb (although there were surprisingly few accidents in proportion to the number of men employed), calling upon every resource of modern large-scale engineering.

The digging was not everything, as the cost of equipment, running to nearly one-third of the construction cost, testifies. The open cuts had to be roofed over, the whole tube sealed and lined, the roadway ballasted, the tracks laid, power and signaling systems installed, a lighting system put in, stations built and equipped, yards provided, repair shops built, among many other chores to complete the enormous project.

Engineers, sandhogs, and contractors had learned a lot from the earlier IRT and BMT (BRT) experiences and applied them to construction of the new subway. In some cases the amount of materiel required was staggering.

About thirteen miles of pipe, ranging from six to twelve inches in diameter, were required for drainage of trackways. Sump chambers with a capacity of from 4,000 to 7,000 gallons were constructed for drainage purposes.

For the walls of the twenty-eight stations, 750,000 square feet of glazed tile were required—enough to decorate 5,500 average-sized bathrooms. There were 142,000 square feet, or about thirty-three and one-third acres, of ventilating gratings in the sidewalks over the structure.

Engineers expected the momentum of trains to change the air in the tunnel every fifteen minutes. There were fifty large ventilating fans, requiring motors furnishing 2,500 horsepower, or enough to operate 40,000 fans of office or home size.

Some 22 million cubic yards of earth and

rock were excavated. This material if spread evenly in Central Park would raise its level four feet. It would take 198,000 freight cars, comprising a train 1,400 miles long or the distance from New York to New Orleans, to haul this material away.

The new subway contained one million cubic yards of concrete, or enough to build a new highway such as the Bronx River Parkway from New York to Albany. The same concrete if cast into blocks one foot square and placed end to end would extend from New York to Buenos Aires.

The work required 6,700,000 bags of cement. They would fill a freight train fifty miles in length or if laid out on a highway thirty feet wide would extend from the Battery to Albany. It would take a fleet of barges forty-eight miles in length to carry the stone, gravel, and sand used in making the concrete.

The steel used in the tunnels weighed 150,000 tons, or three times as much as that in the Empire State Building. That is enough steel to build fifteen first-class cruisers for the navy or five ships the size of the Queen Elizabeth II. It would girdle the earth if drawn into a bar one inch in thickness.

The waterproof fiber in the structure would cover 480 acres if spread out in a single layer. If laid out in a sheet 100 feet in width it would extend from the Battery to Bear Mountain.

The timber in the track ties would cover a floor one inch thick, 100 feet wide, and ten miles long. The power ducts totaled in length 3,200,000 feet. If placed end to end they would reach from New York to Cleveland.

The material used in construction was shipped from 248 plants in 139 cities in thirteen states. The construction work required seven million man-days of labor, as compared with one million man-days for the George Washington Bridge. Construction involved relocation of 26 miles of water and gas pipes, 350 miles of electric conduits, and 18 miles of sewers. It was necessary to rebuild gas and electric service connections to 3,100 houses along the 12-mile route. Another "item" that would be constructed for the new IND was a prototype subway car. The design ultimately selected proved to be not unlike the BMT's all-steel, sixty-seven-foot gem of 1914. Both models employed large, exposed overhead fans and featured both longitudinal and latitudinal seating. While the BMT offered three sets of doors on each side, the newer IND had four sets.

Subway buffs were disappointed when they learned that the new sixty-foot IND car (soon to be labeled R-1) utilized a large front windowpane that significantly differed from its BMT counterpart in that it could not be opened, thus depriving "second motormen" from enjoying the speed-produced breezes as the A Train roared through the tunnel. But the new R-1 was not speedier, more attractive, nor in any way outwardly more magnetic than its counterparts on the BMT, although according to some rail fans it did look better than the IRT's standard car design. However, the R-1, underneath its relatively standard-looking exterior, did offer some innovations.

The doors themselves were designed to permit loading and unloading in the least possible time and with the least possible wear and tear on the passengers. Each car had four double doors on each side, each doorway being three feet ten inches wide. They differed from the IRT car doors in one important respect, however. When they encountered a passenger or other obstruction in closing they did not reopen to their full extent, but stopped where they were. Jocular individuals who held up trains by playing with the doors would thus be thwarted to a considerable degree. On test runs it was found that the station stops, with allowances for loading and unloading under rush hour conditions, ranged from thirty-seven seconds at Times Square to twenty-two seconds at 145th Street and nineteen seconds at West 4th Street. On an average, the new cars could be loaded and unloaded in about two-thirds the time required for the older-type car.

A small detail which became important in

the course of time: the lights in each car were fitted with left-handed threads so that they could not be used in ordinary light sockets and were therefore unprofitable to steal. The heating of the cars in cold weather was directly under control of the motorman. Trains were plainly marked by letters to indicate whether they were expresses or locals. Identification of stations was made easy by the use of five different colors in the lettering and patterns on the platforms, so that once a passenger had mastered the color sequences he knew at a glance about where he was.

As construction of the Eighth Avenue Subway sped to its conclusion in the summer of 1932, it had become apparent that its planners had succeeded in handling the mammoth project with a minimum of complaints from merchants and property owners and a low accident and mortality rate.

"One of the greatest sources of annoyances which the contractors had to contend with was that of 'inspired' accidents," said James W. Danahy, managing director of the West Side Association of Commerce. "A nail sticking up in a board was sufficient inspiration for some persons to rip their clothes and scratch their hands and then demand payments.

"Merchants generally along the avenue took their losses, which were heavy, with a degree of stoicism which was amazing to the contractors. Fewer than twenty merchants or property owners, out of some 1,500 involved, actually brought suits in court against the contractors. In no small way this situation was due to the willingness of the contractors to adjust cases where there was a reasonable degree of evidence that they were morally or legally to blame for the loss."

At last the IND was ready for its world premiere. A total of 300 spanking new cars were delivered for the opening on the twelve-mile stretch from Chambers Street up Eighth Avenue to 207th Street. Before the first passenger dropped a nickel into the turnstile, grand promises were made about the IND's prospects. The new system, in its first year, was expected to carry 114 million passengers and within ten years more than 300 million annually.

The original IND passenger car, R-1 #100 when delivered. It was state-of-the-art in 1932.

The Eighth Avenue System, although only twelve miles long, already was being designed to spread like nerve endings far into the Bronx, Queens, and Brooklyn. All methods of connecting it with the existing BMT and IRT subways had been made and numerous attempts at effecting a permanent unification of the three major systems already were underway. But, for the moment, all eyes were on the IND as its creators and leaders went through the final dry runs prior to the official debut.

The Eighth Avenue Subway was opened to the public at midnight on September 10, 1932. There was no ceremony to mark the opening, and there was no first train. At 12:01 AM platform guards simply removed barrier chains from the turnstiles, the crowds which had been gathering all evening dropped their nickels in the slots and the new line took its place as the third of the city's great rapid transit systems.

Sixteen trains—eight expresses and eight locals—were somewhere in the twelve-mile stretch between the temporary southern terminal at Chambers Street and the permanent northernmost station at 207th Street. Whichever train happened along first at each station became the first train for the passengers at that station.

The nearest approach to ceremony was a gathering at the dispatcher's office in the 42nd Street station of the three members of the Board of Transportation and the highest operating officials of the Independent System. In the group were John H. Delaney, chairman of the Board of Transportation; Commissioner Daniel L. Ryan, member of the board in executive charge of the system; Commissioner Frank X. Sullivan; Colonel John R. Slattery, general manager of the Independent system and deputy chief engineer of the Board of Transportation; Robert Ridgway, chief engineer of the board; and William O. Fullen, chairman of the Transit Commission.

Watch in hand, Mr. Delaney stood by one of the turnstiles, simultaneously trying to talk to the official party around him and to peer at the growing throng outside the gates. He almost forgot to look at his watch, and it may have been 12:02 or 12:03 when he waved to the guards at the gates and said: "Open up."

The crowd surged in, led by seven-year-old William Reilly of 406 West 46th Street, who was born on March 14, 1925, the day ground was broken for the new project. Mr. Delaney, having learned of this, made sure that young William was the first in.

It was a cheerful, noisy throng that pushed through the turnstiles. When they heard the roar of the first train and saw it slip into the brilliantly-lighted station, a volume of cheers and shouts went up that all but drowned the rumble of the wheels.

As the train pulled out, northbound, it was loaded to rush-hour capacity, the passengers still venting their enthusiasm with whistles and cheers that would have been most unusual had they been riding home from work. But the strangest spectacle of all, on this first train out of 42nd Street, was the absence of newspaper readers, the chronic occupation of many subway straphangers.

A single pair of eyes, those of a middle-aged gentleman, were directed to the pages of a morning newspaper. The rest of the passengers were far too busy inspecting the train, from ceiling ventilators to floor coverings.

In the first hour after the turnstiles were opened at the 42nd Street station, a total of 2,808 paid admissions were registered on the automatic counters. Except for the cheering and whistling and the large crowds at every station, the opening of the line was uneventful.

The New York Times reported the IND's debut this way:

"The new Eighth Avenue Subway, which was thrown open to the public at 12:01 o'clock yesterday morning, passed its first real operating test successfully by handling smoothly and efficiently its first rush-hour traffic.

"Members of the Board of Transportation,

General Manager John R. Slattery and Superintendent Philip E. Pfeifer declared that they were satisfied with the initial operation and confident that the new line would be more than adequate to meet the demands of the traveling public.

"The rush hour local service began on a four-minute headway promptly at 7 AM At 9:28 AM a five-minute headway prevailed, to be replaced at 11:28 AM by a four-minute headway which lasted until later, when longer headways became effective.

"The express service went on a four-minute headway after 6:56 AM, with a five-minute headway after 9:28 AM This prevailed until 11:28 AM, when it was replaced by another four-minute headway period lasting until 2 PM

"During the rush hour, express trains, according to Colonel Slattery, were comfortably filled, with fair-sized standing crowds. On the local trains there were, with few exceptions, seats for all riders.

"Colonel Slattery was especially pleased with the way the car doors helped to expedite the loading and unloading of passengers. There are four doors on each side of every car, affording quick access or exit for riders. The conductors were able to open and close their doors in strict accordance with the brief time allotments fixed by the schedule.

"The first operating problem on the new line occurred soon after 2 PM, when a compressed air coupling broke on a south-bound local leaving the Fifty-Ninth Street Station. It caused a delay of about twelve minutes, but normal service was re-established soon afterward."

Unlike the Victorian IRT with its mosaics and nineteenth-century kiosks or the BMT's *mélange* of subways, els, and trolley cars, the IND represented the very acme of modern subway engineering. Its bright, new stations were, as a rule, long and spacious. Instead of mosaics, IND designers resorted to simpler, yet colorful, tiles to spell out the station name. Express lines, such as the A (under Central Park West from 59th Street to 110th Street) and the E and F (from Roosevelt Avenue to Continental Avenue), were among the speediest, lengthiest, and best-planned express runs in the world.

Before the new system had even opened, blueprints had been laid out for a number of other lines that, unfortunately, fell victim to harsh economic times. This additional IND routing included the creation of an enormous junction at South 4th Street in Brooklyn, which was to be part of yet another division of the IND. South 4th Street was to be a six-track express station which would join routes coming from never-completed extensions—an addition to the express tracks east of Second Avenue and another spur coming from local tracks south of Canal Street—in Manhattan. Although the proposed lines never reached fruition, remnants still exist in the forms of unused stations.

One such line would have extended from the six-track express station at South 4th Street in Brooklyn connecting with a planned express stop at Fulton Street and Utica Avenue in Bedford-Stuyvesant.

Yet another ambitious project that never was completed as planned was a spur to the Atlantic Ocean at the Rockaways, which would have run from the IND's Roosevelt Avenue Station in Queens to the beach resort. The Rockaway train's terminal was slated for the mezzanine level, which currently is being used for other purposes.

When it was determined that the Fulton St. El in Brooklyn would be razed, IND planners concluded that the four-track subway under Fulton Street would serve a double purpose. The A (express) Train would head for Manhattan while the locals would, instead, terminate at Court Street Station near Boerum Place and Schermerhorn Streets. Once again the grand plan had to be abandoned and only a shuttle ran from Court Street one stop to Hoyt-Schermerhorn Station. This little-used shuttle ran from 1936 to 1946. The Court Street Station now is the site of the Transit Museum.

The Depression notwithstanding, The Board

of Transportation still was able to make significant additions.

Once the Eighth Avenue line was completed, IND workmen then turned their pickaxes and drills on Sixth Avenue, Manhattan, where the last—and in some ways most trying—stretch of digging took place. According to Groff Conklin, author of *All about Subways*, the building of the Sixth Avenue Subway at Herald Square (34th Street) was unique in the annals of underground planning. "It was," he wrote, "the most difficult piece of subway construction which has ever been attempted."

Because of the labyrinth of tunnels and pipes under the intersection of 34th Street, Broadway and Sixth Avenue, special precautions had to be taken. The Sixth Avenue (IND) line was built over the Pennsylvania Railroad tubes and the Long Island Rail Road tubes and under the Broadway BMT subway and the Hudson and Manhattan tubes. At the time a Sixth Avenue elevated line operated overhead, which meant that it had to be supported during the construction. Meanwhile, the usually heavy vehicular and streetcar traffic had to be maintained and, finally, exceptional care had to be taken not to disturb a huge, high-pressure water main which carried water from the Catskill Mountain reservoirs to New York City. The deep-lying main was buried 200 feet below the surface but was a threat should blasts or low-digging unsettle the water tunnel.

The mammoth Herald Square maze finally was completed in 1940 and on December 15th of that year the IND began operating trains under Sixth Avenue from 50th Street to West 4th Street. It was the last major opening on the IND although a smattering of extensions were built later, including a two-mile route for the GG Brooklyn-Queens Crosstown Local to the 1939-40 World's Fair in Flushing Meadow.

At this juncture, the city was poised for what would have been the greatest leap forward in its subway construction. The new Board of Transportation under Chairman John H. Delaney blueprinted a series of extensions and new subways for every borough—including Staten Island—which, if completed, would have satisfied the city's mass transit needs through the next century. A few of the more prominent projects include:

* Extension of the IND Queens Line (E and F trains) along Hillside Avenue to the Nassau County border at Little Neck Road.

* Extension of the IND Fulton Street Line (A train) to 106th Street Queens.

* Extension of the IRT Flushing Line to Bell Boulevard in Bayside.

* A new Brooklyn-Staten Island subway tunnel from Fourth Avenue and 68th Street, Brooklyn to New Brighton and Tompkinsville, Staten Island.

* Construction of a subway from 53rd Street to 145th Street through Central Park and along Morningside Avenue, Manhattan.

* Construction of a Second Avenue subway from Coenties Slip in Manhattan to Harding Avenue, The Bronx.

These and other programs— including several river tunnels—were sidetracked for an assortment of reasons, most notably World War II, which began eight months after they were proposed. Once hostilities ended in 1945, construction should have begun on several of the projects. The Board of Transportation boasted a robust fiscal surplus and it was apparent that relief of overcrowding was necessary, especially on Manhattan's East Side where the Second Avenue Subway was to be the panacea.

In the meantime, New Yorkers continued admiring the new Sixth Avenue Line.

The Sixth Avenue Subway was by far the most expensive piece of underground work in the world at that time. Although it was only two and a quarter miles long, the outlay for building the structure alone topped $46,800,000, while equipment installed cost about $6,600,000 and the cars needed to run in it added more than $6,250,000. The total cost was about $59,500,000, or between $26,000,000 and $27,000,000 a mile. This compared with costs of approximately $5,000,000 per mile for the construction of the earlier IRT and BMT subway systems, and approximately $9,000,000 per mile for the subway portions of the first Independent Division, which were completed several years earlier.

The most expensive portion of the new line was near the middle, between 33rd Street and 40th Street, where the structure alone cost $8,500,000. Between 47th Street and 53rd Street, the northern section, the cost was considerably lower, being a little more than $5,000,000.

Several reasons accounted for the high cost. First of all, the new line represented a four-track trunk, with connections at its two ends to the remainder of the system. It was built at a period when costs were considerably higher than when the original subways were built, and there was a fairly large amount of Public Works Administration work included. Complicated connections had to be made at the ends in order to keep away from grade intersections.

Following the end of World War II new additions were completed. In 1946 the A Line was extended from its former terminus at Rockaway Avenue, Brooklyn, to a new station called Broadway-East New York. Less than two years later another extension was finished to Euclid Avenue, Brooklyn. Pushing ahead in Queens, the IND extended its route to 179th Street on December 10, 1950.

But there were infinitely more projects on the drawing board, not the least of which was the Second Avenue subway. The saga of the ill-fated Second Avenue subway symbolizes the failure of municipal planning from the post World War II years to the present.

Originally blueprinted in the 1920's, the Second Avenue Line was to be a six-track super subway that would ultimately provide enough ridership to enable the city to scrap both the Second Avenue and Third Avenue elevated lines.

In 1942, the Second Avenue El was torn down accompanied by a firm City Hall promise that a subway would be built underneath. In 1946 the Board of Transportation actually drafted plans for a Second Avenue Subway. The public was primed for the new edition and in 1951 voters passed a $500 million transit bond. Of that, $446 million was slated for the Second Avenue Subway.

As it happened, the cash never was spent on the planned underground. Instead, the funds were diverted to improvements on existing lines. "If we had used the $500 million as originally planned, we might have had a very fine Second Avenue Subway and the rest of the system wouldn't be worth the powder to blow it to hell with," said a TA official at the time.

Meanwhile, overcrowding increased on the East Side's only subway, the IRT Lexington Avenue Line. Fortunately, the Third Avenue El—still operating in the early 1950's—was able to provide some relief for the beleaguered straphangers. It seemed logical that the Third Avenue El would remain operative until a new rapid transit system was built under Second Avenue but real estate interests prevailed over transit planners and in 1955 the Third Avenue El was demolished. Thus, the East Side instantly became America's most intensely populated area with only one subway to service it.

In 1968 Mayor John Lindsay and the Metropolitan Transportation Authority received plans for a 14.3 mile Second Avenue Line. Lindsay and Governor Rockefeller launched the project on October 28, 1972 at Second Avenue and 103rd Street. Three other sections were built; 110th to 120th Streets, 2nd to 9th Streets and Canal Street at the Manhattan Bridge. [In August 1996, I was given a Transit Authority-led tour of the completed tunnel under Canal Street. It has everything but tracks and signals and remains in mint condition.] In 1974 Mayor Abe Beame broke ground for another section of the Second Avenue Subway at Second Street.

By this time, the city was going broke and the Metropolitan Transit Authority conceded that the cost of the Second Avenue subway had quadrupled. It postponed the target date for completion to 1986. A year later, Beame stuck a dagger in the project by leaving construction out of a six-year transit program thereby sealing the tunnels both literally and figuratively.

Where does the New York subway system go from here?

Lawrence Reuter, who became TA president in 1996, said in a 1997 interview with us that the Authority will upgrade a century-old system while adopting new marketing techniques for a new straphanger era.

"What you'll see is a real change of focus as it relates to customer service," said Reuter.

Slowly but relentlessly, the 21st century TA will take the straphangers concerns to heart more than ever since the amalgamation of the BMT, IND and the IRT.

"We're going to give our passengers more information," said Reuter. "We'll have public address systems that people can understand.

"We'll have train delay announcements and loudspeakers that will tell our passengers, 'Next train in three minutes.'"

Reuter made it clear that the subways will explore all available high-technology especially in the realm of signalling. In time, a computerized system similar to that in Vancouver will be utilized. Eventually computers will control the speed and keep trains as close as possible.

"We'll try it first on the 14th Street-Canarsie Line and eventually have a totally computerized system. We'll be taking full advantage of technology."

Reuter asserted that seemingly dormant projects such as the Second Avenue Subway still could be revived in time.

"The Second Avenue Subway is not <u>kaput</u>," Reuter insisted, "We're continuing to look at it. East Side access is our next priority. It's still an issue."

The bottom line: the system enters the 21st century in better style than ever.

Here I am in the bowels of the never-finished Second Avenue Subway in the portion constructed between Confucius Plaza and the Manhattan Bridge. I wonder how long I'm going to have to wait for the train? It would seem forever-and-a-day.

NEW YORK·HUDSON SCENE·AND·SECTIONAL VIEW OF NEW TUBE.

THE NEW   McADOO TUNNEL.

Photo Only COPYRIGHT 1909.
By The H. HAGEMEISTER CO. N.

The "Tubes"—
First Cousin To The
New York Subways

For decades millions of New Yorkers have been oblivious to yet another monumental engineering feat that resulted in a subway running daily along Manhattan's primary vein.

Originally known to Gotham citizens as "The Tubes," this subway is a veritable anomaly in relation to the IRT and BMT lines which surrounded it almost from birth.

Originating at its twin depots—one at Herald Square, the other at Hudson Terminal—"The Tubes" significantly differed from its counterparts in one vital respect, destination.

Whereas the IRT and then BMT both terminated within the city limits, The Tubes

rolled under the Hudson River and then made stops at such "foreign" locations as Jersey City, Harrison and ultimately, distant Newark, metropolis of the State of New Jersey.

The Tubes seemed strange in other ways. Its tunnels emitted a distinctly different—some say it bordered on the exotic—odor that outdid either of its counterparts. Furthermore, in comparison to the IRT its rolling stock was unique, to say the least; and that is not to be construed in a negative manner because virtually everything about the first cousin to the New York subways was appealing.

For starters it should be known that The Tubes were more properly known as The Hudson and Manhattan Railroad Company. That was logical since the line snaked under Manhattan's streets, under the Hudson River and rolled into Hudson County before dashing to Newark.

The full Hudson and Manhattan Railroad Company moniker was soon dismantled by

New Yorkers who alternately referred to the city's most curious subway as either The H and M, The Hudson Tubes or, simply—and most commonly—The Tubes.

Either way it was a winner although the line didn't come easy. How could it since civilized man had never before been able to successfully tunnel a railroad under so vast a waterway as the Hudson River.

Not that noble attempts had not been made, over and over again. DeWitt Clinton Haskin, a Civil War Colonel in the Union Army, was as ambitious when it came to engineering as his name. He was obsessed by the challenge of constructing a Hudson tunnel and believed that he had found the technique to make it work.

The secret was rooted in successful construction of a Missouri River bridge in which a compressed-air-and-caisson method was employed to erect the span's piers. In his definitive history of the Tubes, *Rails Under The Mighty Hudson*, author Brian J. Cudahy recalls the technology employed:

"The technique involved a large inverted 'box'—or caisson—which was positioned at the site of the pier. The masonry pier itself was constructed atop the caisson, which began to sink into the river bottom. Compressed air was fed into the chamber to keep watery slime beneath the open bottom of the caisson out of the interior. Here workmen toiled, under pressure, excavating the downward journey of the caisson, a journey which continued until bedrock, or some other solid material was reached."

Haskin organized the Hudson Tunnel Railroad Company and raised sufficient funds to launch the product in 1874 from the Jersey side of the river. More than 1,000 feet of brick-lined tunnel was constructed under the Hudson before problems overwhelmed the engineers.

In a sense the Missouri River bridge project was deceptive to Haskin because the vertical construction was relatively simple. The problem with the Tubes centered on the horizontal; that is, digging from west (Hoboken) to east (Manhattan). The digging was slow, hazardous and, eventually, stymied by a tragedy on July 21, 1880 when 20 sandhogs were drowned in a blowout.

Haskin began losing his eyesight, his money and the will to continue. But his trans-Hudson tunnel idea already had piqued the curiosity of others and by 1890 a new godfather of The Tubes had taken over.

Long before the IRT was created, S. Pearson and Sons, began orchestrating construction of The Tubes. To speed work, the outfit utilized a more modern tunneling device called "The Greathead Shield," named after the English engineer, Sir James Henry Greathead. The shield eliminated potential blowouts while accelerating river-bottom burrowing. It worked so well that a second tube was planned right next to the original.

For a time optimism prevailed. The tunnel which originated at the Jersey side moved toward Manhattan and seemed close to completion at a target date five years before the turn of the century. Alas, more monetary woes braked progress and construction halted before the tunnel reached its destination near Cortlandt Street in Downtown Manhattan.

The project was put on permanent hold until after the new century was hailed. By then an entrepreneurial genius, William Gibbs McAdoo, and an acclaimed engineer, Charles M. Jacobs, united to re-start The Tubes' engines.

If ever there was an odd couple of subwaying, McAdoo and Jacobs were it. A Southerner by way of Chattanooga, McAdoo had set up a successful law office in Manhattan where his keen business mind adapted to a number of projects. With scant railroad background, he nevertheless became fascinated with The Tubes project and aligned himself with Jacobs who had masterminded the first subaqueous tunnel in New York under the East River in 1894.

Their first objective was determining whether previous work on The Tubes was usable should a third construction attempt be launched. They decided to walk the tunnel, for what it was, in 1901 and then make a determination. The episode later moved McAdoo to write: "The fates had marked a day when I was to go under the riverbed and encounter this piece of dripping darkness and it would rise from its grave and walk by my side. I was determined to give it color and movement and warmth, but it would change the course of my life and lead me into a new career."

The good news was that the existing tunnel would be useful. The bad news was that there was still much to be done such as raising new funds and making a drastic change in the Haskin plan. When the Colonel had devised his trans-Hudson plan the electric railroad as a mass transit device had not yet been perfected. Haskin's idea—looked upon skeptically by many—was to run traditional steam locomotives in The Tubes. Multiple unit electrification of Manhattan's elevated lines did not take place until 1900 but when it proved practical McAdoo and Jacobs instantly understood that their H&M line would be an electrified subway exactly like August Belmont's planned Interborough Rapid Transit system.

In its entirety the grand plan of The Tubes was as awesome as the IRT blueprint. Not only would the H&M connect Jersey City— the first major destination on the line in New Jersey—but also Hoboken and Newark. In Southern Manhattan at the other end of the subway, The Tubes ultimately would burrow west from Morton Street in Greenwich Village to Sixth Avenue and Ninth Street and then ambitiously head north along Sixth to a Herald Square station—actually it was directly under the Horace Greeley statue at tiny Greeley Square—where Broadway and Sixth Avenue intersect near 33rd Street.

(During construction of the IND's Sixth Avenue Line in the 1930s, The Tubes' original 33rd Street station was moved slightly southward to 31st Street.)

Thus, The Tubes would be running parallel to the IRT for a good portion of the respective runs in Manhattan. Redundant but true!

With new money to back the project, McAdoo set his engineering ducks in order and a third start on The Tubes was underway despite still horrendous obstacles. While the IRT opened for business in 1904 Jacobs was trying to conquer innumerable difficulties. It was one thing to dig open trenches in the soil of Manhattan and then erect steelwork and other appurtenances but it was another to tunnel under the grand Hudson. For that reason many critics in the newspapers and out continued to be skeptical about the successful completion of The Tubes.

"Construction was no easy task," wrote Cudahy. "Rock ledge was frequently encountered even in the deepest portions of the river bottom. At one time engineers were faced with the devastating prospect of a formation of reef rock that rose up twelve feet from the bottom of one of the tubes, a tube whose outside diameter was eighteen feet. In other words, while blasting was necessary at the bottom of the tunnel, the top had to be pushed forward through soft mud silt at the same time."

Interestingly, the names of personalities connected with the city's first two subways became household words throughout the five boroughs. Belmont with the IRT and McAdoo with The Tubes. New Yorkers offhandedly referred to the H&M work as "the new McAdoo tunnel" or "the McAdoo system" and when rolling stock was designed, the vehicles were called "the new McAdoo cars."

Deservedly so. Few individuals were so intimately linked with a project as this Tennessean and his sidekick. Jacobs was so intent on letting his superior know about completion of the tunnel that he ordered a temporary telephone installed that linked McAdoo's downtown office with The Tubes. When at last, the last digging was done, Jacobs phoned McAdoo and urged him to come on over and check it out.

An hour later the exultant pair joined hands and carefully negotiated their way from one end of the 5,650 foot tube to the other. The accomplishment later inspired McAdoo to assert, "For the first time in the history of mankind, men had walked on land from New Jersey to New York."

Having survived the under-river trek, McAdoo knew that the time had come to invite the city's influential journalists. With The Boss at their side, they somewhat timidly trod the dirt without negative incident. Now the word was out, McAdoo's Tunnel would, in fact, lead to the first trans-Hudson subway.

Well before the trains began running, McAdoo laid out yet a second section which would link the Delaware, Lackawanna and Western Railroad's Hoboken terminal with Morton Street in Greenwich Village. Clearly, McAdoo and Jacobs were over the hump and the next challenge was putting the finishing touches on the original tunnel and producing rolling stock for the new subway.

In New Jersey planners of The Tubes laid out a series of links with major rail lines. One would be at Exchange Place and the Pennsylvania Railroad and another with the Erie Railroad, just south of the DL&W's Hoboken Terminal.

Three years after the first IRT line opened for business serious test runs were launched on The Tubes. In December 1907 sandbags were placed on the new H&M cars for runs through the Hudson tunnels. The tests were successful enough for engineers to decide to substitute people for the bags.

In the meantime those who had seen the brand, new subway trains were agog with enthusiasm. As impressive as the original IRT rolling stock may have been, the new "McAdoo cars" had a compelling quality all

their own.

The Tubes trains were constructed by two companies simultaneously and both— Pressed Steel Car Company and American Car and Foundry Company—sets were designed by the respected L.B. Stillwell, whose name would become synonymous with passenger cars run by the Erie Railroad.

Stillwell's subway car was at once lightweight, fireproof and well-endowed with doors to permit rapid exit. Each car was 48 feet long, eight-and-a-half feet wide and weighed 64,000 pounds. The dark paint job afforded them a certain mysterious look and, not surprisingly, they were dubbed "Black Cars."

If a subway car could be called handsome, the Stillwell design for The Tubes was it. In contrast to the IRT vehicle the H&M car featured uniquely curved windows along the sides, doors at each end and one in the middle and three sets of windows at the front and back of each car. Virtually every window had a distinct curve, the likes of which were missing on the IRT.

Eight such cars were coupled together on January 15, 1908 at the Sixth Avenue and 14th Street station when McAdoo and a host of dignitaries arrived. The invitations had noted that H&M Superintendent E.M. Hedley would guide the train under the Hudson for the first passenger-filled run.

The cars lurched forward as Hedley pulled on the heavy steel controller handle in the motorman's cab. Tiny tunnel lights flickered past the windows while the cars negotiated curves until the train straightened for its tunnel descent under the Hudson.

Some passengers fixed their gazes on the seemingly endless steel tunnel rings that curved from one wall to the ceiling and down the other wall. Others marvelled at the neat appointments of Stillwell's car while most wondered whether they would reach the Hoboken terminus without mishap.

Not only did the inaugural train make it

A Type "C" "Black Car" at the Henderson Street Yard in Jersey City during 1957. Its classic design was unique among subway cars. The cars measured 48-feet long and eight-and-a-half feet wide. They weighed 64,000 pounds.

safely to New Jersey but then returned to Manhattan in such a rapid manner that all riders took their leave convinced that McAdoo was nothing short of a genius.

Five weeks later—on February 25, 1908, to be exact—McAdoo would orchestrate his final H&M symphony. With suitable fuss and fanfare, he would open The Tubes to the general public but only after involving the Chief Executive in Washington, Theodore Roosevelt.

According to McAdoo's plan, a telegraph machine was installed on the H&M platform at Sixth Avenue and West 19th Street with connections to The White House. McAdoo first ordered all electricity through the third rails shut off. On signal a telegrapher would transmit a message to Roosevelt: "The first official train of the Hudson and Manhattan

Railway Company under the Hudson River awaits your signal and your pleasure. W.G. McAdoo."

Upon receiving the transmission, Roosevelt pressed a button on his desk. This set in motion a signal to The Tube's sub-station where power was then thrown "on" for the third rail. At that point the motorman pushed his controller to the first "point" and the train rolled toward the tunnel.

Like little children—or just plain train buffs, if you will—the distinguished governors of New York and New Jersey, Charles Evans Hughes and Franklin Fort, respectively, excitedly pressed their noses against the front window as the train picked up speed. The entire run to New Jersey consumed ten-and-a-half minutes, which was the projected running time under normal passenger operation.

Evans and Fort were not the only awed dignitaries. McAdoo had captured the imagination of Wall Street and, as a result, the members of the financial community outnumbered the available seats of the eight-car consist. McAdoo added a ninth Stillwell car and still there were standees!

By the time the train reached its Hoboken destination President Roosevelt had wired a congratulatory telegram and more than 19,000 citizens toasted the new trans-Hudson service at the new H&M terminal in Hoboken. Nobody seemed to mind the bitter cold as McAdoo read the president's wire and then herded his entourage back into the cars for the ride back to Manhattan. A commemorative dinner at the chic restaurant Sherry's rounded out the festivities.

The common folk, otherwise known as straphangers, had lined up for the first non-exclusive run and the honor of being the first paying customer fell to Mrs. Barbara Schlatter of Hoboken. The Tubes were in business and McAdoo—who would become Secretary of Treasury under President Woodrow Wilson—had become a civic hero.

It wasn't merely the transit masterpiece that endeared him to New Yorkers but also a skyscraper that rose over the station at Cortlandt Street. The Manhattan terminal was topped by what became known as Hudson Terminal, a massive office complex that would dominate the Downtown skyline along with the Woolworth Building and other skyscrapers.

Ever the hands-on boss, McAdoo showed up at the construction site one day as steeplejacks prepared to hoist a huge steel girder to the top of the building's skeleton. McAdoo summoned a foreman and requested the right to ride the girder as it was pulled skyward. The request was granted and McAdoo, like a surefooted construction veteran, was hoisted to the top where he made his on-site inspection.

After The Tubes reached the line's northernmost point at 33rd Street and the intersection of Broadway and Sixth Avenue, McAdoo had hoped to unite his line with Grand Central Terminal. His blueprints called for a subway extension north under Sixth Avenue, then a curve right (east) along 42nd Street to the link-up under Park Avenue and 42nd Street. Unfortunately, the plan never got off the drawing board, except for a couple of stubs that were to be part of the extended tunnel.

McAdoo's H&M expansion was more successful on the other side of the Hudson. In 1911 tracks were extended to Newark as well as to Manhattan Transfer Station adjoining the Passaic River. It was there that the Pennsylvania Railroad uncoupled its New York-bound steam locomotives and replaced them with side-rod-drive electric locomotives. The DD-1's then completed the run to Pennsylvania Station in Manhattan at Eighth Avenue and 33rd Street. Pennsy riders who preferred heading to Downtown Manhattan merely had to transfer to The Tube trains which were awaiting passengers across the platform.

The Tubes' run to Newark not only was efficient, it was exciting. The straightaway through New Jersey's adjoining Meadowlands enabled the trains to run at maximum speed, particularly after the faster, second generation of cars were added.

Manufactured by Pressed Steel Car Company and assigned the MP-38 label, the new fleet was purchased in conjunction with the Pennsylvania Railroad. Rather than the H&M black, the paint job on the high-speed Newark rolling stock was Pennsy Tuscan Red. While they may have lacked some of the Stillwell amenities they did have more highly-powered motors and distinctive porthole windows in front, reminiscent of the Long Island Rail Road's "Ping Pong" cars.

The sum of all these parts was success. Passengers loved The Tubes for a lot of

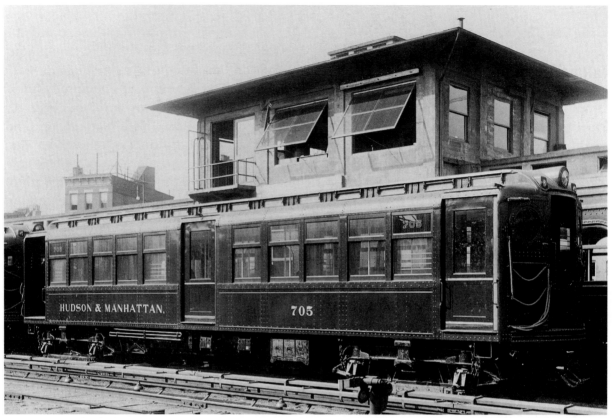

An MP-38 as built by American Car and Foundry Company for the Newark Service at Henderson Street Yard in 1911. A train of MP-38s racing between Jersey city and Newark's Penn Station produced a rate of speed to thrill any railfan

reasons starting with its unique trans-Hudson quality and ending with its service. A stickler for correctness, McAdoo went out of his way to produce a workable system. "The Public Be Pleased" was H&M's slogan and wherever possible its employees tried to deliver.

Ridership response was commensurate with the punctual service and by the start of World War I the number of passengers annually riding The Tubes continued to climb.

Since the IRT's original subway was the only underground railroad available to New Yorkers at that time—construction on the BMT subway and IRT additions took place during the World War I years—city dwellers found the H&M a welcome relief from traffic congestion and an easy, inexpensive way to move from Greenwich Village to the department stores at Herald Square.

McAdoo's stations had a distinctive quality

all their own. The 19th Street depot in Manhattan, for example, featured vaulted ceilings, impressive columns and attractive globe light fixtures with the number 19 embossed on them. Walls were adorned with tile while floors even had spittoons strategically placed near the exits.

Even signage was particularly neat. While the IRT sported distinctive blue and white message boards, The Tubes employed red lettering on a white background. The H&M Christopher Street station, which adjoined the Ninth Avenue Elevated Line, featured a handsome curved marquee with HUDSON TUNNELS signs both above and below the entrance.

No less attractive to New Yorkers was Hudson Terminal itself which had a charm not unlike Pennsylvania Station and Grand Central Terminal. Hudson Terminal became

(above) *The 19th Street station photographed one week after the Tubes service commenced on March 5, 1908.*
(below) *The Christopher Street station entrance. This marquee-type design gave The Tubes its unique image among the New York subways. The Ninth Avenue El station looms in the background.*

the focal point of McAdoo's subway which grew in popularity long after he left Manhattan to work for President Woodrow Wilson.

Ridership continued an upward surge even after completion of the Dual Contracts of the IRT and BMT and by 1927 The Tubes set a record of 113,000,000 passengers. To accommodate the popularity the H&M purchased a new fleet of cars from the American Car and Foundry Company and they remained in service until well after World War II.

Shortly after the onset of The Great Depression ridership began to dwindle. Massive unemployment during the early 1930s was one reason and improved trans-Hudson transportation systems was another. Construction of the Holland and Lincoln Tunnels as well as the George Washington Bridge made it easy for motorists to reach New Jersey. More cars were on the road and fewer riders were in The Tubes.

A crisis was reached in the early 1950s when The Tubes plunged into bankruptcy and measures were taken to find a new operator of the line. Remarkably, during those desperate times both the H&M and Pennsylvania Railroad chipped in to purchase 50 air-conditioned cars from the St. Louis Car Company. The deal, consummated in 1958, was a marvel of its day, particularly since the New York City Transit Authority leaders had long insisted that it was virtually impossible to air-condition subway cars because of intense passenger use.

The spanking new cars—30 were owned by the Pennsy and 20 by H&M—were a marvel of their time and completely refuted the New York TA's claim that air-cooled cars couldn't work under rush-hour conditions.

While the new rolling stock proved to be the salvation of overheated commuters the salvation of the Tubes was found in the Port of New York Authority, one of the world's most powerful transportation units. The Authority agreed to buy and run The Tubes and the Hudson and Manhattan Railway had its name officially changed to the Port Authority-Trans Hudson Corporation, an operating subsidiary of the publically-owned Authority.

Oldtimers still referred to their favorite line as "The Hudson Tubes" or simply "The Tubes," while newcomers have come to call it "The PATH,"—as in Port Authority Trans Hudson—which is the Port Authority's preference.

At first the new ownership was viewed with skepticism by riders in New York and

Trains of H&M "K" class cars and Pennsylvania Railroad MP-51 cars pass each other between Harrison and Newark in 1958.

New Jersey. The general feeling was that the PA was more interested in fostering motor transportation and that the PATH was its transportation orphan which was to be ignored and eventually closed.

This, however, was not the case. The PA introduced a number of tangible improvements including purchase of 206 new air-conditioned cars from the St. Louis Car Company and an extensive rehabilitation of the line from 33rd Street to Newark.

This saddened some nostalgia buffs because the landmark Hudson Terminal fell victim to The Tube's renaissance under the PATH imprimatur. The twin-towered World Trade Center became The Tube's new Downtown Manhattan terminus.

The infusion of still more rolling stock in 1972—Canadian-based Siddeley Company manufactured 46 air-conditioned cars—embellished the fleet even more. It now had become apparent to the riding public that the Port Authority was serious about not only maintaining but upgrading The Tubes.

Although many of the venerable old stations—19th Street and 28th Street—are gone, The Tubes in the late 1990s still displayed the trappings of its earlier life. The skeletal steel rings continue to adorn the tunnels and the distinctive musky odor remains a part of one of New York's underground transportation marvels.

Even one of the early "Black Cars" was preserved. A pair of rail buffs, Alan Zelazo and Bill Wall, brought the 1928-vintage American Car and Foundry Company product to the Shore Line Trolley Museum near New Haven in 1979. Using old blueprints and ancient parts, they and a handful of museum volunteers gave life to the old Stillwell-type car.

Tube fans, like Zelazo and his son, remain numerous because McAdoo's railroad still retains its adorable quality.

The Hudson Tubes—or PATH, if you will—remains as much a Manhattan subway as the IRT, BMT or IND. The difference is that it remains the only one that goes to New Jersey!

The Newark Terminal of the "Tubes" in 1912, long before the H&M moved to the larger, newer Pennsylvania Station in Newark in 1935.

(above) *The mezzanine of the original 33rd Street Tubes station before it was moved South to its present location after construction of the Sixth Avenue Subway. Notice the platforms were under the turnstile area and the stairway leading down to the platform on the far right. Also unique were the H&M-style columns in the mezzanine. They were removed during the rebuilding.*

(next page, top) *The platform area under the mezzanine in its original form. Notice the reference to Broadway on the columns, a feature not present in today's station. As in the subways, vending machines abounded, another convenience victimized by modern times.*

(next page, bottom) *In the early 1960's four "Black Cars" emerge from the tunnel, whose mouth lines halfway between Grove-Henderson Streets station and Journal Square in Jersey City.*

Post-World War Two Growth

Once World War II ended, the city was poised for yet another great leap forward in terms of subway construction but it would be dramatically different from all others.

Since the turn of the century the New York subway's growth was significantly unsteady. The underground system was built in spurts of activity; the original line constructed by August Belmont was followed in the second decade of the century by the Dual (IRT-BRT) System, which more than doubled all that had been built before. Then came a third spurt with the building of the city's own Independent line, the IND.

The IND began operating prior to World War II, at which point all major subway construction was halted "for the duration." Once hostilities had ended in the Pacific, city planners got back to the drawing board and concluded that more subways were needed; the sooner the better. In Brooklyn it was agreed that the IRT Flatbush Avenue Line, which terminated at Nostrand and Flatbush Avenues, should be extended all the way to the sea along Nostrand Avenue, winding down at Sheepshead Bay. Real-estate interests in Manhattan clamored for the razing of the Third Avenue El. It would be replaced by a new subway under Second Avenue. Still other routes were suggested.

However, not until 1951 were the hopes of transit planners and straphangers given realistic encouragement. In November of that year a $500-million transit bond issue was put on the ballot. Promoters of the bond issue clearly indicated that its approval would mean construction of the long-awaited Second Avenue Subway, at a cost of $446 million, as well as a number of other improvements and extensions.

As expected, the bond issue was approved, and the Board of Transportation authorized the line in 1952 for completion in 1957-58. It was to be a four-track line with connections to the Bronx and Queens. The $500-million bond issue was sold through the banks and New Yorkers eagerly awaited the start of construction. They waited and waited and waited. Finally, it became apparent that voter approval or not, the Second Avenue Subway would exist in blueprints only.

The culprit, in this case, was the newly created New York City Transit Authority (TA), which replaced the old Board of Transportation in 1953. Before expediting the Second Avenue project as everyone had expected the new agency to do, the TA decided to review the bond issue. When the review was completed, the TA insisted that the money would be better spent for other purposes, namely, the rehabilitation of existing lines. Mayor Robert Wagner supported the TA's assertion that the subway system had so deteriorated that the funds from the bond issue were needed for rehabilitation.

But many respected critics believed that the TA and especially Wagner had knuckled under to the then powerful Robert Moses, a strident champion of highways over rapid transit. Moses, who was chairman of the Triborough Bridge and Tunnel Authority, among other agencies he headed, had managed to build ribbons of highways from the late 1930s on while the subways stagnated, and was known to have Wagner's ear.

A large portion of the $500-million bond issue was used for the improvement of existing lines, but to this day critics argue that failure to launch the Second Avenue Subway was a crucial mistake and one that has had long-range damaging effects on New York City. Unquestionably the Second Avenue Subway should have been built in 1953 but Moses's influence on Wagner and the Board of Estimate appears to have been too strong to permit widespread new construction on the city's rapid transit lines. What growth there was on the system came in the form of

The first post-World War II IND subway car. Dubbed R-10, it served the "A" Train.

improvements in subway car design (although there was some retrogression in this department, too) with the ultimate goal realized: air-conditioned cars.

The mere thought of air conditioning the city's subway rolling stock was regarded as a pipe dream in the days following World War II, when new cars were again available. The 1946 model (R-10) offered a cooling system that, practically speaking, was no better than the overhead fans featured on the 1914 BRT sixty-seven-foot standard car. If anything, the R-10's smaller fans made ventilation even worse.

But a few years later an advanced subway car called the R-15 made its appearance. Featuring a turtle-back roof, fluorescent lights, multi-colored tiles on the floor, and soft seats, the R-15 boasted a more sophisticated ventilating system. When the car temperature passed 65 degrees Fahrenheit, the cars automatically changed over from the heating to the ventilating system, and the dampers opened. As the

temperature in the air increased, the speed of the fans (embedded behind louvers in the ceiling) increased. If the car temperature fell below 65 degrees, the heat increased accordingly.

On September 9, 1964 the TA displayed the first of an order of 600 stainless-steel cars, R-32 Brightliners. The order, the largest ever placed in the United States, cost $68,820,000. Apart from their attractive appearance, the new R-32s were 4,000 pounds lighter than their predecessors and saved considerable amounts of power. However, the stainless-steel Brightliners relied on thermostat motivated fans and still there was no air conditioning.

Actually, the TA had been testing air-conditioning equipment on the system since 1955. The first experiment involved an IRT R-15 car. TA engineers outfitted Car No. 6239 with four packaged air conditioning units of one-and-one-half tons capacity each. (In a packaged unit the compressor and evaporator are mounted together in an integrated unit.)

(above) R-32 "Bright-liners" Note the update TA logo on the right.

(right) R-15's on the IRT's #7 Flushing Line at 33rd St.

(below) R-17's at the Pelham Bay Parkway Terminus of the IRT. Pelham Park is behind the depot.

R-32 "Brightliner" interior. Hard, plastic seats have replaced the more cushioning rattan.

A year later ten IRT R-17 cars, Nos. 6800-6809, were received from the St. Louis Car Company equipped with six units of one-and-one-half tons capacity. After a relatively short period of time these packaged units were replaced with two-ton units, increasing the air-conditioning capacity of the cars to twelve tons.

Every experiment failed. The air conditioners broke down but were left in the subway cars that remained in service, and eventually were removed and replaced with traditional axiflow ceiling fans. The early air conditioners failed because of a combination of inadequate capacity and car-ceiling mounting, where they were inaccessible for maintenance purposes and yet caused noise and vibration that were at intolerable levels.

By this time TA officials believed they had proven to the public that the subways simply could not be air conditioned. They argued that there was no way to avoid the loss of cooled air though opened doors at the frequent station stops or the high humidity generated by heavy rush-hour crowding. But the public was not convinced. Demands for air-conditioned subways continued and

became even more pressing after the receiver of the Hudson and Manhattan Railroad Company, Herman T. Stitchman, then operating the Hudson Tubes connecting New York City with Hoboken, Jersey City, and Newark, began a series of successful experiments with railroad-type air-conditioning equipment. When the Hudson Tubes were acquired by the Port Authority-Trans Hudson Corporation it ordered 206 air-conditioned rapid transit cars and, suddenly, New York City's TA was again on the spot.

Back to the drawing board went the TA engineers, who concluded that air conditioning could work if the machinery were better designed. To test their theory ten R-38 cars with air-conditioning were ordered and placed in service on July 19, 1967. "If these tests prove successful," said Mayor John Lindsay, "the City will put a top priority on orders for several hundred more so that air conditioned trains will be moving on nearly all subway lines in the next few years."

The tests were a success and in 1968 the city ordered 600 air-conditioned subway cars (200 R-40's plus 400 new R-42's). From that point on the TA had irrevocably decided that air

conditioning would be standard equipment on all subway cars ordered in the future.

Inevitably, a "lemon" would emerge from time to time among the shiny new designs. One of the worst was the R-40, styled by the industrial design firm of Raymond Loewy-William Snaith, Incorporated. The design was an attempt to provide a more esthetically pleasing vehicle and, in some ways, it succeeded.

The R-40's most distinguishing feature was a sharply sloped front end that gave it a sleek, ultra-modern look, a distinct contrast to the TA's generally austere rolling stock. But no sooner did the R-40 go into operation then it became the butt of heavy criticism. In November 1968 the TA admitted that the R-40's design was unacceptable, and an additional $200,000 would have to be spent to rectify the flaws.

While more attractive than previous rolling stock, the R-40 clearly was less safe for passengers. The sharply sloped ends produced a "lip" which seemed to invite youths to ride in

R-40 interior. There's room aplenty—at the expense of seating.

hazardous fashion on the outside of the train. The new car also was conspicuously lacking safety devices to protect passengers walking from one car to another. Following a spate of criticism, the TA installed pantograph gates and safety stanchions adjacent to the body's end-door openings to permit riders to walk between cars without hazard from the sharply-sloped ends. In its final concession that the Loewy-Snaith design was impractical, the TA ordered the industrial design firm of Sundberg Ferar to revise the styling of the last 100 R-40 cars on order to make them similar to the R-42 then under design.

Throughout the post-war years one anachronism survived on the system. In the distant Canarsie section of Brooklyn a grade crossing reminiscent of an Iowa farm village survived the growth and modernization of the BMT 14th Street line. Located at East 105th Street, the crossing gate and a small wooden station building originally served an area of small truck farms. But by the end of World War II Canarsie was becoming heavily populated and the bucolic flavor of the old

94

community disappeared. Finally in August 1973 the BMT submitted to "progress" and closed the grade crossing. A new and very unattractive station was built at a cost of $400,000, which included an overpass above the tracks. Eliminating the grade crossing meant the loss of jobs for four towermen, including one beloved gatekeeper who was accustomed to keeping the gates up when people were running toward the station to catch a train.

Genuine progress was made in the area of train communications when, in 1968, the TA installed two-way radios in the motorman's cabs. Now, when a motorman wants to contact someone over his radio, all he has to do is step on a footswitch and talk into a microphone while keeping his hands on the controls.

One of the most dramatic, not to mention controversial, changes made in the TA's rolling stock was the Authority's decision in the early 1970s to increase the length of trains from what had become the standard sixty feet to a record seventy-five feet from front to back. Heretofore the longest cars had been the sixty-seven foot "Standards" introduced by the BRT in 1914 and used regularly on BMT lines until they were eased out of service in the 1960s.

The new rolling stock was designed for operation on the IND and BMT where tunnels originally had been designed for trains no longer than seventy feet. While all New York subways use the American railroad track gauge of four-feet,-eight-and-one-half inches, the IRT cars are thinner. Their width is eight feet, nine inches. BMT and IND cars measure ten feet wide. The TA's assistant general superintendent, Harold J. McLaughlin, was aware of the intrinsic dangers and ordered TA engineers to devise a machine to detect potential obstructions. The result was a bizarre looking car over 75 feet long—with whiskers!

TA crews at the Coney Island yard constructed the hirsute train from a battered R-1 subway car, No. 192, that dated back

thirty-nine years to the first days of the IND line. Mechanics first cut the old car in half and then welded in what appeared to be an Erector Set midsection, extending the standard sixty-footer to seventy-five feet, the length of the projected new cars.

To probe the subway tunnels for obstructions in much the same way a cat uses its whiskers to gauge whether it can squeeze through a narrow space, the TA mounted wire "whiskers" at the front, center, and back of the old R-1 car. When the "whiskers" touched an obstruction anywhere at the top or sides of the tunnel an electrical circuit closed, causing a buzzer to sound and a bulb to light on a panel board. This enabled the test-car crew to pinpoint the obstruction. On its first two pre-dawn runs the bewhiskered train discovered clearance problems at the upper and lower corners of the car. Most of the difficulties involved concrete catwalks on curves as well as columns, light fixtures, and wires. Old No. 192 had done its job well. A list of 119 obstructions were compiled, which meant that the TA had to spend $400,000 for tunnel modifications to accommodate the seventy-five-foot cars.

Built by the St. Louis Car Company—just before the firm permanently closed its factory—the new R-44 cars cost $211,850 each and immediately caught the fancy of New Yorkers because of their comparative opulence. Seats were three different shades of orange. Fluorescent lights ran down the middle of the ceiling and at each end of the car the panels were made of an attractive imitation wood.

The shiny, clean new trains were equipped with bells that warned when the doors were closing and an interior that was remarkably quiet. Gone were the straphangers' straps. Instead there were five foot eight-inch high bars above the seats. There were also eight vertical poles in each car, well away from the doors to avoid jams at the entrances. "The spectacular thing about the new cars," commented the *New York Times*, "is their silence, which is due to new methods of insulation."

Not everyone was enthusiastic about the new rolling stock. One of the most vocal antagonists was Carol Greitzer, head of the City Council's Mass Transportation Committee. On December 4, 1975 Councilperson Greitzer charged that the city's new subway cars were "unsafe, impractical and overly costly to maintain." Ms. Greitzer based her charges on a report by a consultant engineer, Dr. Martin Huss, professor of transportation engineering at the Polytechnic Institute of New York. Dr. Huss contended that a design problem in the electric circuitry of the cars could lead to fires and darkened cars and pointed out that there had been a number of fires in these cars while they were standing in the yards. He recommended several changes, including emergency brake-pull cords at each end of the cars; a fire extinguisher at each end of the cars; an automatic lock on end doors to function when trains took a curve (included in original plans but not built in), and installation of safety glass between cars.

The TA, which was amassing a fleet of more than 1,000 new cars—R-44 and a newer model, R-46—was predictably furious over the criticism. John G. DeRoos, who had become the senior executive officer of the TA, replied that the new cars were "the best and safest railroad cars of their kind anywhere." DeRoos acknowledged that the cars had problems in the electric circuitry but maintained they were being eliminated.

While the new rolling stock was immediately pleasing to the eye, the commuters in distant areas of Queens and Brooklyn as well as residents of Manhattan's East Side still clamored for more extensions and new lines. Although many New Yorkers had long forgotten the $500-million bond issue for the Second Avenue Subway, others did remember and demanded that the line be built. The IRT's East Side Subway was the city's most crowded line in 1970, though the densest traffic was on the Flushing-Times Square line at peak periods when thirty-six

trains ran each hour at a headway of only 100 seconds. Only a Second Avenue addition could relieve East Side congestion. "You just can't go on doing what the city's done," said Metropolitan Transportation Authority (MTA) chairman, William Ronan.

"You can't go on building office buildings, apartment buildings, without planning for adequate transit. You ought to require that there be transportation just as there must be water, light, sewage and so forth."

Responding to the public pressure, the MTA, supported by Governor Nelson Rockefeller (significantly, a close friend of Ronan) and Mayor Lindsay, produced the most comprehensive plan for subway expansion in more than forty years. It included the following projects:

1. A super-express line in Queens connecting Forest Hills and Long Island City, feeding into the new 63rd Street tunnel.

2. A crosstown link in Manhattan along 48th Street between First and Twelfth avenues.

3. A line along the Long Island Expressway to serve northeast Queens.

4. A line to serve southeast Queens, using the Long Island Rail Road Atlantic Branch right-of-way, including the demolition of the Jamaica Avenue elevated train in the Jamaica business district.

5. Extension of the Second Avenue Subway into the northeast Bronx connecting to the Dyre Avenue and Pelham Bay Lines.

6. Extension of the Nostrand Avenue Line in Brooklyn to Avenue W.

7. A subway extension along Utica Avenue in Brooklyn to Avenue U.

8. A line in the Bronx to replace the Third Avenue Elevated.

9. Relocation and extension of the 14th Street Canarsie Line.

Fortunately, not all construction on subway extensions was halted because of the city's monetary *malaise*. Throughout the early 1970s the clangorous symphony of jack hammers was heard in and around the southern tip of

Central Park in Manhattan where workmen tunneled through porous rock, starting in 1971, to produce two new underground connections from existing lines. One extension continued the BMT's tracks past 57th Street station (Central Park South) on Seventh Avenue, northward through the park, and then, abruptly, eastward to 63rd Street. The second extension moved the IND line northward from 57th Street station on Avenue of the Americas (Sixth Avenue) under Central Park where it eventually linked with the BMT tunnel at a point immediately south of the zoo. The two routes continue eastward under 63rd Street and then in a double-deck tunnel under the East River to Queens.

These and other changes indicated that the Transit Authority had not been playing Rip Van Winkle. It had been far from dormant, even to the point of changing its name, not to mention its leadership. Since 1971, the following individuals have headed the system: Daniel T. Scannell (October 1971 - April 1975), John G. DeRoos (April 1975 - July 1979), Steven K. Kauffman (July 1979 - November 1980), John D. Simpson (November 1980 - August 1983), Daniel T. Scannell, acting, (August 1983 - February 1984), David L. Gunn (February 1984 - March 1990), Alan F. Kiepper (March 1990 - 1996) and Lawrence G. Reuter (1996-Present).

As far as the name change, the TA officially became known as New York City Transit. As for the other meaningful additions, consider the following:

* The TA was able to construct a 63rd Street extension which opened a direct subway link between Roosevelt Island and Manhattan. The project resulted in 3.2 miles of new track being laid at a cost of $868 million. The technology used to build the tunnel was virtually unchanged from that used back during the 1930's. From the original design, the tunnel was constructed with two upper levels for the subway and two lower levels for the Long Island Rail Road. However, the use of the two lines on the Long Island Rail Road level was postponed.

Originally, after ruling out other locations for the new extension, 64th Street was selected. This was directly below Rockefeller University and University officials objected to the noise and vibration that would result from construction. To avoid delays, 63rd Street was chosen as an alternative.

Another major concern was the effect that construction would have on Central Park. Many feared its beauty would be destroyed forever. To help calm these fears, special fencing was built with noise-absorbing material and designed to add beauty to the park. Drill houses were constructed to help limit noise and electric compressors were also used.

The 63rd Street Extension went into service in 1989.

* Yet another major accomplishment was completion of the new Archer Avenue Line. Construction was begun on August 15, 1972 and the first cars accepted passengers on December 11, 1988.

The new Archer Avenue Line extended over two miles and connected the Queens Boulevard IND Line with the elevated Jamaica Avenue BMT Line. This allowed passengers to take either the E trains to midtown Manhattan on the Queens Boulevard line or the J or Z trains on the Jamaica Line to lower Manhattan.

Three new stations were also constructed. The first was the Jamaica-Van Wyck Station, located at the intersection of Jamaica Avenue and the Van Wyck Expressway. The second was the Sutphin Boulevard Station, located at the corner of Archer Avenue adjacent to the Long Island Rail Road. The third new station was the Jamaica Center Station, located on Archer Avenue at Parsons Boulevard.

All the new stations were built with safety and comfort in mind, limiting the number of columns on the platforms and constructing 213,000 square feet of high, suspended ceilings. The lighting in the stations was also highly intense.

For all the comforts provided and the length of track constructed, the city spent a total of

$465 million on the first new subway line to open in the borough of Queens since the Rockaway Line made its debut on June 28, 1956.

*   Not only spending on projects to convenience commuters, the TA also funded restoration projects such as the one at City Hall station.

The total cost of the restoration was $3.5 million. However, $750,000 of this was in the form of a federal grant. New York City Transit allocated $300,000 for the project and hoped to raise the rest of the money needed through the donations of private investors.

Through the 1990s the quest for the "perfect" subway car continued. In 1992 the R-110A, made by Kawasaki, entered service on an experimental basis over the A Division, Number Two Line tracks. Meanwhile, a Bombardier-manufactured prototype car, R-110B entered service on the B Division. The stainless steel trains featured wide doors, automated station announcements and other amenities. Based on tests and the public response, other changes were made for a new fleet under construction for the new century.

By the year 2000 New Yorkers will be riding in the most up-to-date subway trains in the world!

When the subway opened in 1904, local platforms were just long enough to accommodate three-car locals while express station platforms handled five to eight car trains. Almost immediately this proved to be totally inadequate and train lengths increased forthwith. It would be years before platforms on the original subway route were extended to equal the train lengths. Here, the IRT proudly announces trains have been expanded to ten cars.

(above) *Construction of the Seventh Avenue Line connection with the original route just west of the Times Square Station in 1915. Portions are still visible from the station walkway.*

(below) *The IRT being constructed under Eastern Parkway in 1917. The Brooklyn Museum is in the distance and beyond it Grand Army Plaza and Prospect Park.*

(above left) *Motorman's cab of an IRT Lo-V, 1924.*

(above right) *The interior of an IRT Lo-V. Note the experimental loudspeakers.*

(below) *A Seventh Avenue Express to Flatbush Avenue, with Lo-V equipment, entering the Franklin Avenue Station in 1951. By this time its ancient motors emitted a distinct groan, not unlike the mooing of a cow.*

(above) *Construction of the IRT's Flushing Line portal and ramp just east of the Hunters Point Avenue Station in 1916. The Sunshine Biscuit factory looms in the distance.*

(below) *Construction of the massive Queensborough Plaza Station in 1915. Before 1949, the station had four platforms and eight tracks.*

(above) *The Queensborough Plaza station and approach tracks nearing completion in 1917. The Queensborough Bridge, (59th Street Bridge) which opened only a few years earlier, is in the distance.*

(below) *The Queens Boulevard and the art deco 33rd.-Rawson Street station in 1917. Sunnyside was farmland before the el brought homeowners to Queens. This is the classiest el structure on the entire New York system.*

(above) *The 14th Street Canarsie line originally did not connect directly with the rest of the system. Here, we see a brand new BMT "Standard" #2700 being lowered into the subway by means of a temporary track connection at Bushwick and Montrose Avenues in 1924. A crowd of Williamsburg onlookers check out the rare event.*

(below) *Temporary track at the bottom of the same ramp. Note: third rails have yet to be installed.*

(above) *R-4 557 leads a set of similar looking R-1 to R-9's at the Carroll Gardens portal in Brooklyn . This is where the IND climbs over the Gowanus Canal at Smith-9th Street Station. Note the onlooker atop the fence.*

(below) *These are Lo-V cars built in a slightly more modern style in 1938 for express service on the Flushing Line to the 1939 World's Fair. They ended their careers in the early 1970s, having done yeoman service on the Bronx portion of the Third Avenue El.*

(above) *BMT Standards on the Brighton Beach Line near Beverley Road in 1953.*

(below) *R-36 type cars in "World's Fair" paint at the Grand Central Station stop on the Flushing Line in 1964. Auto-type headlights had become standard equipment.*

The end of Car 4664 destroyed in the Williamsburg Bridge disaster on June 5, 1995.

DISASTERS

A railroad so busy, vast and complex as New York City's subway-elevated system could never be accident-proof no matter how many safety devices were installed nor how diligent the work force.

The mere fact that trains operate round the clock—24 hours a day, 365 days a year—suggests that perfection is impossible. The Law of Averages dictates that over a period of nearly 100 years, human error, defective signals and broken switches will causes derailments, if not disasters.

Mile for mile, hour for hour, The Big Apple's underground is the safest railroad in the world, not to mention the most exciting and architecturally magnificent.

But perfect it is not, although its record in the earliest years defied the critics.

When the city's first significant el—the Ninth Avenue Line—premiered in 1870 predictions were rife that locomotives and passenger cars would lose their battle with gravity and regularly plunge off the steel skeleton and on to the sidewalks below.

Eighty years—and 35 billion passengers—later the els' injury record was minute compared to other forms of street level transit. Until 1905, not a single rider had been killed while commuting on elevated lines.

Nevertheless, the elevated structure itself hardly was conducive to confidence. One look at it from a distance produced shudders in the timid. The iron supports spaced from forty to sixty feet from one another did not appear hefty enough to carry the rush-hour loads, let alone the smoke-belching locomotives.

"And the overtaxed structure itself was constantly exposed to vandalism, accident or demolition," wrote Robert C. Reed in his book The New York Elevated. "Even a fire in an adjacent building could tumble down high masonry walls onto the ironwork, which could but offer little resistance."

Fear of falling trains was a natural reaction but, in the light of accident *records, an exaggerated one. Over an entire century a total of three passenger trains—one in Manhattan and two in Brooklyn—hit the streets. That includes the original Greenwich Street experimental line which had a clean slate in terms of keeping its rolling stock where it belonged, above the ground not on the pavement.*

Disasters afflicted the transportation system in an assortment of forms, from derailments to front-to-back collisions. In 1879 a switchman negligently ignored an open switch whereupon two steam locomotives on the Third Avenue Line crashed head-on near 42d Street. It marked the first significant mishap on the elevated system. Two passengers were seriously injured and others hospitalized. But by far the worst disaster of all was the Malbone Street crash of 1918, which also was unrivaled in terms of melodrama, plots—political and otherwise—and sub-plots. The death toll was 97.

A year later a local on the IRT's Bronx Park Line rammed into the rear of an empty train ahead of it at the Third Avenue Line's 175th Street Station causing three deaths.

In some cases history repeated itself. The 1928 IRT wreck, caused by a switch that moved as cars passed over it, was virtually duplicated—with thankfully fewer injuries—in the summer of 1997, only this time on the IND.

Each disaster posed mysteries of its own. Some were solved, others remain perplexing to this day. It is our purpose to present them not as typical of the system but as a rarity on the world's busiest—and safest—web of trains

The Els

The first disaster to traumatize New York's elevated railroad was an aberration in every sense of the word. It was not a wreck, yet the entire system was brought to a halt. It happened in 1888 on the threshold of spring, yet it was the most memorable blizzard in the city's history.

The Blizzard of '88 engulfed the city at a time when its elevated rapid transit lines had become pivotal to the economy. Only a decade earlier (1878) the total annual ridership was 4,000,000. By 1888 the number had skyrocketed to 172,000,000. Snowstorm or no snowstorm, the Manhattan Railway intended to keep its trains moving. At first, though, there didn't seem to be a problem as dawn broke on the island.

A torrent of rain soaked Manhattan's citizens in the morning of March 11, 1888, a day which would progressively grow colder as the afternoon unfolded. By nightfall what became notorious as The Blizzard of '88 was blowing to full force and train speeds dwindled from their normal maximum of 20-plus miles per hour, down to 15 mph, 10 m.p.h. until the locomotives could hardly, move.

While the elevated railroads were prepared for snow removal, they were unaccustomed to a storm of such Promethean proportions. In some areas the wind-driven snow had drifted as high as the tracks of the Manhattan Railway which operated the Second, Third, Sixth and Ninth Avenue Lines, not to mention a suburban branch from 129th Street and Third Avenue.

In one station there were close to a hundred impatient men, boys and about half a dozen women waiting for an elevated. Many had been waiting for three hours or more. While two or three locomotives had pushed down the track, they were still snow-covered. The snow was so heavy and compact that it refused to be crushed aside, which caused the locomotives to bounce over the lumps of snow.

Miraculously, trains chugged through the drifts to handle rush-hour passengers in the early morning hours but snow-plows were fighting a losing battle. Manhattan Railway general manager, Colonel Frank Hain, was determined to keep the trains running until the combination of ice and snow blockaded the lines before Noon.

At Grove Street locomotives again tried to push forward. It was at this time that one of the engines was pushed off the track. One engineer was thrown from the cab, sustaining minimal injuries, while the three other engineers were trapped in the cab as it was crushed by a falling telegraph pole. One received a fractured skull while the other two suffered internal injuries and broken legs.

The little steam locomotives pushed valiantly ahead where they could but, finally, the blizzard triumphed. Engines were forced to a halt as thousands of passengers—one estimate put the total at 15,000—were trapped in the rapidly-freezing cars as gale-force winds assaulted the city.

Others, who were not in the cars, were also "trapped." One woman rushed to the Seventy Second Street Station in the hopes of catching an elevated to see her dying husband. After climbing up the stairs she asked if anyone knew when the next train was coming. Someone responded, "No one knows if the train is coming at all." She immediately burst into tears and collapsed on the station floor. Recovering quickly, knowing there was no time to waste, the lady explained how she had received a call from her husband's doctor telling her to get to Thirteenth Street as soon as possible, as her husband desperately called for her. Not sparing a moment, the lady quickly dashed down the stairs and ran off in the direction of 13th Street.

Another man who was trapped by the storm proclaimed in anguish how, here he was prepared to repay an unpaid note and now there was no way he was going to be able to get to the bank. He continued to blame the elevated railroad for all the trouble he was encountering.

It became apparent to transit officials that a calamity was in the making if ways and means to rescue the commuters were not immediately found. Ladder companies from the Fire Department reached some trains but many were out of the rescuers' reach.

As the storm reached its crescendo some entrepreneur-rescuers actually pushed ladders against the ironwork and allowed entrapped passengers to descend—but for a price! The exact figure depended on the cynicism of the private ladder companies.

According to Robert C. Reed, passengers in a marooned car managed to warm themselves up by dropping a rope to the sidewalk where a neighborhood barkeeper tied assorted bottles of rye, bourbon and rum which then were hoisted to the trapped straphangers.

Col. Hain's goals were, a. To clear the tracks; b. To obtain a semblance of rush-hour service by Tuesday morning and, c. Demonstrate to his customers that rapid transit could emerge from the disaster quicker and more efficiently than ground transport such as horse-cars and other vehicular traffic.

All obstacles considered, The Manhattan Railway delivered. As the blizzard moved into the decrescendo stage, plows assaulted the drifts and by late Monday night there was hope for a breakthrough by rush-hour on Tuesday morning. Once the plows pushed through openings, Col. Hain borrowed a technique employed by the nation's mountain-climbing western railroads. Instead of using the traditional single locomotive, he assigned them in married pairs to take on the difficult assignment of moving the trains.

It was a noble and successful effort. The trains were running again on Tuesday—albeit on an unpredictable schedule—and their above-ground progress was far better than the chaos on the street. Col. Hain and his staff emerged as heroes of the '88 Blizzard.

More than a dozen years would pass before another major el trauma would unfold. It happened after electrification was achieved on the els in 1902—starting with the Second Avenue Line on January 9, 1902. At that point operation was speedier, more efficient and far less polluting—but not accident-free. Less than a year after August Belmont's Interborough Rapid Transit began operating the first subway, the Ninth Avenue El suffered a big-time black eye.

Beginning at its 155th Street terminus adjacent to the Polo Grounds baseball park, the Harlem River and nearby High Bridge aqueduct, the Ninth Avenue Line headed South to its last stop, South Ferry, at the foot of Whitehall Street. Like the other former Manhattan Railway lines, it now was operated by the IRT.

During the morning rush hour in 1905 the entire trip consumed forty-five minutes with two-minute intervals between many stations. Trains rolled south down Manhattan's spine, first along Harlem's Eighth Avenue until they left the 116th Street station.

This was followed by the serpentine "Suicide Curve." It snaked to the right (west), high above 110th Street. It then moved west past Morningside Park— created by Calvert and Vaux who also designed nearby Central Park—and then sharp left for its southward rumble past the apartment houses along Ninth Avenue.

The stations along Ninth Avenue were so close to each other—104th St., 93d St., 81st St., 72d St., 66th St.—that the running time between stops sometimes was only 90 seconds. Platform-to-platform from 59th Street to 50th Street was only a 62-second sprint, hardly enough time for the motorman to get his train at top speed before applying the air brakes.

Under normal conditions, the braking was done before southbound trains approached 53rd Street. It was there that a set of switches moved Sixth Avenue Line trains—which operated over the Ninth Avenue route from 155th Street—on eastward tracks across town to West 53rd and Sixth where they then proceeded on to South Ferry along Sixth Avenue.

Only five years past the turn of the century, the els were the predominant form of rapid transit and—along with the lone IRT subway—were carrying an estimated 250,000,000 riders a year. Business was good, which meant that the rush-hour headway between Ninth and Sixth Avenue trains along this busy stretch of the elevated was exceptionally close.

Responsibility for switching Sixth Avenue trains on to the 53rd Street spur rested with the towerman—in this case Cornelius Jackson—who took his cue from disks which were affixed to the front end of the wooden el cars.

What's more, it should have been clear from the arrangement of the disks which trains remained on the Ninth Avenue straightaway and which should be dispatched to the Sixth Avenue Line via 53rd Street.

Because of the harsh, 90-degree curve, Sixth Avenue motormen were on notice that they were to apply their brakes at 56th Street to afford themselves ample time to slow to a 9 mph—or slower—crawl before the wheels rolled into the switch.

Ninth Avenue trains, of course, could go faster but by the time the cars had bounced over the switch they were to begin their deceleration process for the stop at 50th Street.

As he pulled on his controller and moved the Ninth Avenue train out of 59th Street station, motorman Paul Kelly could clearly see the red lights on the last car of the Sixth Avenue train ahead of him. It was close enough for him to hear the *clunkity-clunk-clunk* of its wheels banging through the switch and over the intersecting rails.

Kelly's sidekick, conductor J.W. Johnson, was responsible for the proper selection and arrangement of the disk so that the towerman understood that this was, in fact, a Ninth Avenue train not another Sixth Avenue el.

With the Sixth Avenue cars curving out of

110

sight behind the tall, balconied apartment house at the northwest corner of West 53rd Street and Ninth Avenue, Kelly added another point on his controller. He assumed without a shadow of a doubt that towerman Jackson had spotted the telltale disk on his front platform and had rearranged the switch to straightaway.

Meanwhile, the streets below resounded with the cacophony of steel on steel as Kelly's train thundered south, moving from a speed of 20 mph to 25 mph and even higher. Had he been traditionally observant, the motorman would have noticed the amber (slow) track signals some 500 feet before the switch. The amber warned that the switch was arranged for a curve on to the 53rd Street track.

From his vantage point in the tower, Jackson stood transfixed as the train bore down on the still-curved switch. Without knowing the precise speed of the oncoming train, Jackson's railroading instincts instantly told him that it was not only going far too fast —by now an estimated 30 mph—but was a disaster-in-the-making.

Motorman Kelly's eyes, which were riveted on the gleaming, steel tracks ahead, suddenly became fixed on the distant switch down the line. Could it be? Was he actually observing a switch that, mistakenly, still was in the turn position? Was his speeding train doomed to a derailment?

The thoughts cascaded through his mind as he simultaneously slammed the steel controller into the "off" position and played the brake handle to "emergency." Unfortunately, the six-car train was too close to the curve to be effectively slowed although Kelly's lead car somehow held the rails.

Kelly gave this account of the crash: "I put on my brakes when I saw that I could not avoid the curve. But the speed of the train was too great to have any effect, and the next thing I knew the accident happened."

Incredibly, the second car not only jumped the tracks but described an aerial loop before plummeting over the side of the el's superstructure and down to the street below.

At the conclusion of its horrific dive, the second car's roof was sliced open like the top of a sardine can. The car's rear platform stuck through the top of the trackbed like a seal emerging from the water while—nose-down on an angle—the front end touched the sidewalk in front of an apartment house.

The third car actually passed the second one and careened off the rails toward 53rd Street. When it thudded to a halt, the third car precariously hung over the abyss, its undamaged front end seeming to peer down on the destroyed second car to its immediate right.

By this time the deafening noise of the crashing steel, splintering wood and breaking glass aroused the neighborhood. Frightened residents, whose windows looked directly out on to the track bed, shrieked as they reacted to the horrendous sight.

One woman, Mrs. James G. Crowe, viewed the disaster from her apartment window. She was relaxing in her bed when she heard a crash. She jumped to her feet and ran for her children. She then heard a second blast. This time she saw part of the train's platform crashing through her parlor windows followed by escaping riders.

Mrs. Crowe recalled, "Most of those who came through the windows were men but there were a few women and the men thrust the women aside as they rushed through the room and down the stairs to the street, with apparently no thought for the safety of any one but themselves. There must have been fifty or sixty of them who escaped this way."

What others saw—apart from the disjointed first two cars—were the last three pieces of rolling stock derailed but virtually unharmed on the wooden ties above Ninth Avenue.

Meanwhile, pedestrians who had been en route to work on the street below, swung into action summoning emergency vehicles. From the cries of the wounded it was evident that the most serious injured were those in the second car whose nose was on the ground.

Almost no one who was in the car which fell from the structure escaped injury.

Passengers crawled out of the car with nothing more serious than scratches and bruises while some of those next to them were mangled beyond recognition.

Ambulances rushed them to nearby hospitals and when the final toll was counted, twelve persons were killed and 42 injured, five of them mortally.

Motorman Kelly survived, maintaining his innocence.

Kelly claimed, "As I approached the tower I looked at the track signals. Both of them—the six-foot and the two-foot signals—showed green disks, which means clear road ahead for Ninth Avenue. As I always do, I looked up at my air, and the next moment when I looked at the track again, just before I reached the switch, I saw that the signals had been changed and that the two-foot signal showed a yellow disk." Which means that the switch was set for Sixth Avenue.

Kelly's explanation of what had happened was that Jackson was, "trying to do him." He said that it was not the first time that Jackson had switched the signal on him. On previous occasions Kelly said he was forced to reverse, costing him time and causing him to get in trouble with the administration.

Jackson, the towerman, insisted that the front car's disk was that of a Sixth Avenue train and therefore he was justified in keeping the switch in its curved position. But Johnson, the conductor, contradicted that claim. He not only asserted that the disk was for the Ninth Avenue run but added additional evidence supporting his sidekick Kelly.

Johnson argued that station guards at each platform from 145th Street on southward would broadcast to the waiting commuters that this was, in fact, the Ninth Avenue train that was rolling into the station. "Some of the men would most certainly have noticed if the train had carried Sixth Avenue markers," wrote Reed.

Final blame however, rested on the shoulders of Motorman Kelly. The Coroner and the officials of the railroad agreed that Motorman Kelly should have seen that the tower signals were set for Sixth Avenue. They contended that since he was running a Ninth Avenue train, he should have stopped it until he got the proper signals to proceed down Ninth Avenue.

Photos of the plunging subway cars made the front pages of the newspapers on September 12, 1905. To many New Yorkers who had become accustomed to tragedy on the streets, the sight of a train tailspinning to the base of Ninth Avenue was as traumatic as anything they could imagine. Naturally, it inspired demands for greater safety on a road that already had an excellent track record.

This record would get even better as the IRT installed state of the art protective devices, one of which was the safety tripper. A steel arm adjoined the tracks near every signal on the system. After a train passed over that section of rail, the arm would move into an upward formation as the signal light turned red.

If the following train ran the red light, a metal strip overhanging the truck would make contact with the tripper. This would activate the emergency brakes, bringing the train to as abrupt a stop as possible under the circumstances.

The tripper was a landmark advance in transit safety technology although it was not one-hundred percent perfect. By manual operation, a trainman could neutralize the tripper enabling the cars to roll through the red signal without being automatically halted. This "key-by" system enabled dispatchers to shorten headways during rush-hours. The assumption, safety-wise, was that the "keying" motorman would be extra-vigilant in terms of the train immediately ahead of him.

That was the scenario on April 29, 1929 along an interesting portion of elevated track on the IRT. Both the Lexington Avenue branch of the subway and the Ninth Avenue elevated line ran on the same tracks, usually one followed by the other.

On this day seven old wooden cars of the Ninth Avenue El were at the 170th Street

Station in the Bronx. The antique rolling stock dated as far back as 1878, 1887, 1888, 1893, 1903 and two from 1904. But they were only seven of the 1,700 wooden el cars in daily use on the IRT.

Right behind was an all-steel Lexington Avenue Subway train stopped at a red signal south of the platform.

Still another train was behind the Lex. This one was awaiting a go-ahead to move across the switch to pick up passengers on an adjoining platform. Before the third train could move, it had to wait for the subway in front to roll ahead out of its way.

To keep the trains moving it was decided to have the IRT express key by the red light. A keyman neutralized the stop signal and the motorman promptly pulled his controller forward.

At this point the events take on a mysterious quality. The motorman had to be aware that his speed should have been—for safety purposes—limited to the lowest point on his controller. Yet he totally ignored this rudimentary practice. Furthermore, there was no visibility problem and the Ninth Avenue El's rear car had its red warning lights functioning. The local should easily have been seen ahead.

The impact itself was not enough to send any of the cars from the tracks and the fire that resulted in the last car was put out quickly but it still sent the estimated 3,000 passengers into a state of panic.

Andrew P. Corcoran, the Motorman for the IRT who was assigned the duty of key man on the foot platform, explained what happened moments before the crash. "I was on duty at 170th Street and Jerome Avenue on the platform along the side tracks about fifteen feet south of the station," Corcoran said. "Cullen's train came by. He opened the door and said, 'Hello.' I said 'Hello' back, and then looked ahead and saw that traffic was backed up from 157th Street. This was at the peak of the rush. I told Cullen, 'I'm going to key you by; look out for that elevated train ahead of you.' Cullen said, 'All right.' I keyed him by and I saw Cullen put his controller on multiple, meaning full speed ahead. All at once, when Cullen was about a car length behind the elevated train, I heard the air brakes. I can only think Cullen's mind was not on what he was doing, but it did seem to function before the crash, for he set his brakes."

Another witness, Harold Kuhner, 19, was in the last car of the elevated train. This is what he saw. "The elevated train stopped," he said. "I looked out of the rear door and saw the motorman of the subway train. The horrible look on his face I will never forget. He seemed to be trying frantically to stop the train."

When Motorman Cullen was found in the wreckage his hand was still pressed to the emergency brake lever and the motor controller was in reverse.

Why the motorman disregarded the mandatory safety practices is unknown. He pulled the controller to high speed position and ploughed into the flimsy wood cars ahead and died in his crushed cab. Three other fatalities resulted from the collision that stirred public opinion and demands for an end to the key-by practice.

Just two days later the Transit Commission banned keying-by but the edict was just as abruptly cancelled thanks to the lobbying of the subway-el barons. Keying-by remained *de rigueur* on the system and, thankfully, no other major el disasters followed.

The very first elevated line built in Manhattan inspired fear among New Yorkers that at some point a train would be derailed and plunge to the street below. This terrible event, described above, actually took place on September 7, 1905 on the 9th Avenue Line. At the intersection of 9th Avenue and 53rd Street a local went off the tracks and one of its cars plunged to the sidewalk below (right). The result was the worst wreck on the elevated lines in the history of New York transit. Inspectors are shown checking the ruins.

*Because of accidents like this 1928 rear-ender at 113th Street and 8th Avenue—
on the 9th Avenue Line—the public clamor for safer cars increased.*

(above) *Because the early elevated trains were partly made of wood and lacked "anti-climbing" devices at each end, collisions could have horrific results. An example is the telescoping of trains on the Third Avenue Line, October 21, 1919. The car on the left (#923) was scrapped but the other (#1762) actually was repaired.*

(left) *One of the joys of riding the El in mild weather was standing on the open platforms at either end of the train. Conversely, they also could be dangerous when there was a collision, as on June 15, 1930. This rear-ender occurred on the 6th Avenue Line at Chambers Street in Manhattan.*

(below) *Sometimes all-steel subway cars ran on the same track as the older, wooden, elevated rolling stock. This was fine, as long as they kept their distance. But in June 1923 a steel IRT Subway car (#4654) rammed a wooden elevated car at the junction of Jerome and 9th Avenue lines south of 167th Street, with devastating results.*

An April 1920 switching mishap on the Ninth Avenue El just north of the Rector Street station.

A derailment on Belmont's experimental monorail in Pelham Bay Park.

Brooklynites surround and overlook this wreck on the Fifth Avenue El south of Atlantic Avenue. It happened in June 1923, confirming the fears of those who worried about El cars plunging to the street.

The Malbone Street BRT Wreck

At 6:45 P.M. on the evening of November 1, 1918 Irving Melton, a tailor who lived in the Brighton Beach section of Brooklyn, picked up his evening newspaper and scanned the headlines. Melton was sitting in the front coach of the five-car Brighton Beach local-express which was taking on passengers in the Park Row terminus of the Brooklyn Rapid Transit Company at City Hall in Manhattan.

It had been an exciting day and Melton didn't know where to turn first for his reading. The Allied offensive in France was crushing the Kaiser's armies and it appeared that, any moment, World War I would come to an end. Soon, the sons of Irving Melton's friends would return from overseas. But another story on Page One furrowed his brow.

Motormen and train guards of the Brooklyn Rapid Transit Company had walked off their jobs and were on strike. In order to maintain service on the heavily-travelled lines, the BRT said it would recruit employees from other positions and give them instant training as motormen. The company assured riders that there would be no interference with schedules. Melton glanced up from his newspaper and everything seemed normal. Commuters were pouring into the rickety wooden cars. Conductor Michael Turner and train guard Samuel Rosoff watched as the more than 900 passengers came aboard. Turner jerked the handle and the gate swung closed with a loud report.

The route of the Brighton Beach local-express traced the spectacular growth of New York City since the turn of the twentieth century. The train would roll over the Brooklyn Bridge and on to Fulton Street in the Downtown shopping area of Brooklyn. It would eventually switch to southbound tracks at Franklin Avenue in the posh Bedford-Stuyvesant area and cut a swath through the newly developed communities of

Flatbush and the fishing village of Sheepshead Bay. Finally, it would end its long run at Brighton Beach at the southern tip of the city.

A series of intricate curves along the route bedeviled motormen. One in particular traumatized even the most competent motorman— the approach to the Malbone Street tunnel in Flatbush. Engineers had designed the Brighton Beach Line so that it dipped from an elevated run at the Franklin Avenue and Dean Street Stations south to a street-level platform at Consumer Park, and dipped still further until it reached the Malbone Street tunnel less than a quarter-mile away.

About twenty feet from the mouth of the concrete tunnel the tracks lurch sharply to the right, and fifty feet later swerve just as dramatically to the left, carrying the trains into the Prospect Park Station. As S-curves go, there were few sharper or more perilous in the world—a fact that was quite evident to the management of the BRT. To neutralize the danger, it emphasized to all motormen that the train's speed along the tunnel approach must be limited to six miles per hour. A sign posted well in advance of the tunnel underlined the regulation.

For motorman Edward Luciano (identified in some dispatches as Edward Lewis) the Brighton Beach local-express represented a formidable challenge and a threat. Dark, slender, and ambitious, the twenty-three-year-old Luciano had worked for the BRT for three years, first as a train guard and then as a dispatcher. When he reported to the dispatcher's office at 5 AM, he learned that only minutes earlier the Brotherhood of Locomotive Engineers had called its strike. Luciano was ordered to act as a motorman.

He had mixed emotions. On the one hand, he sympathized with his colleagues and their aspirations, but on the other hand, he realized that the BRT had vowed to break the strike and would recruit inexperienced men like himself to run the trains at a considerably higher salary than he was making as a dispatcher. The death of Luciano's three-year-old daughter a week earlier, from influenza, and the unpaid funeral bills, coupled with the threat of reprisals against workers who didn't help break the strike, convinced him to go along with the company's demand.

The BRT, whose motto was "Safety Always," normally required that its motormen undergo a minimum of sixty hours of training before they piloted a train on a regular run. But in this case the railroad barons were willing to overlook the rules if it meant crushing the strike. When Edward Luciano jerked the controller to start his first official solo trip as a motorman, his experience consisted of two hours instruction, one-thirtieth of the minimum requirement.

Luciano's first trip was on the BRT's Culver Line. As routes went, it was relatively easy, even for a novice. And since Luciano had been a dispatcher along the line, he was more than casually aware of its pitfalls. But when his ten-hour stint was finished and he was preparing to head home, he was told to switch over to the Brighton Beach local-express and guide the train from City Hall to the shore.

The Brighton Beach Line was a mystery to Luciano. What's more it was nightfall, and he did not have time to study maps of the line nor consult with veteran motormen who could have warned him about its dozens of switches, hairpin curves, the new tunnel construction at Malbone Street and the dreadful S-curve. As he waited in his cab at the Park Row station, all Luciano could think about was the end of the day and the moment he could go home and unwind.

Rush-hour passengers, confounded by strike delays, were anxious to get home for a weekend's rest. And the signalmen were just as anxious to get the Brighton Beach local-express back on schedule. "Take her out quick, you're ten minutes late," the station master bellowed at the already jittery Luciano. He tugged hard on the bulbous wooden handle of the controller. The motors groaned and the wheels screeched as they brushed against the curved steel rails that swung onto the Brooklyn Bridge.

The first stop would be Sands Street in Brooklyn at the other end of the span. Darkness had enveloped the city on this balmy November evening and fatigue was disrupting Luciano's concentration as the train reached the crest of the bridge and approached the long downhill to Sands Street Station. It was a descent that required sensitive braking to prevent the wooden trains from speeding out of control. Luciano tried to use the brake handle but the complicated formula for air pressure baffled him. The *click-clacks* of the wheels against the rail openings accelerated far beyond the normal speed. Irving Melton, who was scanning his newspaper, stopped reading as he realized the train was plummeting down the incline.

An abnormally sharp right-hand curve awaited the local-express at the entrance to the Sands Street station. By now, Luciano had lost control of the train but it managed to whip around the curve with the confidence of a speeding roller coaster. Before the motorman could regain control of his machine and bring it to a terrifyingly abrupt halt, two cars had overshot the station.

It was now 6:50 PM Luciano had been working for fourteen consecutive hours, but he knew he had only to reach the Brighton Beach terminal and his stint would be complete. The tracks curved on to Fulton Street and, this time, Luciano's confidence returned. The braking system was coming to him. He put the controller on high and, in the distance, he could see the Franklin Avenue station switch tower.

A switchman awaited the Brighton local-express. When it rolled into full view, he would pull the long wooden handle in his tower and the rails would swing into place allowing the train to switch off the main line and turn right in the direction of Brighton Beach.

Suddenly the switchman noticed the train was thundering down the track at an abnormally high speed. Thinking it was a City Line train, he did not pull the lever and, no doubt, saved the train from disaster at that juncture. Having temporarily lost control of the local-express once again, Luciano finally brought it to a stop far past the cut-off.

By now riders were either paralyzed with fear or furious with the motorman. When the train was backed up to the Franklin Avenue station, they eagerly alighted. Before it reached the Malbone Street tunnel, more than half of the 1,000 passengers had left the train rather than gamble on the motorman's ability.

George Horn, a husky marble cutter, was leaning against the iron gate on the end platform of the train and recalling his wife's premonition ("I dreamed you'd be in a bad accident today," she had told him). Still, he decided to stay on the train. When Horn related his wife's words to a companion, the other laughed. "What the hell do you think can happen to you on the el?" Horn refused to enter the elevated car. "I feel safer out here," he said remaining on the open end platform and watching his friend walk inside—to his doom.

Irving Melton found it difficult to concentrate on his newspaper. He gazed up at an advertisement hanging over the front window: TRY GRAPE NUTS, THE FOOD THAT YOU'VE HEARD SO MUCH ABOUT. IT SAVES WHEAT, SUGAR, FUEL, AND WOOD. A REAL WAR TIME FOOD. SOLD BY GROCERIES.

Less than six feet from Melton, inside the motorman's cab, Luciano looked at his watch. He was ten minutes late. Obsessed by a desire to make up lost time, he disregarded caution and barreled the train at top speed into the next station, Dean Street, then crashed on the air pressure with such volume that the train nearly swayed off the tracks. Ironically, he actually stopped the train too soon, forcing some riders to trudge from rear cars forward to the station platform. A few people screamed hysterically and conductor Michael Turner began walking toward the cab to warn Luciano. But too many passengers were

exiting to allow him to leave his post, so Turner remained at the gates and hoped for the best.

By now, everyone on the train was aware that the Brighton Beach local-express was not in competent hands. At Dean Street the train was still plying a straightaway along the elevated tracks but soon it would descend toward the tunnel. Dozens of passengers refused to continue the journey. When the motorman started the train before all departing passengers had alighted at the Dean Street station, several men vaulted the iron gates and fell to safety on the wooden station platform.

Those who hadn't learned their lesson at Dean Street had one last chance at Park Place, where the train once again overshot the platform. Despite attempts to make up for the lost time Luciano was fighting a losing battle. He could see the lights of a train behind him and he was worried. As far as he knew, there was a straightaway before him. But it was dark and Luciano, a Culver Line man, was ignorant of the Brighton system. The hill leading down from Park Place would bring him to the Consumer's Park Station, which was so small trains stopped only by request, and then the sudden turn right into the blackness of the Malbone Street tunnel and the S-curve.

The long leather straps hanging from the ceiling began to dance crazily inside the car as the train moved down the incline. Irving Melton had made up his mind. "Tell him I want to get off at Consumer's Park," he ordered train guard Samuel Rosoff.

Without hesitation, Rosoff tugged on the overhead cord three times, ringing a warning bell in Luciano's cabin. But it was too late. Before he realized it, Luciano had permitted his train to surge out of control toward Malbone Street below. With each yard of track, the wood-and-steel caravan gained speed until it rocked past Consumer's Park station so fast its platform signs and lights melted into a blur to the passengers.

A woman leaped from her seat and

smashed her fist against the thick wooden cab door, pleading with Luciano to slow down. It was no use. He played with the brakes but the complicated braking system eluded him in his panic. The train was now doing forty-five miles per hour as it passed a tiny yellow light that reflected a sign: SIX MILES AN HOUR.

Those who remembered how the train managed to negotiate the Sands Street curve off the Brooklyn Bridge prayed that another miracle would save the Brighton Beach local-express. And for a couple of seconds it appeared that just such a miracle would occur. The front wheels of the first car clung tenaciously to the tracks as the train screeched around the first curve. Dozens of standing passengers were hurled to the floor.

When the lights of Luciano's front car picked up the threatening curve, he hit the brakes again with all the energy at his command, but the mounting speed proved too much for the old cars and the brakes lost all hold on the wheels. While the front truck of the lead car managed to survive the gravity pull of the swerve, it was too much for the rear wheels. They surmounted the tracks, plunging the rear platform into the side of the tunnel with a deafening report. Passengers were catapulted off the train and thrown against the new concrete wall.

Once the first car jumped the track, it carried the second with it. The front of the second car leaped upward, smashing its roof against the tunnel ceiling while its wood frame crumbled into thousands of splinters. Amid frenzied cries from the 400 passengers, the train still plunged forward to its ultimate doom.

Deafening crash followed upon crash as the second car was decapitated from its floor up. Plate-glass windows turned into bayonets, impaling the helpless passengers. The third car had so much velocity behind it, it fused with the second. The fourth smashed its front against the tunnel wall with such force it ripped its coupling off the fifth car, which miraculously came to a halt without a scratch.

In a matter of seconds the Malbone Street tunnel had become a cave of horror and death. Fresh crimson covered the faded dark red paint of the cars. Agonizing shrieks pierced the air and carried out to Malbone Street where a ticket-seller at Prospect Park Station heard them and bellowed for police and firemen.

When the police arrived they were confronted with chaos. The train had wiped all lights off the tunnel walls. Automobiles were requisitioned and driven to the tunnel where their lights at least partially illuminated the disaster. But they arrived too late to save those who at first had escaped injury only to be felled minutes later by an ironic mistake.

When the train crashed it uprooted the third rail, shorting out the circuit. Electricians in the BRT powerhouse spotted the short circuit, but mistakenly suspected it was the work of union saboteurs. They were ordered to restore current in such emergencies. The juice was revived on the third rail as countless survivors made their way over the tracks toward salvation. Without warning, the current electrocuted dozens of survivors in an eerie lightning-blue flash of light. Within minutes, the rails shorted out again, but this time the electricians suspected more than foul play and kept the power off.

Sitting at the head of the front car over the wheels that held the track, Irving Melton survived the pulverization of the train. When the shock of the impact had abated, he got to his feet and remembered he had a small flashlight in his pocket. It still was working but he wondered whether it made sense to keep it on. Wherever he turned, the beam picked up dismembered bodies and several passengers still alive but trapped beneath debris.

Melton tugged at a survivor. Soon others joined in the desperate rescue operation, until 250 of the most seriously injured were carried to safety on Malbone Street where they awaited transportation to hospitals. Within the hour, relatives descended upon the site from all points of the borough. The curious drifted down, some to offer aid, others to capitalize on the disaster. Human jackals invaded the tunnel and corpses were later found with their ring fingers chopped off.

Doctors and ambulances were hard to find because the city already was in the grip of an influenza epidemic. George Horn, whose wife had had a premonition of the disaster, writhed on blood-stained Malbone Street awaiting help. He had suffered a fractured skull in the disaster. His friend, who had insisted upon sitting inside the train, was dead.

In lieu of ambulances, private cars and fifty volunteers from the Women's Motor Corps helped transport the most seriously wounded to hospitals. The ninety-seven dead were lined up in the Snyder Avenue police station and in the lobby of the Ebbets Field baseball stadium, three blocks away.

When Luciano's train plowed into the concrete tunnel wall, the motorman, like Irving Melton, was saved by the front truck, which somehow clung to the tracks. The motorman's cab further protected him from the flying wooden flak. Finally Luciano staggered from his cab, physically unscathed. But the shock held him in a vise. Unable to release his grip on the brake and motor handles, he clutched them tightly as he fumbled his way through the carnage toward the mouth of the tunnel.

Slowly, the intensity of the disaster penetrated through to him. He began a hysterical trot, then a run toward his house. When he arrived home, he sobbed in his wife's arms: "Today is All Saints' Day. They must have spared me."

Unaware of the full extent of the disaster, Luciano's wife prodded him. "What about the other people?" He told her everything, but when she urged him to give himself up to the authorities he refused. Through the night they argued until, finally, he relented.

He surrendered himself and was subsequently indicted for manslaughter. Similar indictments were brought against top BRT officials. Brooklyn's district attorney sought to prove that the men who had ordered the inept Luciano to pilot the train had sentenced 97 people to death. Some reports had the number of dead at 102 or more. It marked the first time a railroad management was brought to account for a fatal accident.

Luciano insisted throughout his trial that the brakes had failed. BRT officials contended that the young motorman was incompetent. After six months of legal wrangling, the trial ended and all of the accused were acquitted.

The Malbone Street crash gave rise to demands for more safety measures. The BRT responded by coming up with an automatic time tripping device, Similar to what the IRT already utilized; A thick metal arm activated the braking system of a train that ran through a red light or similar cautionary signal, over the prescribed speed limit. Should the train exceed the desired speed, the trippers would swing into action, activating the brakes.

Just such a system is in operation now along the route of the old Brighton Beach local-express. Today they call the line the Franklin Avenue Shuttle. It begins its run at the Franklin Avenue Station, with a short hop to Park Place, Botanic Garden (then Consumer's Park) and, finally, Prospect Park.

The only thing missing is Malbone Street. That's not there anymore. The name conjured up such fear in New Yorkers, it was changed to Empire Boulevard.

(next page, top) *A view from the treacherous "S" curve inside the Malbone Street (now Empire Boulevard) tunnel following the November 1918 crash. Notice the clean look of the-recently-completed tunnel wall leading into Prospect Park Station.*

(next page, bottom) *Miraculously, the fifth car of the ill-fated Brighton local-express survived the disaster but the debris surrounding it hints of the calamity which took place in the tunnel near Prospect Park.*

Ironically, some of the wooden el cars involved in the Malbone Street disaster remained mostly intact while others were virtually obliterated in the crash that cost 97 lives. These cars were stored in the 36th Street yards after the wreck.

The Times Square
IRT Mystery Crash

As always, the Times Square Station was a maelstrom of activity in late afternoon on August 24, 1928. IRT locals and expresses plied the four-track main line up and down Broadway. Rubbing shoulders underground were the heavily-trafficked Brooklyn Manhattan Transit's Brighton, Sea Beach, West End, and Montague Street (tunnel) trains, each of which stopped at Times Square.

An underground arcade, extending from Broadway and 43rd Street to Seventh Avenue and 40th Street, linked the main IRT and BMT routes as well as the IRT's 42nd Street Shuttle that bounced between Grand Central Station and Times Square. Through these portals thousands of commuters were funneled at 4:55 PM that summer afternoon when the IRT southbound express from Van Cortlandt Park in the Bronx lurched through a mild curve and into the complex station under 42nd Street and Seventh Avenue.

Motorman William McCormick applied the brakes on the steel cars. The ten-car train screeched its way to a normal halt and as soon as the doors opened passengers dashed for the few available wicker seats.

At that precise moment Mounted Patrolman

John F. Ward of the New York City Police Traffic Division was riding his horse southbound down Seventh Avenue from 42nd Street toward the corner of 40th Street and Seventh Avenue, then the site of the Metropolitan Opera House.

Patrolman Ward was accustomed to hearing the incessant starting and stopping of the subway beneath him. His ear was trained to detect the unusual but there was, at 4:58 PM, nothing especially strange about the sounds emanating from the checkerboard steel subway grating alongside him at the curb. Nothing, except the fact that the IRT downtown express from Van Cortlandt Park had not pulled out of the station. Considering the rush hour and the urgency to maintain headway, it was highly unusual for a train carrying 1,800 passengers, as was the case with the downtown express, to remain sitting in the Times Square Station.

Underground, and unknown to Patrolman Ward, IRT maintenance men had held the express at the terminal because of a problem that appeared to become aggravated by the hour. A switch in the tunnel eighty-five feet south of where the express tracks re-enter darkness beyond the station had been betraying defects as successive trains thundered over the tracks. At this point several individuals became involved in determining the fate of the downtown express.

Harry King, an IRT towerman, was on duty in the signal tower immediately south of the Times Square Station at 40th Street under Seventh Avenue. The tower contained an interlocking machine of twenty-three switch and signal levers, but King was concerned with only three of the levers. One was the switch on the downtown express track, eighty-five feet south of the platform. King actuated the switch by operating Lever 17.

Of the many switches on the IRT system, the one south of the Times Square station was among the most strategic and therefore potentially hazardous. Its prime function was to shunt extra rush-hour trains uptown from Times Square. The transfer was accomplished in this manner:

A rush-hour extra—a "gap train"—would complete its southbound run to Times Square. It then would proceed past the station and approach the switch operated by Lever 17. The towerman would activate the switch, shunting the train to the left off the express track and onto a special "gap" lay-up track from where it would then be switched onto the uptown express track and resume operation.

One such gap train had preceded the Broadway express into Times Square Station that fateful Friday. After its passengers were discharged the train was to proceed to the switch and then cross over to the lay-up track. Towerman King activated Lever 17 but it would not work.

When King was certain that the switch had failed, he immediately notified his superior, IRT maintenance foreman William S. Baldwin. Baldwin was stationed at 34th Street and Seventh Avenue at the time. Accompanied by his assistant, signalman Joseph Carr, Baldwin arrived at the Times Square tower in a few minutes. Meanwhile, the gap train was held at the platform until the switch could be repaired. Immediately behind the gap train sat the regular Broadway express, waiting for a red stop light to turn yellow, signaling "proceed with caution."

Having inspected the defective switch, Baldwin determined that the gap train could be shunted over to the lay-up track if he himself manually operated the switch from track level. Baldwin warned King not to touch Lever 17. "I did not touch the switch," towerman King later insisted. Baldwin then ordered his aide, Carr, to go to the emergency box and manually crank the switch and "key" the waiting gap train, which was to be shunted into the northbound service.

Having concluded that it would be safe to manually dispatch the gap train leftward on the switch, Baldwin shouted to Carr that the procedure could begin. At this point Carr held the switch key down as the train moved forward. The flanged steel wheels hissed and screeched as they rolled out of the station toward the troublesome switch now locked into the reverse position. Baldwin and Carr peered through the semi-darkness of the tunnel, their eyes riveted on the precise point where the curved switch rail hugged the straightaway and prayed that it would hold.

Moving at approximately five miles per hour, the train heaved on to the switch, its two foremost right wheels leaning against the curved rail. Carr heaved a sigh of relief while keeping his hand firmly on the key. The train easily negotiated the defective switch and moved onto the lay-up track.

The red signal which had halted the southbound main line Broadway Express at the entrance to Times Square Station flashed to amber as the gap train swerved left out of sight at the other end of the station. Motorman William McCormick pushed his brake handle forward to its release position, pressed down on the controller (accelerator), and pulled it one notch, so that the train softly rolled into the Times Square Station.

By this time, Mounted Patrolman Ward had ridden his horse into the shadows of the Metropolitan Opera House. Almost directly beneath him the southbound express had pulled to a halt and discharged and ingested its passengers. Once again Baldwin had to take command and make a decision; either continue the practice of manual operation of the switch and hope that it would hold fast as it had for the previous train, or take another option by "spiking" the defective switch.

Spiking (driving a regular railroad spike into the wooden tie alongside the switch, thereby locking it into place) was common railroad practice and ensured that the switch would not drift from its proper position. It would have been a feasible alternative in this situation were it not for the need to continue switching gap trains back to the uptown tracks. Baldwin was persuaded that the manual system, having worked for one train, would continue to operate safely—at least for the southbound express, and probably for

trains that would follow—until repair crews arrived.

Motorman McCormick leaned forward in his cab. He saw that all the block signals ahead of him were in red lights; he could not proceed until they changed to amber or he received hand signals at track level from Baldwin.

Carr looked to his boss and got the order without hesitation. Baldwin told him to key the waiting southbound express past the switch. They beckoned to Motorman McCormick. Given the go-ahead hand signal, McCormick again tugged on his controller, gathering speed as the express moved toward the station portal.

Towerman King and a motorman, Michael O'Connor, were in the 40th Street switch room at the time. O'Connor had entered the tower waiting to take charge of the gap train for the northbound (uptown) rush-hour run. Mounted Policeman Ward was heading south along Seventh Avenue toward 39th Street.

Motorman McCormick's train lumbered out of the well-lit station into the black portal. As it approached the switch, the express had gathered momentum and was moving from ten to fifteen miles per hour. Less anxious than before, Baldwin and Carr waited at the crossover where Carr held down the switch key.

Less than a half-mile ahead, the lights of the Pennsylvania Station 34th Street express stop flickered as McCormick tugged his controller another notch faster. To his right was the downtown local track. In front and to the left gleamed the switch connecting with the layover track. Just beyond the switch was a concrete and steel barrier which separated the downtown express tracks from the layover area.

Satisfied that the gap train ahead of him had cleared the switch without incident, McCormick confidently worked his express toward the 20 mph mark as he reached Baldwin and Carr. The wheels on the front truck of the first car did a thundering *paradiddle* as they rolled safely through the switch toward 34th Street. The pattern was repeated by the rear trucks and then the front trucks of the second car. Baldwin and Carr were noticeably relieved as car after car of McCormick's express negotiated the switch and roared southward. As the eighth car thunked over the switch the train was doing 20 mph. Baldwin couldn't wait until the last two pieces of rolling stock cleared the switch so he could make another attempt at getting it back into normal working order.

He trained his eyes on the intersection of straightaway and curved switch rails as the front truck of the ninth car spun ahead. In the two seconds between the crossing of the first truck and the arrival of the second truck on the ninth car a faint but fearsome noise assailed Baldwin's ears. It was a hissing sound, like the exhale of a giant. To a trained railroad man such as Baldwin, the *hiss* was the unmistakable sound of escaping air from the switch valve. Horrified, Baldwin realized that the switch was moving from straightaway position to curve (over to the layover track) as the rear truck of the ninth car approached it.

"I knew what was going to happen," Baldwin later said, "but I was powerless to prevent it."

Baldwin's worst fears were justified. The switch had completely moved from straight to curved position as the rear trucks approached. While eight cars of the express continued to plow ahead through the tunnel, and half of the ninth car lunged forward, the rear of the ninth car drunkenly swerved left over the curved portion of the switch.

For an agonizing split second, the ninth car was engaged in a tug of-war with itself; one half pulled south on the downtown tracks while the other half swerved east on the switch curve. The strain was unbearable and, finally, the rear trucks leaped the curved switch track with a horrific jolt. Its wheels now cutting an ugly swath across the wooden ties and uprooting the rails, the rear truck seemed not to want to give. Suddenly there was a terrific jolt, whereupon the front

quarter of the ninth car was torn from the rest of the car.

Remarkably, the wild-swinging front quarter of Car Nine remained coupled to the eighth car, but only for the briefest agonizing moment. Then it was flung against the concrete-and-stone partition immediately beyond the switch. Its passengers already shrieking in horror, the severed train was pulverized as it crashed into the twenty foot-high abutment separating the north and southbound tracks. Simultaneously the lights had gone out in the rear three-quarters of Car Nine, which whipped left, throwing itself against several steel supporting pillars.

Immobilized by the horror before their eyes, Baldwin and Carr watched helplessly as the tenth car, pulled forward by the train's momentum, crashed into the tangled rubble of the ninth car. The uprooting of the third rail instantly created a bizarre succession of lightning-like flashes as the tenth car buckled and bent like a bow. Amid a crescendo of screams, the last car of the doomed express finally sagged over to become a mass of ruins.

The scene thirty seconds after impact was grotesque. Looking like a battered piece of tin, the ninth car was scattered in bits and pieces along the track. Its forward part was lying sideways, a few airpipes and valves sticking out of the corridor. "It had been twisted," said one early viewer, "as one would twist a piece of paper. Its interior was diminished to a space through which a small man could hardly crawl. The center was only a foot or two in width."

So vicious was the blow of steel car against steel pillars that two twenty-foot vertical barriers were sheared from their bases by the impact and bent in a wide curve where the front of the derailed ninth car had hit them. Leaning against the partition, the rear of the ninth car only partially survived. One side of it was intact; the other was scattered somewhere in the tunnel.

Convulsed by the explosion of its forces, the subway tunnel was alternately pierced by excruciating screams, glowing with eerie flashes from the third rail, and obscured by swirling dust and dirt as if a volcanic eruption had begun to subside. Were it not for the carnage that accompanied the derailment, an objective viewer would have been arrested by the awesome beauty of the underground pyrotechnical display.

Above ground Mounted Patrolman Ward heard the thud and crash of the ninth car as he rode his horse past Seventh Avenue and 40th Street. He wheeled his horse around and raced to the subway entrance at the southbound corner to the rear of the Metropolitan Opera House. Leaping off his horse, he raced down the subway steps. Ward surmised that an accident had taken place, but he had no idea of the extent of damage until he tried to get on to the station platform.

Panicked by the thunder and lightning in the tunnel, passengers waiting on the Times Square station platform stampeded toward the exits. The scene at the wreck site inside the tunnel was a distillation of agony, panic, confusion and infinite heroism. The earliest rescuers reported that the victims were so badly crushed that, in many cases, identification was impossible. Many of the survivors on impact were killed during the ensuing panic over escape routes. Several bodies in Car Nine were found wedged at one window, indicating that the victims had struggled one against the other to escape through the small opening at the top of the window.

One of the first to reach the scene was Magistrate Hyman Bushel, who heard the dull roar of the smashing cars while walking along Seventh Avenue. He rushed down into the subway entrance at 40th Street only to be confronted by chaos. "The sight was so terrible," said Bushel, "that I stood for a time in awe. I was incapable of doing anything. There were horrible cries, all lights were out, and there was the pungent smell of smoke.

"I saw people hurry over to the wrecked cars and take out persons who were dead and others who seemed to be dying. It was a terrible sight."

If there was any solace for rescuers, it was in the absence of a major conflagration. "There was no fire, thank God," said Assistant Fire Chief "Smokey Joe" Martin, "although there was a flare or flash at the start. We did not have to fight flames, and this enabled our men to get right to work helping to get passengers who were hurt or frightened out of the place."

Mounted Policeman Ward, who at first assisted passengers off the station platform, now rushed to the scene of the collision. Using his flashlight, Ward searched for victims, pulling out dead and injured from the wreckage of the crumpled ninth and tenth cars. He guided those who still were mobile through the darkened subway to the south end of the Times Square platform and to the street.

By this time the first batch of ambulances from Bellevue, St. Vincent's and New York Hospitals were on their way to the scene. Ward was immediately aided by Detective John J. Broderick, head of the Police Department's Industrial Squad. In his first trip to the street with the injured, Broderick carried an injured girl under one arm and a man under the other, while another girl clung desperately to his neck as he struggled onto the street.

A phalanx of taxis was already at hand to help the wounded, and in no time at all the Police and Fire Departments had coordinated their rescue efforts. Less than ten minutes after the initial impact of the ninth car against the concrete wall, Lieutenant John O'Grady was on the scene with the first Police Department Emergency Squad. He sent an alarm for all reserves and every available ambulance. Within fifteen minutes police lines had been established from 35th Street to 42nd Street and Seventh Avenue, and a short time later 200 policemen were on duty at the scene.

Less than fifteen minutes after the wreck had taken place, Mayor Jimmy Walker was escorted into the tunnel where he comforted the injured and conferred with IRT officials.

Forsaking dinner, the mayor then went to the hospitals to visit with survivors of the crash.

Meanwhile, reporters from the city's dailies combed through the Times Square Station, interviewing passengers who survived the wreck and other witnesses. Many of the most coherent statements were offered by passengers in the forward cars, immediately brought to a halt by Motorman McCormick. He had sensed the calamity as soon as he felt a reverberating thud in his compartment. Some of the on the-spot observations of onlookers follow:

An Interborough guard, who declined to disclose his name, said: "It was horrible. I was hurled almost the entire length of my car and knocked out. When I came to I found a woman lying dead beside me."

Lawrence Kerney, who was on the third car of the southbound express, said: "There was something wrong with the train all the way down from Seventy-Second Street. There was a heavy, constant grinding and the train was lurching from side to side. Some of the passengers thought something was wrong, but none of the Interborough people took any notice of it.

"Suddenly there was a terrible smash. Lights went out. The train shook like a leaf. There was some screaming and a rush began toward the windows. But on the whole most people kept their heads. The women were cooler than the men.

"I was one of the last to leave the train, helping as much as I could in lifting dazed passengers down so they could be taken out of the emergency exits. On my way out I saw three dead men near each other."

According to Lillian Harvey, of Eastern Parkway in Brooklyn, "We were riding only a short while when I heard a great noise and then the car I was in turned over. A man grabbed me by the arm and pulled me out through the fifth car."

Thomas Guilfoyle, U.S. Treasury agent, was passing the subway entrance at 40th Street and Seventh Avenue when he heard the crash and raced down the stairs.

"I could make out the car forms in the darkness. I ran over to one of the cars, broke a window, and began taking passengers out to the platform. It seemed to me that at least two of those I helped pull out of the car windows died on the platform," he recalled.

"In all I assisted fifteen passengers, men and women. Most of them seemed badly hurt. Those who were capable of limping or being helped up stairs I got in the open air.

"By the time I arrived on Seventh Avenue with the first two or three passengers the police and others were commandeering automobiles to send the injured ones to the various hospitals.

"From what I heard some of the passengers say, the train they were on was traveling fast. They said there was a sudden crash, followed by several explosions and then darkness.

"Passengers who were frightened but not hurt added to the confusion by shouting and attempting to push their way out. It was more than half an hour after I ran down the stairs that there was anything like order.

"I drove three children to the Polyclinic Hospital. As I was carrying a little boy, he suddenly went limp in my arms, and I realized that he was dead. About thirty injured people were driven in private cars and commandeered taxis to the hospitals before ambulances reached the scene."

Mounted Patrolman John F. Ward said:

"I realized the accident was a bad one and knew that an alarm had already been sent in. I got to work trying to get out the living as quickly as possible. From every window as near as I could make out were protruding hands and arms. Some of the windows contained wedged forms of two or three, none able to move.

"Everyone seemed to be shouting as loud as possible. Wherever I saw an arm or head I pulled. In most cases, I am glad to say, those I succeeded in getting out of the train were alive.

"After most of the injured were removed from the cars came the work of getting out those who were unconscious or dead. It looked to me as if some had been killed by being crushed.

"It seems like a miracle that more were not killed. When you realize that the sudden crash and the extinguished lights added terror and maddened those trapped in the cars, I wonder that the list of dead did not have hundreds of names."

Dave Oliver, a newspaper cameraman, was standing on the Times Square platform at the time of the crash.

"I was on my way to the Pennsylvania Station and I was just cursing my luck for missing the train which was first pulling out. I was watching the train disappear, when suddenly I heard a screeching of what sounded like a train's brakes. Then there was an explosion. Everything went dark. I heard a women scream and then groans. Smoke and overpowering fumes began to fill the station. Several women fainted on the platform.

"My first thought was pictures. I fought my way as close to the downtown end of the platform as possible. By the time I got there the lights were on again on the platform and down the track. I was able to get a little room and set my camera up long enough to photograph the wreckage.

"Most of the smoke had cleared away. I guess they turned the power off. I could see the train down the tracks. It was bent and twisted. One car was broken in two like a stick of wood. The pillars supporting the subway roof were torn down. The whole scene was a tangle of twisted steel."

Peter Molitor, a twenty-four-year-old chauffeur, was in the seventh car of the doomed train. Although suffering from a sprained ankle, he remained on the train, helping the passengers to safety. As he sat on the curb waiting for an ambulance, he said: "The crash and stopping of the car was so sudden that everyone in the car must have been either injured or badly shaken up. It was like a madhouse when the lights went out. Everywhere I could hear shrieks. Those who were not shouting for help were sobbing. There were a number of children in the car

and their cries could be heard above the others.

"I was near a window, and taking out a wrench from my hip pocket, smashed the window glass. We were near the platform and I managed to push out those nearest me. It was very difficult working in the dark. Now and then someone would strike a match, and the tiny flare showed a struggling, heaping, milling crowd in the car. I never saw anything like it in all my life, and never want to again."

The chief medical examiner, Dr. Charles Norris, was on the scene fifteen minutes after the accident. He was one of the first to go into the subway.

"I don't know how many were killed," Dr. Norris said soon after the crash, "but I know it's a nasty accident, one of the worst in the city's history."

Police, firemen, and bystanders were so involved in rescue operations that few took time to determine precisely what caused the accident. IRT President Frank T. Hedley conferred with company employees and inspectors of the New York City Transit Commission and, for the moment at least, announced that the cause of the wreck was a defective switch.

Colonel John F. Slattery, a commissioner of the Transit Commission, was more precise. He said that presumably the switch had been thrown too swiftly or had been defective. Commissioner Slattery didn't realize it at the time but he had carefully delineated what soon would be the major mystery to be solved by the IRT, the Transit Commission, and the district attorney.

The immediate response was to blame the IRT official nearest to the accident. Acting in advance of any findings, District Attorney Banton placed responsibility for the accident upon maintenance foreman Baldwin. Charged with homicide, Baldwin was released on $10,000 bail. However, there was evidence that he might be innocent of any culpability in the accident. For Baldwin, the first ray of hope came from the Transit Commission, itself, which released an official finding on August 25, suggesting that the derailment might have been caused by the switch being thrown as the train was passing over it.

Towerman King maintained that he had no control over the train once Baldwin, his superior, appeared. "I've been told not to talk," King told a reporter, "but I will say that I did not touch the switch."

It seemed unlikely that Baldwin had erred. He had thirty years of railroading experience, fourteen on the IRT. His future would be determined by District Attorney Banton's investigation to fix responsibilities for the 16 deaths and 100 injuries to passengers in the disaster. Steadfastly, Baldwin insisted that he never threw the switch. The district attorney's task was to determine first whether the switch was thrown and, if so, which of the three suspects—Baldwin, Carr, and King— did it.

The first witnesses were called on August 29. Baldwin denied that he nor Carr had done anything that would have caused the switch to shift. King and motorman Michael O'Connor acknowledged being in the switch tower at the time of the crash and within reach of the switch levers, but they denied having touched any of the levers.

Within twenty-four hours Banton revealed that he had made several definite determinations. One was that the switch had not been thrown by manipulation of the switch lever in the tower. He added, however, that on the wall back of the levers was a row of buttons, pressure on which would operate the switches by compressed air. Signal experts agreed that it would have been possible to throw the switch, even with the weight of the train on the crossover, by use of the proper button.

The investigation suggested two possible causes of the crash:

1. Someone may have tampered with the emergency button in the tower.

2. The entire electrical or mechanical system controlling the switch may have been out of order.

"A third possibility," Banton said, "is that some one may have taken the twenty-five-pound drum covering off the switch mechanism at trackside. But there is little likelihood that the third possibility occurred."

On August 31 an anonymous letter to the district attorney revealed that King was, according to the technical IRT job description, a train clerk, not a towerman. IRT President Hedley explained: "King is a train clerk but he is also a fully qualified towerman. Part of the time he works as a train clerk in the tower and part of the time he acts as towerman." Testifying on September 17, King admitted that he never had received special instruction in the handling of the switches, but pointed out that Baldwin, who was on the scene, warned him not to touch the switch lever.

King described the heavy roar he heard when the ninth car jumped the switch and crashed into the partition, then added an extremely pertinent piece of evidence. Minutes after the accident, Baldwin ran into the tower and exclaimed: "Someone must have touched that lever!"

King insisted that he had not done so. Nevertheless, he came under further scrutiny on September 18, when Gilbert Whitney, signal engineer of the Transit Commission, who had inspected the wreck site two hours after the collision, testified that it was "extremely doubtful" that Baldwin could have operated the switch. He added that the probability was that the switch was thrown by someone in the signal tower. Whitney further testified that someone in the switch tower would have required only five seconds to throw the switch lever and push the emergency button after Baldwin's hand signal to the motorman had been given. While the switch lever was in proper position when Whitney examined it after the wreck, it could have been placed there after having been wrongly operated.

Recalled to the stand, King argued in his defense that he had not touched the switch lever. On September 21 King was called to the stand for the third time. His testimony, though abbreviated, was crucial.

King testified that he had been in New York since November 1926 when he had left Baltimore where he had lived for five years after coming east from Iowa. When his statements were found to be inaccurate Homicide Court Magistrate Corrigan ordered King's arrest on October 4, charging second-degree manslaughter in connection with the Times Square subway wreck. At the same time the magistrate dismissed the homicide charge against Baldwin.

At his grand jury hearing King admitted that he had lied about his name. It was not King but, rather, Harry C. Stocksdale. He also revealed that he had once been convicted in Baltimore for cutting another man with a knife. Magistrate Corrigan told the court:

"I am forced to the conclusion that the switch was moved by someone throwing the lever and pressing the emergency button in the tower. The only people in the tower at the time of the accident were Harry King, the towerman, and O'Connor, the motorman who was waiting to take the 'gap' train.

"The testimony proves that the only way in which the switch could possibly have been moved at the time of the accident was by the use of the lever plus the emergency button in the tower. It follows that someone in the tower house must have caused the movement. There is no reason to suppose that O'Connor interfered in any way with the lever. King swore that O'Connor did not do so.

"If O'Connor did not do it, King did. Moreover, King's demeanor and his testimony were not satisfactory. His cross-examination based upon investigation conducted by Inspector Valentine of the Police Department shows that King's testimony before me was false in many particulars. His name is not King, but Stocksdale. He was not born where he said he was; he did not live the life he described. He was convicted in Baltimore of stabbing a man with a butcher knife.

"I am forced to the conclusion that in defiance of Baldwin's order he moved the lever, pushed the emergency button and caused this wreck."

It now was up to the grand jury to confirm or deny Corrigan's theory. The indicted towerman held firm in his denial that he had defied Baldwin's order, and no evidence could be obtained to prove otherwise. Finally, on November 19, 1928, nearly three months after the fatal movement of the switch, the grand jury made the decisive move to dismiss the complaint of second-degree manslaughter against the towerman.

To this day, railroaders debate the cause of the accident. One school of thought endorsed by a local transit expert is that the problem was not in the tower but at trackside. "A disaster would have been averted," he said, "if the switch had, as the rules stipulate, been spiked." But it was not and no further evidence was forthcoming. All that was definitively known was that the switch did move and, on Friday afternoon, August 27, 1928, more than 100 passengers were injured and 16 were killed in New York City's second worst subway disaster.

(next page, top) *A split switch accident similar to the one at Times Square. This one however, developed in the still-to-be completed Montague Street tunnel on February 9, 1918. The car involved is a brand-new BRT "Standard" 2208. No passengers were on board.*

Terror on The Tubes

Its tiny, musty-smelling tunnels have given The Hudson Tubes a surreal look every since the subway linking New York and New Jersey was opened on February 25, 1908.

Curves that seem to defy passage snake through Lower Manhattan and parts of the New Jersey route. Over the years many passengers who have viewed them from the front window of the first car have been alternately dazzled that the cars even negotiate them, thrilled by the experience and even frightened.

The fear rarely is justified. Despite the omnipresent S-curves, 90-degree turns and criss-crossing trackage, The Tubes' safety record has been admirable over more than three decades, both under the earlier Hudson and Manhattan Railroad regime as well as the present Port Authority.

But one tragedy above all cast a pall on the H and M. It took place early in the Spring of 1942 when Adolf Hitler's Panzers were marauding across Europe and Uncle Sam still was reeling from the Japanese sneak attack on Pearl Harbor.

America had mobilized and citizens such as Christensen Timpe of Jersey City had vowed to do their all for the war effort. On Sunday evening, April 26, 1942, Christensen left his house at 63 Poplar Street and headed for his job at the Brooklyn Navy Yard.

Louis Austin Vierbuchen already had reported for work. The 48-year-old motorman had spent more than 20 years with The Tubes. He was looking forward to retirement and rest within two years but now he was doing what he did best, piloting his train between Newark and New York.

He had begun his Sunday tour of duty at

4:42 PM and completed three round-trips before leaving for his evening meal at 7:40 PM Precisely how Vierbuchen occupied his time during that interval and his return to the train is pivotal to the episodes that would transpire.

According to a *New York Times* dispatch, Vierbuchen was alleged to have admitted in a written statement that he ate nothing during his meal time but had five beers.

Published reports indicate that 9:32 PM was the time the motorman was due back at his train yet he didn't take his cars out of Newark until 10:32 PM He activated the motors, heard the familiar staccato whine and moved the six cars across the bridge spanning Newark Bay.

After a stop at nearby Harrison, the six-car train began its straightaway gallop across New Jersey's meadows toward Manhattan's skyscrapers in the East. The more than 200 passengers alternately read their newspapers, dozed or peered out of the windows at the many freight cars parked at sidings along the route.

Nobody paid much heed to the speed because one of the Hudson Tubes' major assets was its *giddyap* run from Harrison to Jersey City, first outdoors on a banked track, then a plunge into the portal and stops that included one at Exchange Place in Jersey City.

By this time the straight tracks had given way to a labyrinth of switches, curves and crossovers that required motorman vigilance as well as deft brake-handling on the part of Vierbuchen.

To limit speed outside Exchange Place, the H and M had mandated a 12-miles per hour maximum speed. This would enable the train to safely negotiate the switches west of the station platform before coming to a stop. A time signal—with the 12-mph figure—was affixed to the tunnel wall to reinforce in the motorman's mind that potential danger loomed ahead.

It was in full view of Vierbuchen who, after so many years on the system, knew the route and its rules by heart. Nevertheless, on this run his Manhattan-bound train approached Exchange Place at an exceptionally high and frightening speed.

In fact some riders said they believed the train was at maximum speed as it "lurched and jolted" toward impending doom.

Other passengers later told Hudson County assistant prosecutor William T. Cahill that "the train swayed and rocked at possibly sixty miles an hour." If true, that would place it at 48 mph over the limit approaching a perilous turn. Other riders reiterated that the train's behavior was abnormal compared with its usual measured meander into Exchange Place.

"It seemed as if we were speeding up as the train was about to enter the station," said Ben Agron, a passenger from Brooklyn.

Vierbuchen's six-car consist was more like a torpedo bursting over the tracks. Swaying crazily in the tunnel, it had already knocked the 12 mph speed limit marker off its fixture and plunged across the tracks and into the station. The initial shock produced by the combination of high speed and train trucks trying to negotiate the tracks under extreme duress caused the motorman's car to uncouple from the five behind it.

"I was standing at the rear of the first car," Agron remembered. "It sounded as if the car jumped the track."

Gaping in horror, Vierbuchen watched his train career 100 feet alongside the platform to the east end of the station, demolishing signal equipment and uprooting the third rail as it dove out of control. It finally ground to a halt and within seconds, caught fire.

Meanwhile, Car Two somehow managed to remain on the rails but the third telescoped into the second with an agonizing jangle of steel on steel forcing its rear end to smash into the concrete of the three-foot station platform.

Even worse—were that possible under the unfolding circumstances—the fourth car became dislodged from its link with the third, climbed upward, sheared off its trucks and mounted the Exchange Place platform like an enormous, mythical sea monster leaping out of its natural watery habitat. Once settled on the platform, the car lurched forward, pushing, as the *New York Times* noted, "a runway for itself through the concrete" before grinding to a stop.

Miraculously, the last two cars remained on the track although Car Five was nearly parallel to the car that only seconds earlier had been pulling it.

What had earlier been a rather mundane commuter run had turned into a jumble of broken glass, twisted steel and flashing light. Terrorized straphangers tried to regain their senses and comprehend what had happened and, more importantly, what to do.

"When the crash occurred and the lights went out some of the people around me screamed to get out," said Andrew Sabol also of Brooklyn. "The door wouldn't open so I smashed a window and carried four people our through it."

Passengers evacuated the first car as flames tore through its body, blackening it throughout. "Women and children screamed and men pounded the doors which would not open," reported *The Times*. "Steel and wood debris was scattered over the scene and dense smoke filled the poorly ventilated tube, the station of which was plunged into semi-darkness by the crash."

The acrid mixture of smoke and electrical fumes coupled with destruction of the station's ventilating system compelled firemen, doctors, nurses and police to don gas masks and water-soaked handkerchiefs before descending to the tumult in the tunnel.

When rescue workers reached the scene they were greeted with more than human misery. The physical plant had been wasted by the out-of-control cars which had smashed into conduits carrying 6,000 telephone trunks through The Tubes. The severed trunks cut off telephone communication between Lower Manhattan and Northern New Jersey.

"I found myself on the floor," recalled passenger Ben Agron. "When I came to, I got out the door."

Many were not as lucky. Five persons died in the wreck. Three of them—Rube Greenberg, Anna Stephen, Allen Williams—were from New York City and one, Morris Huttler, from Providence, Rhode Island. The lone New Jersey victim was Christensen Timpe. There were 222 injuries and one who emerged virtually unscathed was motorman Vierbuchen.

Jersey City police chief Harry W. Walsh was to tell Judge Anthony Bottin in the city's First Criminal Court that when he first looked upon Vierbuchen in the Exchange Place Station after the wreck he decided to have him examined by Dr. James Norton, the police doctor.

"I concluded he warranted examination as to his sobriety," Chief Walsh said.

The motorman told the police, "Something blew up."

At the crash site firemen had extinguished the blaze and probed through the wreckage along with a score of other rescue workers. Trapped amid pretzels of steel and wood in the fourth car, a 13-year-old girl screamed for help. Firemen armed with acetylene torches arrived and while the teenager remained conscious, they cut through the wreckage and extricated her, saving the youngster's life.

In time H and M crewmen were able to back the two rear cars from the scene. Wrecked beyond repair, the second, third and fourth cars were taken apart and hauled away.

Vierbuchen's lead car was relatively undamaged.

The wreck traumatized passengers and trainmen alike. On May 5, 1942 a Hudson County grand jury in Jersey City returned six indictments against Vierbuchen, five charging manslaughter in connection with the deaths and one charging the motorman with operating a train while under the influence of liquor.

Among the witnesses who testified were Police Chief Harry W. Walsh of Jersey City and J. C. Van Geison, superintendent of the Hudson and Manhattan Railroad.

Vierbuchen's defense counsel countered that his client was not responsible for the wreck. The attorney said the motorman was not responsible for the disaster. He charged that The Tubes "equipment is obsolete."

Assistant Prosecutor William T. Cahill of Hudson opposed bail for Vierbuchen asserting that he once had been convicted on May 13, 1929 of driving a car while intoxicated.

Perhaps the saddest story from the wreck's fallout involved the trainmaster who dispatched the ill-fated consist to Manhattan.

On May 5, 1942 John H. Vogel, 54, had been scheduled to appear as a witness before the Hudson County grand jury in connection with the investigation of charges against the motorman. Vierbuchen had been assigned to duty by Vogel.

For five days prior to his scheduled appearance Vogel had not been home. He later told detectives that he had not reported for work in almost a week and had been sleeping in hotels around Newark until May 5th when he went to Weequahic Park in Newark.

Vogel later allowed that he had been worrying about the wreck, the five dead and more than 200 injured. He added that he had been unable to get the thought of the accident out of his mind and that his superiors had criticized him in connection with the wreck.

A 30-year veteran of the Pennsylvania Railroad—of which the H&M was a subsidiary—the distraught trainmaster did not show up as scheduled before the grand jury.

Instead, he remained in Weequahic Park and soon pulled out a razor blade and proceeded to slash his throat and wrists.

The attempted suicide was halted by a policewoman who found him at 10:30 in the morning, weak from the loss of blood. He was taken to City Hospital where he later revealed his tale of depression and guilt over a disaster that still haunts oldtimers who remember when PATH was still The Tubes.

(previous page, bottom) *An incredible aspect of the 1942 Hudson Tubes crash at Exchange Place Station in Jersey City was the catapulting of a car on to the concrete platform. Inspectors view the wreck's aftermath.*

(above) *As a result of the Tubes' Exchange Place disaster, five passengers were killed and more than 200 injured. A Jersey City policeman, his face covered with grime, collects hats, shoes and other victims' belongings.*

The Astor Place Flood

The old, abandoned John Wanamaker department store buildings sat like overblown mausoleums in Manhattan's Greenwich Village area on a hot Saturday, July 14, 1956. Adorned with cast iron, the New York City landmark was built in 1862 by A. J. Stewart.

The two Wanamaker buildings dominated Astor Place. They reached only five stories but spread over a whole block—9th and 10th Streets and Fourth Avenue and Broadway—with the store actually comprising a north and a south building, connected by a bridge. The plot of land itself was steeped in history, most of it turbulent. At the building site, Broadway takes an abrupt westward turn. The bend occurred because a stubborn New Yorker named Hendrick Brevoort wouldn't allow city planners to cut down his favorite shade tree that stood in the line laid out for Broadway in 1807.

Old Brevoort kept making trouble for the city fathers, which explains why there is no 11th Street between Broadway and Fourth Avenue. Brevoort adamantly refused to allow any cuts through his farm. Hence, a portion of 11th Street never was opened.

137

More controversy erupted at the eventual site of the Wanamaker store in May 1849 when two rival actors—Edwin Forrest and William Charles Macready—became embroiled in a dispute over which of the pair was the better Hamlet! The argument escalated into a bloody riot, and when the dust had cleared Astor Place was strewn with 200 dead and dying.

In 1876 A. J. Stewart sold the building he had erected to a firm called Hilton, Hughes and Company. John Wanamaker bought the property in 1896 and developed it into one of Manhattan's most successful department stores, which included a newer annex. But business sagged in the years following World War II, and in late December 1954 the Wanamakers abandoned the buildings, which were bought from the Wanamaker family in January 1955 by a syndicate headed by David Rapoport, a lawyer. Rapoport decided to raze the old landmark and erect an apartment development.

This seemed like a splendid idea because the prospective tenants would not only be adjacent to Greenwich Village, which was enjoying a renaissance, but also be conveniently close to two of the city's main subway lines. The IRT Lexington Avenue Line, a four-track express-local route, operated in a tunnel under Fourth Avenue, while the BMT Broadway Line, a similar four-track run, flowed in a north-south direction under Broadway. The IRT Astor Place Station was within shouting distance of the Wanamaker building, as was the BMT's 8th Street local stop.

Late in the winter of 1956 demolition work on the original Wanamaker building was begun by Lipsett, Inc., a New York-based firm. On Friday afternoon, July 13, 1956, Lipsett's wreckers had completed scaffolding around the building and were cutting up pipe in the subcellar. Julius Lipsett, the company's vice president, later would tell questioners that the building had been inspected at 4 PM on Friday, and basement areas, where acetylene torches that had been used to cut

up pipe, had been wetted down to prevent fires.

Lipsett maintained a full-time watchman service at the site. Nothing of a suspicious nature was reported during Saturday morning or afternoon. Sam Piparo, an employee of the United Service Detective Corporation, was on duty outside the Wanamaker building that morning. According to Piparo, he noticed a peculiar smell emanating from the onetime department store. Piparo did nothing, theorizing that the odor came from burned articles on the floor left behind by workers the previous day. His job, he insisted, was to watch the outside of the building. "I had nothing to do with the inside," he later said.

Precisely what happened inside the abandoned department store will remain a moot question forever. Fire Commissioner Edward F. Cavanagh, Jr., theorized that a spark from an acetylene torch ignited a piece of flammable material minutes before closing time on Friday afternoon. The smoldering material went unnoticed by the workers, who then left the structure for the weekend. "It is very likely," said Cavanagh, "that the fire was going all Friday night and Saturday."

At 5:46 PM on Saturday the flames became visible and the first fire alarm was sounded by an unnamed passerby. By that time the subcellar and basement areas were, as Commissioner Cavanagh described it, "a raging fire." As hook-and-ladder companies arrived at the scene, it soon became apparent that more than two alarms would be required to extinguish the rapidly increasing blaze. By 9 PM the conflagration was so intense that firemen were ordered out of the building.

The immediate strategy was to confine the fire, but it had spread too rapidly and was generating a crippling amount of smoke, especially from the basement. Before midnight thick smoke rolling out of the lower reaches of the structure had caused five firemen and a radio reporter to be taken to hospitals while others were treated at the scene.

The quarter-inch glass windows of the old store sometimes resisted a single hose for as much as ten minutes, with other jet streams being necessary to break them. Eventually almost all the arched windows—twenty-one in a row from the avenue sides, thirty on the side streets—were broken out.

There were other problems. The old store was full of spaces concealed by partitions, where the fire would lurk and then make a surprise breakout. There also was a 40,000-gallon fuel oil tank, with some oil inside.

In addition firemen had to defend the surrounding area. Besides a bridge linking the northern and southern buildings of the store, there was a tunnel at the cellar level. Firemen inside the southern structure successfully held the blaze away from the northern end with the help of double steel fire doors.

Danger from smoke inhalation and the possibility of a wall collapse led to evacuation of a nearby rooming house. Thirty-four occupants of the building at 57 Fourth Avenue, at 9th Street, were ordered out by the police on advice from the Building Department at 4 AM.

During the early hours of the fire little concern was given to the state of the two nearby subway lines, the IRT and the BMT. Both had been operating normally in the early evening. But as firemen poured millions of gallons of water on the Wanamaker Building the situation dramatically changed. The underground seepage to the Lexington Avenue Line grew to hazardous proportions at 11:50 PM, as a five-car southbound Pelham Local approached the Astor Place Station. At that moment the roadbed at the station dropped four feet.

Fortunately, the motorman detected the dip in the tracks seconds before he brought the train to the platform. He pulled his brake to emergency position and stopped the local before pulling all the way into the station. Since the train was adjacent to the platform—although a considerable distance from its normal stopping point—the conductor opened the doors to permit the passengers to exit. This they did without panic, despite the fact that four feet of water now covered the tracks and was rising rapidly to station-platform height.

Moments later the ground beneath the third and fourth cars of the Lexington Avenue local caved in, dropping the end of each car four feet and leaving them in a semijackknifed position. The time was 11:55 PM Twenty minutes later, at 12:15 AM Sunday, the Transit Authority ordered all traffic on the IRT Lexington Avenue Line halted between Grand Central Station and Brooklyn Bridge.

The Wanamaker Building still was blazing and there was no indication when the fire would be brought under control. What troubled TA engineers most of all in the early hours of Sunday morning was the imminent flooding of the BMT's 8th Street Station. Water was rapidly filling the two underground basements next to the station. Two double-opening glass doors provided an entrance to the platform from the old building. In a desperate effort to bolster the barrier, TA workers lugged sandbags and timbering, improvising a second "wall" behind the glass doors. They then waited and hoped that it would hold until the fire was extinguished.

As long as the barrier held fast, the BMT trains could continue running. The TA dispatched two pump cars to the BMT station. They sucked out 2,400 gallons of water a minute and were effective as long as the glass-door barrier remained solid.

At 8 PM on Sunday the heavy timbers began creaking under the strain, and soon the water, which had reached a height of five feet behind the glass doors, smashed down the portals and spilled a torrent of water on to the BMT platform where workmen had been busy with the pumps. The water spilled over the platform and hit a live third rail, causing a cloud of steam. Service in both directions on the BMT Broadway Line between Canal Street and 34th Street was discontinued at 8:20 PM. Now two of the busiest subway lines in the world were completely halted by the cascading effects of the millions of gallons of water poured on the fire.

Nevertheless, the tide had turned. Arthur J. Massett, acting chief of the Fire Department, announced on Sunday night that the fire was under control, twenty-five hours after it had first been reported. By that time more than 600 firemen of the department's entire complement of 11,000 men had fought the blaze. They had worked in three shifts and 187 of them had been treated for smoke poisoning.

By early morning, Monday, July 16, the legion of firemen knew that they had won their battle. Now the TA faced one of its most awesome challenges: the rehabilitation of the flooded stations and undermined roadbeds and the restoration of service on the eight affected tracks, four on the IRT and four on the BMT. Officials at City Hall told Mayor Robert Wagner that it would take at least one month before full service could be restored on the IRT Lexington Avenue Line. The BMT Line, which suffered considerably less damage, was expected to be ready sooner.

Now that the water from the 50 million gallons poured on the fire had stopped flowing onto the tracks, TA engineers tackled their first major problem on Monday afternoon—removal of the stranded IRT Pelham local cars from the Lexington Avenue tracks.

To hasten the job, the TA crew took several gambles. At 3:30 PM the TA requested that a ten-car train be brought up from the south to attempt to pull out the first two stranded cars, which had remained on the level, and the third car, which had dived into the washout. Its motors straining under the pressure, the rescue train gradually pulled the three cars to safety. Nathan Brodkin, chief engineer with the TA, examined the remaining IRT car, No. 6554. Its front was down in about seven feet of water, while its rear had risen to about six inches away from the tunnel roof with its eighteen-inch cross beams.

After sizing up the situation, Brodkin ordered a work train, powered by four motor cars, down from the north. A huge chain, thirty feet long, was rigged to the 85,000-pound car. The final rescue operation began at 5:19 PM when the motorman in the work car turned on the juice and the chain tightened. Would it hold? Would the $105,000 subway car remain on the warped tracks or would it derail, further complicating the salvage operation?

"Go ahead," shouted Brodkin, "take her away!"

Engines groaned as the work train slowly but relentlessly pulled at the half-drowned IRT car. It crunched and squeaked, but within fifteen seconds it was out of the morass and back on the level rails. "We've won the battle," the gray-haired Brodkin cheered.

But there were other battles to be fought. As soon as Car No. 6554 was rescued, ten men began carrying away loosened rails past the pool of mucky water while chanting the "Song of the Volga Boatmen."

Next, the TA had to strengthen the station foundation weakened during the ordeal. At 8 P.M workers completed cutting a six-by-four foot hole through the paving on Fourth Avenue near 8th Street to allow concrete and timber to be passed into the tunnel for the underpinning job. Meanwhile, tracks had been cleared on the BMT, and limited service was resumed.

On Tuesday, July 17, at 9 A.M., the Fire Department officially declared that the Wanamaker fire was extinguished, although it was not called "closed" because a dozen firemen remained as a watch line and three engines still were pumping water from the building. Nevertheless, TA workmen were readying concrete for a Wednesday pouring operation.

Before this could be done excavation of a hole eighty feet by thirty feet, averaging five feet in depth, was necessary under the steel ledges supporting the first and second rows of subway columns. Mechanical screw jacks, were installed beneath the most critical columns. Drills and shovels broke up debris, which was removed by a work train and by a crane that reached down with a clamshell bucket from a hole dug into Fourth Avenue and 9th Street, eight feet by four-and-a-half in diameter.

On Wednesday, July 18, 500 cubic yards of concrete were poured down a chute from the street access hole. Workmen shoveled it under the column benches for the new foundation, encasing the jacks as well. Then the TA crews installed ties, rails, and a crushed-stone roadbed, as well as new signaling equipment.

Late Wednesday afternoon Brodkin and his boss, TA Chairman Charles Patterson, stood on the flood site and confidently predicted that full IRT service would resume by 8 AM on Friday, July 20, nearly a month before many believed possible. Early the next morning (Thursday) new tracks were installed on the new roadbed.

Sure enough, on Friday morning the first train, led by Car No. 6643, rolled into the Astor Place Station. It had headed south from Grand Central at 12:02 AM, five days and twelve minutes after the undermined roadbed of the Lexington Ave. Line had crumpled gently beneath the local.

It was one of the Transit Authority's finest hours. "About the time an ordinary railroad would be deciding when to call a conference to decide what to do about it—about that time, we had it done!" said a proud TA worker.

Cleaning up the Astor Place washout.

The Roosevelt Avenue IND Mixup

By New York City subway standards the G, (formerly GG Brooklyn-Queens Crosstown) Line is an oddity. Unlike other main routes on the IND (or B Division Group II), all of which enter Manhattan at some point in their runs, the curious G wends a circuitous trail. Its starting point is in middle-class Forest Hills, Queens. It rolls to its other terminus in the reviving Red Hook-Park Slope section of Brooklyn, without entering Manhattan.

The line had opened in part in 1933 and was fully completed in 1937. The G carried its passengers on local tracks alongside the speedy E and F express trains at the start of its journey at 71st Street-Continental Avenue.

The expresses, en route to Manhattan, exchange passengers with the G at two important junctions: Roosevelt Avenue in Jackson Heights (Queens) and Queens Plaza in Long Island City. Since the E and F lines were the most heavily-traveled New York subway lines, a considerable number of passengers crossed the platform at Roosevelt Avenue where local and express met.

The G picked up and discharged another large passenger load at Queens Plaza, where the local then turned away from the main express run. Both E and F continued on under the East River to Manhattan while the G plunged beneath Newtown Creek, swerving southward to Brooklyn. The crosstown local moved through such old Brooklyn communities as Greenpoint, Williamsburg, Bedford-Stuyvesant, Clinton Hill, and Fort Greene before reaching another major local-express junction at Hoyt and Schermerhorn Streets near the Fulton Street downtown shopping center. Then, a few stations beyond, in an oddity for the IND system, the G moves up and outside for a short but thrilling climb along the highest elevated run (87.5 feet) of any line—the concrete viaduct over

Brooklyn's Gowanus Canal. The Smith-9th Street Station is perched atop the viaduct.

From the Transit Authority's fiscal viewpoint, the most vital section of the G operation was the densely-packed rush-hour run from the local's starting point at 71st Street-Continental Avenue to Queens Plaza, where it split off from the expresses. After leaving Continental Avenue, the local picked up large numbers of passengers at such Queens stations as Sixty-Seventh Avenue, Sixty-Third Drive, Woodhaven Boulevard, Grand Avenue, and Elmhurst Avenue before reaching the express stop at Roosevelt Avenue. Those were stations that a passenger like Anna Bovino passed every workday on the route to her office at the CBS building in Rockefeller Center.

Anna Bovino was a typical G passenger on the morning of May 20, 1970. Her husband, Frank, drove her to the 71st Street Continental Avenue station, where she boarded the local. On this morning Ms. Bovino, 36, thought she would take the leisurely local run all the way to Queens Plaza and then catch the express to Manhattan.

Anthony Haynes and Abraham Williams, Jr., comprised a typical G crew. Haynes, 50, was the motorman in charge of piloting the train to Brooklyn, while Williams, 37, a conductor, opened and closed the doors and maintained a safety vigil for his motorman and passengers.

Haynes and Williams began their workday at the IND's Jamaica yard, where they climbed aboard the G for the rush-hour run. Their first passengers poured in at 71st Street-Continental Avenue. It was 7:13 AM By Woodhaven Boulevard, three stops later, the local was crowded with passengers, among whom was one Timothy Cronin. A regular passenger, Cronin was disturbed when he noticed the G was remaining with its doors open at Woodhaven Boulevard station for an abnormally long time.

At the Woodhaven Boulevard station motorman Haynes had experienced a malfunctioning of the brakes on his first and second cars (a "married" pair set of 4501-4500 R40s). A road-car inspector, Francis Farmer, 45, happened to be on the disabled train. After Haynes conferred with Farmer, it was decided to cut the brakes out of the first two cars and operate the train from the third car. Car inspector Farmer told motorman Haynes to contact the desk train master at the command center later. Haynes decided the local train would have to be taken out of service. This meant that all passengers were to be discharged, after which the train would be shunted along the local tracks to a siding and then to the repair shop.

Conductor Williams informed the passengers that they must vacate the disabled train and wait for the next local. All riders but one heeded the order. Timothy Cronin remained on the train, assuming that it would have to stop at Roosevelt Avenue, which is where he wanted to get off. There he would catch the Manhattan-bound express.

Meanwhile motorman Haynes and conductor Williams worked out strategy for piloting their wounded local to the IND infirmary. Car inspector Farmer cut the brakes out on the first and second cars, a procedure often used by the Transit Authority when the lead car was disabled and a train had to be shunted out of service. Farmer also told Williams to stand at the front car and use his flashlight to signal Haynes the condition of the signals ahead. A wave of the flashlight was the only means of communication used by this train crew. Farmer remained on the train to assist the motorman if further mechanical difficulties were encountered.

Once its doors were closed, the local lurched forward and rolled westward toward Roosevelt Avenue. At this point, stowaway passenger Cronin approached Farmer and asked him to have the motorman drop him off at Roosevelt Avenue. Farmer reluctantly agreed; he couldn't, after all, leave Cronin alone in the train as it made its way to a siding track. The car inspector opened the third-car motorman cab door where Haynes was operating the train. "I was surprised to

see the motorman running the train from the third car going at the normal rate of speed for trains operated from the first car," Cronin said later.

Before the crippled train was moving again TA dispatchers had quickly arranged to prevent a major jam of locals behind the disabled G. In cases where a stalled local blocks the tracks the following locals are rerouted onto the express tracks. In this case the operation took place at a switch at the west end of the 71st Street-Continental Avenue Station. The rerouting operation enabled the locals to continue moving westward on express tracks until the disabled train cleared the regular local tracks. Rerouted locals would be switched from express tracks back to the local tracks just west of the Roosevelt Avenue Express Station.

This meant that all rerouted westbound locals would bypass the Sixty-seventh Avenue, Sixty-third Drive, Woodhaven Boulevard, Grand Avenue, and Elmhurst Avenue Stations. They would stop at the Roosevelt Avenue Station on the express track and then proceed over the switch in order to return to the local track en route to Brooklyn.

Motorman Haynes guided the disabled G along the local tracks to Roosevelt Avenue without obstruction, since all other trains ahead of him had cleared the track. As the train lumbered toward Roosevelt Avenue Station, Williams kept his eyes on the tracks ahead of the train. Farmer soon opened Haynes's cabin door and asked him to allow Cronin to get off at Roosevelt Avenue.

Once Cronin had alighted, the disabled local was set in motion again and rumbled toward the darkened tunnel ahead. Approximately 50 to 100 feet beyond the end of the platform lay a crossover, enabling trains to switch from express to local tracks. At this point a new and disturbing element complicated Haynes's operation.

Unknown to the motorman, who lacked communication with the TA's central command center, a rerouted local had pulled into Roosevelt Avenue on the express tracks.

It discharged its passengers, took on new ones, closed its doors, and then proceeded according to the command center instructions to the switch where it would cross over to the local track.

Precisely why Haynes was unaware of the switching local remained an unanswered question. The Transit Authority later established that all signals were operating properly and that the motorman ignored a double-red (red-over-red) "stop-and-stay" signal at the west end of the station. This signal protected movements over the crossover just ahead.

Haynes pulled on his controller in the third car and the local moved forward out of Roosevelt Avenue station toward the switch. Suddenly conductor Williams, up front, saw the local train swerving right from the express track, directly into the path of the disabled G. Williams rushed behind the empty motorman's cab in the first car and reached for a red wooden knob attached to the emergency cord. He yanked the cord downward with all his might.

Normally such a maneuver automatically set the train's brakes in "emergency" position, thereby bumping the local to a quick stop. But this time the cord had no effect at all, for the brakes in the first two cars had been cut out and were inoperable. Conductor Williams watched helplessly while his local bore down on the train ahead as it rocked over the cross-switch, veering on to the local track.

Haynes's local rammed the fifth car of the passenger-filled G with a horrible force before it completed the turn onto the local track. The impact was so severe that the rammed steel car leaped from the tracks and hit the tunnel's concrete wall that separates local and express tracks. Anna Bovino was sitting next to the window of the smashed train when the crash occurred.

"I went flying in the air," said Ms. Bovino. "It was like dreamland. I think I must have been unconscious, but not too long."

She had been lifted from her seat and hurled into the aisle against a pole. Her glasses were ripped from her face as she fell to the floor in the darkness that enveloped the scene. Meanwhile, the fifth car had been split open at the middle, as if struck with a giant ax. One side of the car was almost completely ripped away.

"Witnesses said the scene in the tunnel just after the crash was one of twisted metal and shattered glass," according to a dispatch in the *New York Times*. "The only sounds were the cries and moans of the injured and the hiss of escaping air from broken brake hoses."

Motorman Haynes's train had gathered enough speed by the moment of impact that the two cars were fused together following the collision. Hours later, even after workmen had begun to use acetylene torches to cut away sections of the contorted cars, it was difficult to tell one train from the other. The crash killed two persons and injured approximately seventy others.

Service on the line was spotty for the remainder of the day while TA crews removed the tangled mass of metal from the tracks. By the next morning the tracks were usable and normal service was restored in time for the rush hour. But the question of why it had happened remained perplexing. "The main thing," said Mayor John Lindsay, "is to make sure that the public gets every fact in this tragedy so that we can know why the safety mechanisms—the mechanisms that are supposed to keep this sort of thing from happening—why these safety mechanisms failed."

Probers began at the beginning. They investigated the disabled braking system. They questioned car inspector Farmer's role in having motorman Haynes move the train from Woodhaven Boulevard Station. They wondered why there was such poor communication between conductor Williams and his motorman in the third car.

David Lubash, attorney for the Rank and File, a dissident group of largely African-American and Puerto Rican transit workers, blamed the TA's emergency procedures for the accident. "Permitting the operation of that train out of the third car was just asking for trouble," said Lubash. Equally bitter was Bronx Borough President Robert Abrams who charged the TA with "abandonment of preventive maintenance."

Mayor Lindsay immediately organized a Subway Service Watchdog Commission, an unpaid group of fifteen city residents. The commission launched an independent study, which concluded that "bad engineering and poor maintenance" were responsible for the collision. However, differing views were offered by the Metropolitan Transportation Authority's probe and another conducted by the Queens grand jury.

While the Queens grand jury deliberated the case for more than two months, the MTA's investigative panel made its decision with minimum delay. On May 24, four days after the crash, and before conductor Williams appeared before the grand jury, the MTA panel officially blamed Haynes, Williams, and Farmer for the accident, attributing the disaster to human failure rather than mechanical mishap. Haynes, whom the MTA said had acted irresponsibly in operating the train from the third car without proper supervision, and Farmer, who ordered Haynes to do so, were suspended. Williams was not.

"Motorman Haynes, in starting his train without any signal from his conductor at the head end of the train, clearly violated rules governing such emergency procedures," the MTA concluded. "This was the immediate and principal cause of the accident." In addition, the board said, Haynes had operated the train through a red signal. That was the key to the disaster.

As for inspector Farmer, the board said he "had exercised improper authority over the motorman in directing the motorman to call the trainmaster at the command center at a later time and to proceed with the movement of the disabled train."

The findings of the seven-member panel were criticized by the Transport Workers' Union, which accused the MTA of going for a "hasty" report in order to get headlines. Instead, said the union leaders, it was "inexcusable neglect in maintenance and operating procedures" by the MTA in general that caused the accident and was responsible for generally poor subway service.

The mayor's panel largely agreed with the union. "The MTA, and its subsidiary, the Transit Authority, tried to cover up their own negligence by issuing white-wash press releases," the panel charged. The specific charges issued by the commission included the fact that the braking system of the disabled G local was inadequate.

Just eight days later, on July 8, the Queens grand jury released its findings, charging that both sides were equally to blame, but refusing to indict anyone for criminal negligence. The grand jury's thirty three-page report, based upon testimony of twenty witnesses, pinpointed several causes of the collision:

1. Employees who "have repeatedly demonstrated manifest disregard for standards of safety," creating "a substantial and unjustifiable risk of harm."

2. Failure by the three-man crew—Haynes, Williams, and Farmer—to communicate effectively.

3. Inherently dangerous automatic braking equipment. The accident would not have occurred, said the grand jury, if the train had not broken down in the first place.

Now the ball was in the court of Metropolitan Transportation Authority chairman, Dr. William J. Ronan. The man in charge of the new superagency which oversaw the Transit Authority had been accused by many of being insensitive to the problems of subway riders.

At a news conference following the release of the grand jury's report, Ronan assured the press and the public that the Transit Authority would take quick and proper action to rectify the faults in the system as spelled out in the report.

The manufacturers of the car braking system, Ronan said, had been told to redesign the brakes so that the malfunction that led to the accident would no longer be possible. In addition, all TA trains were being immediately supplied with two-way radios to ensure better communication between motorman and conductor. New rules on operating from other than the first car were instituted.

And finally, the MTA chairman said, there would be a review made of the hiring practices of the MTA and the Transit Authority, as well as a thorough check of the personnel records of people assigned to such crucial jobs as motorman and conductor. It was disclosed by the grand jury that Haynes, the motorman, had violated safety rules on twelve previous occasions in his nine years with the Transit Authority.

"With any accident, except for one caused by an act of God," Ronan concluded, "I assume it could have been prevented. I am never satisfied that everything is being done to make the subway reliable and safe," Ronan said, closing the incident.

There is, however, one footnote to the crash. On the day a G local crashed into another one, killing two passengers and injuring seventy-one, MTA Chairman Ronan was doing something to make the subway more reliable and safe.

He was in England, inspecting a newly-designed train.

Havoc at Union Square

The headline in the *New York Times* on Thursday August 29, 1991 said it all: IRT MOTORMAN IS CHARGED IN 5 DEATHS; CRASH SHUTS LINE AND TIES UP CITY.

The macabre headline also begged two questions: how and why did so grisly an accident take place at a time when the Transit Authority's high-tech safety precautions had reached a point of near perfection?

To better understand the causes of the derailment that wrought havoc a few hundred feet from the IRT's station at 14th Street and Broadway in Manhattan, one must first trace the curious behavior of Train 4-2333.

At 11:36 PM—three minutes after the scheduled departure time—the ten-car Downtown (#4) Express was ready to start its run. It began when the small, horseshoe-shaped object known as the reverser—or key—was inserted in the neutral position. Two other positions were available, forward and reverse.

The brakes were then charged to ensure that there was sufficient air to properly operate the pneumatic system and then the reverser key was shifted to forward. The headlights were turned on and the motorman then pulled on the controller to start the trip southward through The Bronx.

The controller provides three speed options. When tugged forward to the first or "switching" setting, the train slowly rolled forward at from three to five miles per hour. To accelerate it is pushed into the second, or "series," position which moved the cars at from 15-18 mph. For top speed—more than 35 mph—it is edged into the final, or "multiple unit," position.

At the beginning of the run, one can see the panorama of The Bronx on a late summer's night. The #4 line rumbles south along an elevated structure before descending into a portal and underground into the subway. Since in this instance it was almost Midnight, none of the cars were particularly crowded.

But the few riders and others who would board the express would soon realize that something was not right about this run. One of them was 22-year-old Jerry Yambi of Fort Sill, Oklahoma who was visiting relatives in the Kingsbridge section of The Bronx. Another was the conductor on NYCTA Train 4-2333.

After the express gained full speed, the conductor—who was in the sixth car—watched in surprise as the motorman failed to bring the ten cars to a braking mode for entrance to the Mosholu Parkway Station. According to the conductor, the train overran the platform by five cars. He notified the operator of the situation and added that the train would have to remain stopped long enough for the passengers to leave through the five cars still adjacent to the platform.

Four stops from the route's start, Yambi was standing at the front of the Kingsbridge Station platform. He could see the train's headlights and hear the vibrations of steel-on-steel as the express approached him. "There was something wrong from the beginning," said Yambi.

Instead of bringing his train to a normal stop before the platform's end, the operator allowed the first car to overshoot the platform. Yambi had no choice but to enter the second car which was accessible.

The next stop was Fordham Road. As the #4 rolled into the station, Yambi noticed that its speed was faster than normal and when the train finally was brought to a stop it had overrun yet another platform. "Two cars from the front passed the platform," said Yambi. "Yet the doors opened and (for the first two cars) there was no platform. People had to walk back two cars to get off."

Concerned about the erratic stops, the conductor of train 4-2333 warned his colleague that he would not take the train further if normal procedures were not observed during the rest of the run. At Bedford Park Boulevard—according to the conductor—another disturbing incident occurred. This time the train stopped within the platform confines but the motorman missed the "spotting boards," which are fixed signals on the station platform indicating to the conductor where the train must stop to ensure that all doors of the train are abreast of the platform.

Nevertheless, the conductor was able to open the doors and the run continued toward Manhattan. Concerned passengers, such as Yambi, seemed reassured enough to remain on the #4 as did other late-night commuters.

Significantly, the conductor—though admittedly unnerved by the motorman's actions—took no further warning action through the Grand Central stop.

But the 12.5 mile trip from Woodlawn Station to Union Square would be riddled with unnerving moments. A police officer noticed that the train began rolling briefly before the doors closed at 125th Street Station.

That station in Harlem marks the beginning of an express run with the only stops at 86th Street in Yorkville, 42d Street at Grand Central Station and then 14th Street at Union Square.

Such a straightaway invites a speedy run by subway standards which, at that time, was no more than 50 mph. Yet even hardened riders of the underground were concerned that the #4 was going beyond its limitations as it careened downtown.

"Crazy fast" was the way passenger Yambi described the speed of the train.

Ironically, when it pulled into Grand Central the express slowed to a crawl upon entering the station and then slowly proceeded to the number 10 which marked the stopping place at the head end of the platform.

It was now a few minutes past Midnight as the motorman inched the controller into its top-speed position. The next stop for the #4 would be 14th Street. Under normal conditions this is a fast-paced run as the #4 blurs past the 33rd 28th and 23rd Street local stations before barreling into the Union Square express stop.

But on this night conditions were not normal on the Lexington Avenue Line. General Order 1416-91 had been issued by the Transit Authority to alter both the speed of the southbound trains as well as the normal route of expresses. Overnight work on the express tracks meant that the #4 would have to be switched to the local track before it entered the 14th Street Station.

Under the circumstances, standard safety procedures would enable the train to handle the re-routing without mishap. As the train moved through 23rd Street and approached the crossover, the motorman would be confronted with signals. They would be arranged to slow his train to an acceptable speed that would enable the ten cars to negotiate the turn on to local tracks.

At about 12:12 A.M. the train sped into the dark south of 23rd Street. TA signalmen at the Grand Central Tower had arranged the switches and signals at 14th Street Crossover 135 for the re-routing. The first signal encountered by the train was #136 about 900 feet north of the switch. The signal flashed green.

The second signal, #134, was 400 feet north of switch 135. The signal flashed yellow over green with an illuminated "D". Defined in railroad terms it meant "proceed on main route prepared to stop at next signal expecting a diverging route."

Finally, there was Home Signal 132, located 40 feet north of Switch 135. It was red over red, an unmistakable order to stop and stay. Sight-distance tests later conducted revealed that all three signals were clearly visible for sufficient proper braking. With more than two years of experience as a motorman, the operator understood all the procedures.

For a month there had been a standing order for express trains to switch to the local tracks. The operator should have been accustomed to that order because he was on his regular route.

Instead the train relentlessly plunged through the tunnel, passing the first two signals, then approaching the double-red lights at a speed far in excess of the switching limit with no appreciable braking to decelerate the ten cars. The motorman apparently had the controller in high-speed mode because after the derailment the propulsion device was found in full-power position.

The conductor and several passengers were now acutely concerned that Train 4-2333 was rolling at a life-threatening speed but it was too late for anyone to take any precautionary action. Now the fate of the #4 Express

remained with wheel flanges, the crossover—and luck.

Astonishingly, the front truck on the first car (1440) managed to hold the rails—first swinging hard right through the crossover and then hard left—negotiating the switch and saving the motorman's life. At this point luck ran out on Train 4-2333.

The Laws of Gravity and Physics worked against Car 1440's rear truck as its wheels ground over the rails in the switch and bounced madly through the tunnel in an eastward direction. This, in turn, caused the lead truck of Car Two (1439) to follow.

Supernatural sounds of crashing steel intermingled with screams echoed off the tunnel walls as the derailment reached its point of no return. What followed was a chain reaction of horror starting with the soon-to-be-annihilated first car.

Once its rear truck de-railed Car 1440 struck a bank of overhead support columns, an air compressor and its aftercooler which were located north of the 14th Street Station platform. It then collided with the concrete crash wall adjacent to the local track. The wall acted like a giant knife, shearing the embattled piece of rolling stock in half.

"I thought it was the end of the world," said George Salazar, a Brooklyn security guard who was in the fourth car (1436) which was thrown sideways across the track.

At his station in the sixth car (1434), the conductor first heard a crashing sound, followed by others whereupon his car abruptly stopped on its tracks. Upon regaining his senses, the conductor tried to contact his motorman on the train radio but received no reply. He then sent a Mayday signal to the IRT command center.

Among the first rescuers to reach the scene—at 12:24 AM, 12 minutes after the derailment—were six Fire Department units. They would be followed by almost 200 other rescue workers including the Transit Police, the Police Department and the Emergency Medical Service.

By this time the major damage had been

done. The front of the lead car had been severed from the rest of the train, coming to rest with its front wheels jutting in the air about eleven yards from the Union Square platform. The rear of the mangled car was severed and entangled with the compressor room.

The second car (1439) fared better than cars three (1437) and four (1436). As *The New York Times* reported, "The cars jumped into the air and were crushed together in a tangled metal mass. They came to rest perpendicular to the tracks."

In fact the derailment was so violent that the identity of the cars baffled some of the investigators. "It's a mangle of steel," said Sgt. Luis Medina, a spokesman for the Transit Police. "It's hard to tell which car went where."

Rescue teams were horrified by the panoply of both physical and metallic wreckage. Bodies were strewn about with one landed on top of a subway car. A police emergency team found a shoe with a foot in it lying on the track.

"Everyone was thrown," said Joseph Dowers, a passenger from Crown Heights in Brooklyn. "I ended up crumpled up about three to four feet from the front of the train."

Five passengers were not so lucky. The fatalities were Jimmie Robles, 9-years-old, of Brooklyn; Victor Lewis, 36, of Manhattan; Audrey Pascal, 39, of Brooklyn; Delores Pryce, 37, of Brooklyn, and Richard Limehouse, 41, of Far Rockaway, Queens.

Some 20 other riders were admitted to hospitals as well as eight police officers and six firemen who were overcome by carbon monoxide spewed by generators placed on the tracks to power emergency lights and equipment to cut passengers free.

The five fatalities occurred almost immediately upon derailment and could not have been prevented by rescuers. According to the post-mortems, four of the deaths were caused by "blunt-force injuries" to the bodies of the victims while the fifth was caused by "extensive blood loss following the amputation of the victim's right foot."

At first there was believed to be a sixth fatality, Steven Darden, a 33-year-old Transit Authority worker. Darden was pinned under the wreckage and thought to be dead. But a rescuer saw his arm move and stayed in the oppressively hot tunnel for three hours aiding the wounded employee. He was fed fluid intravenously until rescue workers could pry him loose and take him to St. Vincent's Hospital. Darden suffered a fractured arm and trauma.

The motorman—not unlike Edward Luciano in the Malbone Street Disaster—walked away unscathed and was picked up near his home in the Bronx five hours later. He told police he had had three beers after the crash. New York City Police Commissioner Lee P. Brown said an alcohol test showed that he was legally drunk. Brown also said the police believed that he was drunk at the time of the accident. This was based both on the alcohol test and reports from passengers on the erratic run of Train 4-2333.

The National Transportation Safety Board's investigation tracked the motorman's movements for more than five hours after the crash. According to the NTSB report: "The operator left the train and walked up to the street level above the subway station to Union Square Park. After purchasing a 16-ounce can of beer at a nearby delicatessen, the train operator sat in the park and consumed the beer while watching the emergency response activity. He returned to the delicatessen two more times, buying and consuming a can of beer on each occasion. After 2 1/2 hours, the train operator left the park, walked approximately 30 blocks to Grand Central Station, and took a train toward his home. He purchased and drank another beer before arriving at his apartment, about 15 minutes' walking distance from the subway station."

After the police located the operator at 5:35 AM, he was taken to the NYPD 13th Precinct, where he remained during the day. Although NYCTA company policy requires post accident blood alcohol and urine screening tests and the operator had given consent for such tests to be conducted, the New York District Attorney had determined that a court order must be obtained before taking a blood sample from the train operator. Obtaining the court order delayed taking the sample until 1:05 PM.

As for the subway system itself, the result was chaos.

The Lexington Avenue Line was shut from Bowling Green Station to 86th Street which, according to *The Times*, sent "thousands of commuters scrambling to find other ways to get to work."

Damage to both the tunnel and equipment was extensive. In addition to the wrecked cars, two switch machines including all associated hardware and switch rails, were destroyed as were numerous signal code, line cables and the third rail in the vicinity of the accident. Additionally, 14 support columns between the express tracks and nine columns between the express and local tracks were destroyed.

The National Transport Safety Board took on the case and established some heretofore overlooked points. One of the most pertinent was the train operator's activities for the 24 hours preceding the accident. The NTSB said:

* He began work at 11:59 P.M on August 26, 1991.

* He finished his shift at 7:44 AM on August 27, 1991.

* Instead of going to bed, he "cleaned the house."

* During the day he had three glasses of whiskey.

* He had dinner and went to bed at 8 PM, awakening at 10:30 PM.

* He took a cab to work, claiming to have arrived at 11:10 PM.

(The conductor countered that the motorman did not arrive until 11:30 PM)

Thus, sleep deprivation had an effect on the motorman's performance.

"At the time of the accident," noted the NTSB report, "the operator had been on duty about 30 minutes and had slept only two-and-a-half hours before reporting to work after 11 PM on August 27."

The Board concluded that "the maximum amount of sleep" that he could have obtained in the just over 24 hours between beginning work on August 26 (11:59 PM) and the time of the accident was four-and-one-quarter hours.

"Therefore," the NTSB concluded, "it is evident that the train operator was not only intoxicated but also sleep-deprived when he reported for work the night of the accident."

Which raised another question: why wasn't the train dispatcher who is required by rule "to determine whether crewmembers are fit for duty and to remove them from service if they are not," aware of the motorman's condition?

One reason was that the TA's manuals did not clearly define what constitutes "fitness for duty." The NTSB report added that "a more informed evaluation by the train dispatcher would have revealed signs of the operator's intoxication."

Still, the disaster might have been averted had the conductor followed through on his threat to stop the train had its erratic behavior continued. "As a minimum," said the Safety Board report, "the conductor could have called the (TA) command center and reported the circumstances or requested guidance."

But the TA rules at the time were not sufficiently specific and the conductor could very well have doubted that it was within his authority to halt the #4 Express.

Taking the above factors into account, there still was a possibility of stopping the train automatically had the signaling been more effective and had the train been kept on the straightaway because of its excessive speed.

As a result the Transit Authority revised a key Rule, 109 (m), to read as follows:

"When for any reason, it is necessary to divert a train from its regular route, the switch must not be set for the diverging move nor the signal for that route cleared until the train has stopped, unless the tower operator can see the train and has observed that its speed has been reduced to that allowable for the crossover movement."

If this rule had been in effect, Train 4-2333 would have had an escape route, continuing on the straight track but with the trip arm placing the train's braking system in emergency.

And this brings us back to the questions at the start of this chapter—in light of the high-tech safety system, how and why did this accident occur?

The Safety Board concluded the following:

* *The operator failed to comply with the signal system and the general order because he was impaired by alcohol and sleep-deprived.*

* *The NYCTA failed to provide additional training that may have enhanced the train dispatcher's ability to recognize the possible impairment of train crew members.*

* *NYCTA management failed both to clearly define the authority and responsibility of the conductor and the train operator in the NYCTA's operating rules and to adequately train the employees.*

* *Rule 109(m), which was critical to this accident, was incorrectly written and ambiguous.*

* *The NYCTA's operating rulebook had been updated since 1979 to include changes such as those made to the signal system.*

* *The signal system's grade-time measuring feature for crossover movement was not designed to provide sufficient braking distance for the train's maximum attainable speed when an operator had failed to comply with a signal indication.*

Once the debris was cleared and pillars and other structural supports rebuilt, the IRT line was restored to normalcy while the professionals sought ways and means of preventing a similar accident under identical—or nearly identical—circumstances.

In this instance "human failure" was part of the problem, but it could have been neutralized by means of science—specifically a fail-safe signal system.

To this end, the NTSB made the following recommendations to the Transit Authority:

* *Provide retraining for all supervisors who had received shorter versions of the present substance abuse training course. Also, provide periodic refresher training in drug and alcohol detection for supervisory personnel, such as dispatchers, and other NYCTA employees who are required to monitor the fitness for duty of operating crewmembers.*

* *Revise and update the operating rulebook to include clearly defined duties and responsibilities for operating crewmembers and information on all aspects and indications of signals not previously addressed.*

* *Establish responsibility in the operating department for developing, ministering, and interpreting rules.*

If there were sweet uses of the adversity caused on the night of August 28, 1991 it was that the IRT became a better, safer, and more efficiently run system than it was before the havoc at Union Square.

Unfortunately, it was not the last of the major accidents on the New York underground system.

The Unlikely Uphill Rear-Ender

To some nervous straphangers, a ride in a subway car over an East River bridge is a downright frightening experience.

Some commuters are traumatized by the height; others by the seemingly tenuous appearance of ancient skeletal bridge steelwork managing to hold so many heavy vehicles including an eight-car train. Many riders remain concerned about the respective ages of spans such as the Williamsburg and Manhattan Bridges, each of which is approaching its 100th birthday.

If a simple ride over the waters separating Brooklyn and Manhattan can be scary, imagine what it was like early on the morning of June 5, 1995 when two eight-car trains collided on the Williamsburg Bridge, hundreds of feet above the ground (and water) below.

Logically there was no reason for any rear-end collision to occur at that time nor place in this mysterious episode.

For starters, the motorman, 46-year-old Layton Gibson, was experienced, reliable and fully aware of the system on which he was piloting the J Train.

A colleague described Gibson as a motorman who could "hit the board"—bring the train to a stop so that it was perfectly aligned with the platform—all the time. "He was a good motorman," said fellow worker Jaime Diaz, "no doubt about that."

Gibson's route extended from the Jamaica Center Station in Queens to its Manhattan terminus at Broad Street near the Financial District. Along the ancient elevated structure modern, stainless steel trains thundered through neighborhoods such as Woodhaven (Queens), and East New York (Brooklyn) before moving over Brooklyn's own Broadway toward the Williamsburg Bridge.

The last stop before the East River crossing was Marcy Avenue. From the end of the platform, Gibson could see the bridge spires, the dome of the historic Williamsburg Savings Bank building and even the facade of the landmark Peter Luger's steak house farther west along Broadway where an el spur once carried trains to water's edge and the ferry to Manhattan.

Approaching the incline toward the bridge, the operator had to ease his train around an S curve—to the right, or north, toward Greenpoint and then abruptly to the left, or west, toward the Lower East Side of Manhattan—at the slowest available speed. That was easy enough since even had he illegally moved his controller into "high" the train would not have gained enough momentum until it had passed through most of the curve.

Furthermore, a collision on the uphill portion of the bridge trackage was unlikely because of the angle of elevation which automatically would slow the train (Law of Gravity) and the built-in signal safety devices including the automatic tripper which would activate emergency brakes should Gibson's train run a red signal.

Finally, there was the "dead-man's" position on the motorman's controller. If, for example, the operator suffered a heart attack while running a train and his hand slipped off the speed-activator, the controller was designed to instantly spring in an upward position and thereby automatically set the emergency brakes.

And, yet, despite these assurances, on a clear June morning with no apparent distractions Layton Gibson's train climbed the steep grade, ran the red, tripped the emergency brake and still telescoped into a stopped M train in front of it.

How could such long odds be defied?

To fathom why the tragedy occurred one must first understand that no matter how many built-in safeguards are implemented, it is impossible to construct a one hundred percent foolproof system; not as long as human beings are involved with operating the trains.

Even motorman Gibson, beloved and admired by co-workers, had a blemish or two on his record. According to the National Transportation Safety Board, Gibson suffered a two-day suspension in January 1992 from a December 3, 1991 incident "during which he stopped his train short of a station, leaving two cars outside of the station limits." He also had a reprimand "for sleeping in a darkened room while he was on duty during a Midnight shift on January 18, 1989."

The subject of sleep is pertinent to the disaster because the J Train operator was working a shift that began at 2:30 AM and ended later in the morning. For any motorman it is a difficult time because of physiological demands. Accordingly, one colleague reported that Gibson had problems at night trying to stay awake while running his train. In the NTSB report she said that on one occasion he mentioned that he had "barely made it this trip" because he had trouble staying awake.

Despite Transit Authority policy, crewmembers on the Midnight tour were known to "take naps at work," as one operator put it. Fatigue, it seems, was part of the woof and warp of the early morning shift.

Nevertheless, Gibson betrayed no signs of difficulties as he moved the train from station to station heading to the Williamsburg Bridge. "Nothing was out of the ordinary," said the conductor of Train 531 J.

The Broadway Local completed two round trips and now headed toward Broad Street for the crew's final run. It left Jamaica Center on time at 5:31 AM while dawn broke over Queens. As the sun climbed, the J rumbled across the Queens-Brooklyn line taking the sharp ninety-degree turns between Cypress Hills and Crescent Street with ease.

At Lorimer Street an off-duty motorman boarded the first car after exchanging greetings with Gibson. According to the other, Gibson seemed "awake and alert." Yet, after two more stops he would meet his death, apparently neither awake nor alert!

Under normal conditions the only train that might have impinged on 531 J's schedule was an eight-car M (as in Myrtle Avenue Line) unit that began its morning run from the Metropolitan Avenue depot at 5:48 AM After rumbling toward Broadway-Myrtle Avenue junction, the train made one final stop at Central Avenue before entering the curious spur that snaked it around old Bushwick houses and linked with the main Broadway Brooklyn line that carried the trains through Williamsburg.

This placed the M on the Manhattan-bound local tracks in front of the J. At this point a passenger riding in the first car of Gibson's train recalled an incident as Train 531 J approached Myrtle-Broadway station. Henry Simon, a 28-year-old truck driver, later said that the J stopped abruptly because it was too close to the M in front of it. But no other untoward incidents were reported and the two trains plied their route along the el over Broadway.

The M train was a safe distance ahead of 531 J until the M unloaded its passengers at the Marcy Avenue station and rolled toward the Williamsburg Bridge. At this point an interloper—a TA work train—would play a decisive role in altering the respective runs of the M and the 531 J which followed.

After pulling his controller forward for the bridge climb, the M train operator detected the work train on the same track about 30 car lengths ahead over the East River. Alternately putting his power on and off, the motorman inched his way forward stopping at red signals and then inching forward to signal J2-120 which halted him with another red before the center of the bridge.

The M was comprised of R-42 model cars built in 1968 and 1969 and rebuilt from 1987 to 1989. Meanwhile, Gibson's train had pulled into Marcy Avenue with no suggestion of any difficulties ahead. When all passengers had cleared the doors 531 J's conductor closed them and at 6:10 AM the faint whine of the motors and the screech of steel flanges against steel rails could be heard as Gibson took his train around the curves and over the bus-filled Bridge Plaza below.

If, as suspected, Gibson was so drowsy he was close to being asleep at the controller, it would have been possible to alert him. Rule 40 (m) of the NYCT operating manual stipulated that train operators must immediately notify the command center when they are stopped at red signals. However, it was later learned that this rule often was misinterpreted by employees.

Nevertheless, when the M stopped at the red signal on the bridge, the motorman could have notified command center which, in turn, could have radioed Gibson of the trains ahead. This potential message could well have served to force him to a more alert mode. However the M's conductor never announced that the train had stopped at a red signal. With curves behind him and the climb ahead, Gibson pulled his controller into the high position. Under normal conditions it was the natural thing to do. "He handled it like anybody else would have done," said the off-duty operator who was sitting diagonally across from the motorman's cab. "He was accelerating all the way because you got eight cars and you are going uphill."

That would have been the right thing had there not been a stopped work car ahead on the bridge not to mention the M train with brakes locked behind it. Nor would this have been a concern had Gibson's eyes been clearly focused on the track ahead. In the clear morning light both the caution signals and the stainless steel eight-car M train should have been visible to him on the bridge.

However, neither was apparent to 531 J's conductor. Secure in the knowledge that his business was done until the train rolled underground into the Essex Street Station on the Lower East Side of Manhattan, he closed the door behind the conductor's compartment in the third car to relax. He gazed down at Brooklyn's Kent Avenue which paralleled the East River and to the right where the massive Domino Sugar factory sat below.

The off-duty train operator sitting across from Gibson's cab opened a newspaper, his attention riveted to the headlines on page one.

More concerned was a Transit Authority road car inspector travelling to work in Manhattan. Standing by the rear window in the next-to-last car on the stopped M train, he could see through the storm door of the last car and to the track coming up from Bridge Plaza.

With an increasing sense of fright and disbelief, he watched the J Train move with speed up toward the M. "He was coming pretty quick," the road car inspector later testified. "At least 30 miles an hour."

Precisely how fast the train was moving was impossible to tell at the time. None of the trains on the New York subway-el system carried speedometers but a 30 mph estimate was realistic under the circumstances. Whether the eight-car local could be stopped in time was another question.

Exactly 279.35 feet separated the automatic trip arm at signal J2-128 and the rear of the M local. Had conditions been normal, Gibson already would have seen the red light and brought his train to a stop.

Instead, as the road car inspector remembered, he saw "the train coming to hit us."

Still there was the working tripper. Sure enough, as Train 531 J threateningly rumbled past the red signal, the metal strip overhanging its truck hit the tripper setting off the dreaded *chow*, the blast from the air brakes, signalling trouble ahead.

The fail-safe tripper had worked when the J train was rolling at approximately 34 mph. Now the question was, could the emergency brakes bring the onrushing train to a halt in time?

Had the incident taken place in 1918 when the signal system originally was installed on the Williamsburg Bridge, the answer might have been in the affirmative. Or even had the episode taken place at the time of World War II. The safety system in 1995 was based on the acceleration and braking capacity of subway cars which were built before the war.

Another problem was the spacing between signals. Throughout the Transit Authority lines the average spacing is about 350 feet, allowing for safer emergency tripper stops. But on the Williamsburg Bridge in June 1995 it was only 265 feet!

This was insufficient. There were not enough seconds to allow a full stop from the moment the stop-cock was tripped by the arm at track level and the air brakes went on to the moment the onrushing train reached the local ahead of it.

Those with an ear for the rails knew that doom rode the bridge tracks. One of them was the off-duty operator who dropped his paper the moment he heard the *chow* signalling that the emergency brakes had been activated. He claimed that "within three seconds" of the *chow* the J train ploughed into the M. This was corroborated by the J's conductor who called it "a matter of seconds" between the *chow* and the crash.

"You could hear the automatic stop, the brakes slowing him up," said Julio Castro, 42, a passenger in the front car. "I just knew something bad had to happen."

The J's brakes were working but not fast enough. They had slowed the train down by at least half but it was too late. Like a battering ram, the eight-car local bashed the stopped M, pushed its rear truck off its center casting and raised the car body about six feet into the air as it telescoped about 17 feet into car 4664. The time was 6:12 AM.

Those sitting in the lead car of the J train, 4461, could almost anticipate the disaster ahead from the combination of sounds and sights around them. One was Henry Simon, 28, a truck driver on his way to work. He said:

"The train was going pretty fast. The first thing I noticed was it seemed like we hit a real, hard bump. The noise was like an airplane crashing. The feeling was like an earthquake. The impact threw me back on the floor. The whole thing caved in."

No less horrified was Victor Morales, 29, who was travelling in the front car of the J. "I was sitting in the front and the whole car just came in at me. I saw the whole car coming toward me. To me it seemed like the train never tried to stop. I couldn't move. I just froze. From the impact, everybody just fell to the floor and everybody started running."

Freddie Ramos: "It felt like we hit a wall."

Although passengers in the last car on the M and first car of the J were most directly affected, others reacted with equal anxiety. One was Hermann Stampol, 48, of Ridgewood, Queens, who was in the next-to-last car on the M and apparently daydreaming prior to the collision.

"All of a sudden," he recalled, "that daydream turned into a nightmare. I thought someone set off a bomb. There was smoke and debris everywhere, and the train smelled like smoke."

Layton Gibson never left his motorman's cab.

Since no video replay or any other recording devices were available at the time, one can only conjecture about the operator's last seconds on earth as he took his train around the turn over Williamsburg Bridge Plaza and up the span's incline.

He had been awake long enough to pull his controller into high but not alert enough to respond to caution and stop signals ahead. Yet he—or his body—appeared to have held the deadman's switch in the down position so that the train was able to gain momentum even as he presumably dozed in his cab.

Had Gibson been awake, he would have noticed the amber and then red lights, not to mention the rear red lights on the M local and, being a veteran motorman, he would have taken appropriate action. Even after the *chow* sound had alerted other railroad employees on the two trains, it seemed not to rouse Gibson to evacuate his compartment to escape the impact and almost certain death.

According to the NTSB analysis of the wreck, Gibson simply was either sleeping or in a post-sleep stupor and, therefore, unable to rouse himself to precautionary action.

"The position of the J Train operator's body after the accident supports the finding that he probably feel asleep," said the NTSB report. "About seven seconds elapsed between the time that the J Train went into emergency braking and the time of impact.

"When a train goes into emergency braking, the brake system emits a distinctive noise, recognizable by any crew member. Both the conductor and the off-duty operator on the J Train reported hearing the *chow* sound of the emergency brake.

"Had the J Train operator been alert, he would have been able to detect that a collision was imminent and probably would have tried to vacate the compartment to avoid injury. However, investigators found his body in his seat and no indication that he had turned or moved to leave the compartment.

"His failure to take action in a life-threatening situation strongly suggests that he was either asleep or had just woken up and was too disoriented or sluggish upon waking to respond."

Gibson was killed on impact, the only fatality as a result of the collision. But there were many wounded—some serious—and it required an amazing rescue job involving the police, firemen and workers from all municipal agencies including the Emergency Medical Service.

An eyewitness from the street below originally activated the emergency crews to action with a 911 phone call five minutes after the collision occurred. The first rescuers arrived on the scene at 6:22 AM, five minutes after the alert and only ten minutes after the crash.

Their immediate problem was finding ways and means of reaching the injured passengers stranded on the bridgework high above. Firemen threw up five ladders to the trackbed and gingerly lowered the injured—most with back, leg and neck injuries—one at a time on bright, orange stretcher buckets or aluminum mesh baskets.

A dozen passengers and two crewmembers suffered minor injuries on the M Train. Luckily it was an off-hour and nobody was sitting or standing where the J telescoped through into the last car of the M.

Gibson's cab was totally crushed leaving no survival space. A total of 50 passengers on Train 531 J suffered minor injuries but two other passengers who were standing behind the motorman's cab suffered serious injuries.

Cramped conditions made evacuation extraordinarily difficult, compelling many of the injured to wait in frustration in the trains. Some of the injured waited up to two hours sprawled across train seats or on stretchers.

The Daily News reported: "The soaring height added fear to the misery of some victims. Some turned panicky when they turned from their stretchers and glimpsed the Brooklyn shoreline far below, and several were treated for hyperventilation."

Informed of the disaster, transportation officials ordered the bridge closed. This, in turn, caused a domino effect for motorists and commuters. "New York City hasn't seen a traffic nightmare this bad in many, many years," said Assistant Transportation Commissioner Oscar Sierra.

The wounded included the rolling stock. All eight cars on the J Train suffered some degree of damage, particularly the lead car. Four cars on the forward train were in need of repair, especially the last car which, as the NTSB noted, "suffered massive carbody intrusion."

As for the human wounded some 47 ambulances and a transit bus were employed to take the 55 injured to 11 area hospitals.

Even before the last of the injured was removed from the bridge—three hours and 43 minutes from the time of the wreck—critics were jumping all over the TA for not having sufficient safety precautions to prevent such a calamity. One of them was, former subway columnist Jim Dwyer, then writing for *New York Newsday* and more recently the *Daily News*. Dwyer pegged his argument to the fact that the city had invested some $14 billion to fix the transit system. He wrote:

"I don't care if the dead motorman was whacked out on crack or sober as a judge: A subway train ran out of control on a bridge 150 feet over the East River.

"That train should have been stopped by a combination of the signal system and the subway-car brakes that recently cost us $14 billion to buy, rebuild and repair.

"Instead, it nearly ended up in the East River."

A sweeping investigation followed along with charges and countercharges, some political, some scientific but, unfortunately, the chief protagonist in the mystery could not provide any input because he was dead.

One interesting theory concerned the ability of the R-40 car's brake shoes to bring the train to a stop in time.

Originally equipped with cast-iron brake shoes, the R-40s were rebuilt during the 1980s and the brake shoes were changed to a composition type. The NTSB reported that the new shoes "required the NYCT to modify or replace many brake system components, including the variable load valve."

It is believed by some analysts of the system that—no matter what the compensatory moves—the composite brakes could not work as effectively as the earlier cast-iron version.

The state Public Transportation Safety Board blamed the accident on poor emergency brakes. But the NTSB found that train equipment "neither caused nor contributed to the accident."

There were more contradictions. A Metropolitan Transportation Authority probe of the crash found that Gibson was awake at the time of the crash. But the NTSB said a sleep expert determined that the motorman had dozed off. Alcohol and drugs were ruled out as factors.

The NTSB asserted that the J Train could not have stopped in time, because there was too little space between signals. That led the TA to order that subway cars be rewired to slow their acceleration.

Without question the unlikely, uphill rear-ender had profound ramifications for the city's subway and el system.

Stung to the very core by the episode and determined to regain the public's confidence with a higher level of safety standards, the MTA ordered a significant number of improvements. The agency decided to add speedometers to the cabs, modernize its signals, lower the top speed of its trains by altering car motors and post new cautionary restrictions throughout the system's right-of-way.

The result has been a slower and safer system but, as events would demonstrate, not completely accident-proof.

The interior of Williamsburg Bridge disaster car 4461, facing the motorman's cab

A Double-Dose of Switching Madness and Déja Vu

Switches have been standard railway equipment for so long that they have been taken for granted by passengers in the manner of rails, couplings and wheels. They are there; they do their job and that's that.

Subway riders rarely give switches a second thought as trains rumble over them as casually as they would over a mile of straight, welded rail.

Yet, every one of the 1,700 switches in the New York subway system has a built-in "imperfection." Gaps at the crossing point where the rails meet allow train wheels to move through either the straight track or curve as the case may be. That gap—or "imperfection" in the rail—could, theoretically at least, cause derailment.

Nevertheless, a correctly-aligned switch should be one-hundred percent safe. This is particularly true when one considers the appropriate guard rails installed with the switch to insure against wheels jumping the track. Furthermore, the Transit Authority regularly monitors its miles of tracks and switches as an added precaution against such accidents.

But, as demonstrated in an earlier chapter—The Times Square IRT Mystery Crash—an improperly-thrown switch can cause horrific damage, particularly if a train is crossing through at the time of the switch's movement.

Nevertheless, in the 69 years since the 1928 wreck under Seventh Avenue and a date with fate in 1997 advances in switching and signalling technology had significantly improved the safety quotient on the subway system—but not to the point of unequivocal perfection.

This fact was proven on the night of July 3, 1997 in the tunnel under Harlem's St.Nicholas Avenue, just north of the IND 135th Street Station where tracks were inspected on a weekly basis.

While most New Yorkers prepared for their annual Independence Day celebrations on the following day, a small group of night-shift workers and Southbound revelers headed through Harlem on the Downtown A Express.

Glorified in song—Duke Ellington's rendition of *Take The A Train*, written by Billy Strayhorn—The A Train had been virtually free of meaningful accidents since its inaugural run in 1932.

Originally linking Washington Heights with Downtown Manhattan at Chambers Street, The A Train was acclaimed by transit buffs and ordinary straphangers alike for its speedy express runs between 59th Street-Columbus Circle and 125th Street in Harlem.

It was an historic line when it was built; forming a new artery the entire length of Manhattan Island and being the first step in an extensive new subway system which would eventually serve four of the five boroughs of the city.

But by 1997 The A Train had lost some of its pre-World War II glamour although it still served a useful, if less esthetic, purpose to New York's commuters.

Few of the 100 aboard the IND Express on that Thursday evening in early Summer were thinking much about transit history as The A Train left the lights of 145th Street Station in the distance and gathered speed in the darkened tunnel.

As the clock in the 135th Street Station recorded 10:20 PM, the eight-car train comprised of 40-ton, R-44 model cars built in 1972 by the St.Louis Car Company *click-clacked* toward the local stop.

Travelling at the normal speed of 25-30 miles per hour, The A Train was to pass through the station without stopping, on its way to its next express station at 125th Street.

Just north of the platform the A Train passed over a switch which was in its normal straightaway position. The switch connected the southbound tracks to a spur where trains could be stored during non-rush hours or for other reasons. The spur tracks continued south through the 135th Street Station.

Since the A Train was on its regular run there was no reason for it to be on the spur and, therefore, the switch should never have been moved to the curved mode since The A was rolling along its traditional downtown lane.

As the Express approached the station at 10:20 PM each car produced the oft-heard *thunk-thunk-thunk* sound of train wheels barreling through the switch. That is, every car but the eighth and last of the consist.

Between the time the front truck of the eighth car smoothly negotiated the switch and the rear truck reached the crossover, the switch moved from its correct, straight, position to the curved arrangement.

Suddenly, the rear trucks hugged the switch and began moving crazily toward the spur. But since the 75-foot-long train continued moving forward it quickly pulled the rear trucks off the tracks.

The ensuing events were eerily similar to those which occurred on the IRT in 1928 under Times Square. Passengers' ears were assailed by deafening sounds of a monstrous steel and aluminum train bouncing out of control through the tunnel.

Once the rear trucks headed toward the spur Car Eight began travelling almost sideways. Immediately, it slammed into a cement-block partition separating the express tracks from the spur and knocked out two vertical columns while brushing the top of the grimy tunnel.

"Suddenly, everything started to spin around and then it turned dark," said Isaac Tarik, a 22-year-old sophomore at Manhattan Community College. "There were sparks flying and there was all this smoke. All the electrical cords from the train wrapped around my neck and I was bleeding everywhere. I was, like, in shock."

When Tarik gazed at the train's mangled eighth car he gaped in astonishment. "There was no other side of the train," he said.

The *New York Post* reported that a woman with blood rushing down her face was standing in the middle of a car screaming.

Although most news sources indicated that the last car was empty of passengers, *The Post* revealed that Tarik was "sitting in the subway car that was split in two."

According to *The Post*, Tarik freed himself from the wreckage, spotted a subway employee searching for victims and called for assistance. He was helped to the 135th Street Station platform. "I'm amazed I'm alive," Tarik told *The Post*. "And I just keep thanking God."

Rescuers and city officials did likewise when they reached the site of the impaled subway car. *The New York Times* noted that the broken, 40-ton car was "a jumble of mangled metal, broken glass and sheared off cables."

Sped to the crash scene, Mayor Rudolph Giuliani was astonished when he was informed that there had been no fatalities. He had been led to the tunnel where the crumpled eighth car sat in two pieces—one 60-feet long and the other 15-feet long—and somberly shook his head.

"It was one of the most remarkable things I've ever seen and one of the most frightening," said the mayor. "The entire last car was severed in half, smashed up like an accordion. They're enormously lucky that no one was killed or hurt seriously."

A total of 14 passengers were injured of which eight were treated at Harlem Hospital.

A transit track worker, Angelo Bodoy, was no less stunned by the sight of the demolished vehicle. "It was amazing," he said. "Amazing. I couldn't believe it. I've never seen one of these trains in this condition."

No sooner had emergency workers arrived on the scene questions were being asked, most notably how could an accident such as this happen?

"There are two hypotheses," Giuliani explained. "One of them that a switch malfunctioned so that although the first seven cars got through, the eighth car was knocked off the track.

"The other possibility is that something malfunctioned in the car. They won't know the answer to that for a couple of days at least."

Transit Authority Senior Vice-President Joseph Hofmann was cautious about fixing blame. "We're looking at everything," he explained. "We're looking at the infra-structure. We're looking at the car. We're looking at the track."

At first probing, nobody seemed to factor in the appearance of four transit workers who were doing what was described as "routine maintenance" near the 135th Street Station at the time of the derailment. Their work was regarded by some officials as so routine that the TA had not issued slow-speed orders for that stretch of track.

None of the workers had warning lights to alert the motorman that the maintenance people were in the vicinity. Of all the crash theories, the one involving the workers was considered among the most far-fetched. Meanwhile, the TA shut off power between 59th and 145th Streets and dispatched what would grow to an army of 500 transit workers to both rescue the passengers, pore through the wreckage and then remove the damaged train so that normal service could be resumed.

All four lines—A, B, C and D—were halted north of 59th Street after the accident and remained inactive through Thursday night and into Friday while emergency crews and investigators moved around the crash site.

Reporters on the scene found transit workers in helmets and safety goggles carrying out what *The New York Times* described as, "a bizarre kind of demolition derby, trying to clear the tracks by attacking the last car with blowtorches."

The Daily News noted, that "The scene at the station looked like something from a summer movie thriller. The area was packed with TA trucks and vans."

Working in twenty-minute shifts because of the stifling conditions, maintenance workers cut chunks of the deformed train so that the car could be lifted off the tracks. Acrid smoke and steamy heat produced a strange odor which *The Times* described as smelling "like too many fireworks."

Although giant fans drew away smoke, workers regularly streamed from the wreck for fresh air and water. TA ironworker Larry Lynch said that 100-degree temperatures in the tunnel and fumes from equipment gave workers headaches and spells of nausea. "I had to come up every twenty minutes for air," said Lynch.

A diesel-powered wrecker train pulled up on which workers placed tan-and-orange seats, charred insulation, railings and other debris from the demolished eighth car whose shiny silver roof was crumpled like aluminum foil.

Throughout the Fourth of July laborers cleared the tracks and by 8 PM, in time for the expected crush of riders expected for the East River fireworks, the A, C and D trains were rolling again.

"The Pony Express came through in time," said Lynch, who had toiled in the sweltering tunnel for nearly twelve hours, "and that's something, considering the mess it was down there this morning."

Once the damaged pillars were shored up and the last bits of debris were removed, authorities—including Mark Garcia, lead investigator for the National Transportation Safety Board—began filtering through the clues that would explain the wreck.

At first probers focused on the switch, which still was in working order, as were the tracks leading to and from it. Through the first few days, the sleuths focused on mechanical failure rather than human error. However, interviews were conducted with the four maintenance workers who had been performing track work in the area at the time.

Then, a break of sorts came.

One of the four workers fixing a routine switching problem at the station allegedly opened the wrong valve box and accidentally activated the switch for the wrong track just as the eighth car of The A Train passed over the turn-off. At least that's what the TA maintained.

Both TA investigators and probers from the State Public Transportation Board pinpointed the cause of the crash as the signal maintenance worker's mistake. The worker had eight years experience on the subways and a clean record. Other track workers argued that they never saw the control-box cover removed. An official of the Transport Workers Union supported that claim. However, the National Transportation Safety Board also was on the case conducting its own investigation.

In September 1997 the NTSB concluded that the cause of the accident was human error. "All our tests indicated that there was nothing wrong with the signals," the NTSB asserted, "or the equipment."

However, the NTSB revealed that one of the trackside workers had in fact inadvertently handled a box that controlled the switches. All Indications were that the top of one box had been opened and the (switch) caps had been turned.

"From all appearances," the NTSB declared, "he (the worker) pushed the plunger on the wrong box."

Nevertheless, the Authority still had to wrestle with the problem of eliminating a repetition of such a dangerous maneuver. The solution was a campaign to paint control valves and the switches they operate the same bright color so they will be clearly visible inside the tunnels.

And so, it seemed, the second switch disaster in more than six decades would lead to another long period of time without repetition but in 1997, at least, the Law of Averages was working against New York's subway system.

Only *eleven days* after the Harlem derailment the last car of an IRT Brooklyn local met an almost identical fate as Car Eight had on The A Train!

There were, however, significant differences:
* The second derailment occurred on the A-Division not the B-Division Group II.
* The train was going appreciably slower.
* The most damaged car was considerably smaller than the one on the A Train.
* The wreck occurred while the train was on a curve not the straightaway.

At approximately 1:13 AM on July 15, 1997, the Number Two southbound train left the Franklin Avenue Station in the Crown Heights section of Brooklyn. Beginning at the subway system's northernmost terminal— 241st Street in The Bronx—the Number Two had wended its way along the perimeter of Bronx Zoo and into the southern part of the borough.

It linked with the Number Three tracks at 135th Street in Harlem, moved south under the north rim of Central Park and became an express at 96th Street on Manhattan's Upper West Side. From there it raced down the island on some of the fastest subway express trackage in the world before tunneling under the East River to Brooklyn.

From Clark Street, the first stop in Brooklyn, the Number Two headed to its ultimate destination, the junction of Flatbush and Nostrand Avenues, near Brooklyn College. It was a slow, almost laconic, run that moved under Eastern Parkway before the southward turn toward Flatbush.

As he pulled his train out of the Franklin Avenue station, the motorman saw the amber signal ahead which limited his speed for the switch ahead. The rails already had moved into position so that the moment the front, four-wheel truck reached the switch, the forward set of two wheels would move right and take the curve, crossing over and away from the straight tracks.

At 15 miles per hour, the Number Two gracefully made the turn with each of the first nine cars accelerating under Nostrand Avenue toward the President Street Station.

The front truck of the tenth and last car also rolled through the switch in normal fashion. At that moment, a handful of the 120 passengers had gotten out of their seats to alight at President Street but none in the last car. It, rather fortunately, was empty.

"Suddenly, we heard a big noise: *Boom!*" said 27-year-old Jean Pintro, who was thrown from his seat and banged his head in the process.

The "big noise" was the result of the switch having moved from its curved position to straightaway. Instead of making the right turn, the rear truck proceeded east as if it were part of the Number Three Line heading for New Lots Avenue in East New York.

Being pulled in two directions, Car Ten jumped the rails and slammed into a concrete wall separating the tracks of the Number Two and Three Lines. The impact of the reinforced wall against the car's midsection was like a gigantic blow to the train's superstructure.

"It left what looked like a giant karate chop in the middle of the car, bowing it slightly," reported *The Times*.

The crash activated the emergency brakes which halted the train in a matter of seconds. But that hardly ended the terror for passengers in the nine cars untouched by the derailment. Lights went out, air conditioning failed and straphangers could only guess at the cause of the thunder underground.

"I was sitting there paranoid like the train might be hijacked," said one passenger. "I was hoping ain't nobody coming through here to rob me."

The emergency call produced an invasion of rescue workers who herded passengers into the first five cars before evacuating them from the darkened tunnel. Meanwhile, the TA halted all train service to the seven stations on the southern leg of the Number Two and Five Lines while launching special shuttle bus service for an estimated 15,000 commuters whose morning rush hour transportation would be disrupted.

Once the four injured passengers were treated, subway officials turned to the perplexing question of how such an unlikely derailment could take place especially in view of its similarity to the Harlem collision.

For starters, those probing the crash eliminated one element that was primary to the early switching failure; human error. There were no workers in the vicinity of the Crown Heights derailment as there were at the Harlem site where a maintenance worker was accused of throwing the wrong switch.

What inspectors learned was that the culprit was a simple track relay device.

More than 11,000 relays are sprinkled throughout the system. They are used to trace the whereabouts of trains. The relay also can trigger an automatic stop and send other signals to a conductor. In this case the relay should have indicated to a nearby control center that the Number Two Train had not cleared the switch over to Nostrand Avenue.

Thinking that all ten cars of the Flatbush-bound train had completely passed over the switch, workers at the control tower supposedly gave permission to the following train to pull into the Franklin Avenue Station. Since the second train was bound for New Lots Avenue, the towerman was said to have changed the switch to straightaway apparently misinformed by the defective relay that all was clear.

Ironically, the switch had only been installed three hours before it had failed. According to the TA a pin in the device was bent and that caused the relay to malfunction.

Unable to determine whether the defect was caused in manufacture or whether the relay was damaged during storage, investigators nonetheless sought to insure that a similar incident would not occur.

The solution was to tack a small, white plastic shock indicator onto every relay in stock. If the light turned red, it meant that there was something wrong with the relay and that a worker should not install it.

In retrospect, the dual switching accidents turned out to be the most remarkable of coincidences; million-to-one shots, if not more.

"The only similarity between those two accidents are the results," concluded Leroy B. Spivey the TA's vice-president for system's safety. "Both trains went over a switch and went on different tracks. But the causes were very, very different. When you start talking about lessons learned, you have to focus on the causes."

Another lesson learned was rudimentary.

No matter how safe you may think a high-tech subway system may be, there always is room for error.

Either human or mechanical.

(above) *The street collapsed on Broadway and 38th Street while the BRT subway was being constructed in September 1915. Note the sagging streetcar tracks.*

(right) *In 1921 a pulverizingly difficult way was found to extend the IRT Subway beyond its Nostrand and Flatbush terminal in Brooklyn.*

Motorman

Dispatcher

Station Master

TRADITIONAL UNIFORMS

Platform man

Special Officer

Announcer

OFF THE BEATEN TRACK

Art in the Subway

One January morning in 1957 a woman telephoned the Transit Authority public relations office at Jay Street in Brooklyn and told publicity man Joe Harrington that she had been admiring the beautiful mosaics in the subway systems.

"What do they mean?" she asked. "Why do you use them?"

Harrington, a former newspaperman who usually had an answer, was dumbfounded. "What mosaics?" he replied with a mixture of concern and curiosity. "In our subway?"

Once he was assured that the caller was hardly a prankster, Harrington said he would immediately get on the case. He contacted Walter Cozzolino, the TA's senior architect, who confirmed that mosaics existed on the subways. "But," said Harrington, "he didn't know what they represented and why they were installed."

Joe next approached Adolph Bergbom, assistant secretary of the TA, who pored through his files and unearthed further clues. Bergbom's search revealed that the first contract for the first subway (IRT) specified that each station was to be embellished with a landmark of the neighborhood. But he had no further details.

Harrington checked with George Horn, then an IND motorman who, in his spare time, made special studies of practically everything connected with the subway system. Horn had no definite information, nor did Irving Finkel, the TA's chief of designs. After contacting a host of IRT employees and passengers, most of whom were not even aware the mosaics existed, Harrington concluded that this simply must be recorded as "the Great Subway Art Mystery" and eventually turned his attention to more mundane publicity work.

No official records had been kept of the handsome bas-reliefs and mosaics that grace both IRT and BMT stations, but transit specialists combined on their own to decipher the picturesque symbols and offer several conclusions.

This much is known. When the city's first

subway, the IRT line from Broadway to upper Manhattan, was planned its financial backer, August Belmont, Jr., ordered $500,000 spent to decorate the new stations. The ceilings were separated into panels by wide ornamental moldings and rosettes. Norman brick was used on the wall bases, above which was glass tile or glazed tile followed by a faience or terra-cotta cornice. Ceramic mosaic was used for the decorative panels, friezes, pilasters, and name-tablets.

The decorative panels adorned at least sixteen stations. "They are," said an IRT brochure issued when the subway was opened, "instructive and decorative, as well as practical, and will have their effect on public taste just the same as anything else that tends to uplift and refine." According to subway historian and map expert John Tauranac in *Historic Preservation* magazine (1973), some outstanding examples of subway art: include:

1. Canal Street, IRT Seventh Avenue line: Mosaic, Spire of St. John's Chapel. Renowned for its 215-foot spire, St. John's Chapel was opened in 1807 as part of Trinity Parish and located on Varick Street near what was to be the Canal Street subway station. During the first half of the nineteenth century, St. John's boasted a large parish. But in 1865 Commodore Cornelius Vanderbilt, president of the New York Central Railroad, bought land in the area. He erected a freight depot in 1867 and the neighborhood spun into rapid decline. In time St. John's lost its congregation and was razed in 1918 while IRT trains sped underneath.

2. Fulton Street, IRT Lexington Avenue line: Bas-relief, Robert Fulton's 150-foot Steamship Clermont. Although a Connecticut Yankee named John Fitch actually invented the steamship twenty years before Fulton built the Clermont, Fitch encountered money problems that sank his project. In contrast, Fulton persuaded Robert Livingstone to give an advance for the Clermont and, in return, named the steamship after the Livingstone estate on the Hudson River.

3. Grand Central Station, IRT Lexington Avenue line: Mosaic, Bell stacked Locomotive, New York Central Railroad. When the IRT Lexington Avenue line was extended northward in 1918 the train mosaic was installed in the then new station.

4. Columbus Circle, IRT Broadway West Side line: Mosaic, Christopher Columbus's caravel Santa Maria. The great Italian navigator's flagship was featured in the IRT's original promotional brochure in 1904 after the mosaic was completed at the 59th Street Columbus Circle station.

5. 116th Street, IRT Broadway West Side line: Mosaic, Seal of Columbia University. The Columbia University emblem features a woman, symbolizing Columbia, sitting on a throne with three children at her feet, symbolizing her students. The Hebrew word for Jehovah is above her head and within the circle of the seal is Columbia's Latin motto which, translated, reads: "In Thy light shall we see light."

6. Borough Hall, Brooklyn, IRT Seventh Avenue-Broadway line: Mosaic, The Hall of Records. In this handsome work a spire of what once was Brooklyn's City Hall pierces the clouds. The building was completed in 1848 and was the site of ceremonies marking Brooklyn's transfer from an independent community to one of the five New York City boroughs.

7. Chambers Street, IRT Seventh Avenue-Broadway line: Mosaic, King's College (Columbia University) 1760-1857. The institution then was located between Murray and Barclay streets and stretched from Church to Chapel streets. The mosaic depicts the academic garb introduced to the colonies by Myles Cooper, King's second president. Chambers Street, after which the station is named, itself was named for John Chambers, the first lawyer admitted to the bar in the province of New York.

8. Brooklyn Bridge, BMT Chambers Street: Bas-relief, Brooklyn Bridge. The subway version of the bridge must have caused designer John Roebling to turn over in his

grave. The bas-relief shows cables from the bridge running vertically to the roadway. Actually, the Brooklyn Bridge cables emanate fanlike from the towers to the roadway, not vertically as in the subway picture.

9. Astor Place, IRT Lexington Avenue line: Bas-relief of a Beaver. John Jacob Astor, who made his fortune out of furs, mostly beaver, was once the richest man in America. Born Jacob Ashdour, Astor started life in America as a baker's boy. He later sold pianofortes and soon entered the fur business. In time he was to be called "Landlord of New York."

10. Clark Street, Brooklyn, IRT Broadway-Seventh Avenue line: Mosaic, Brooklyn Heights Waterfront, circa 1900. Bustling now as it was then, the Brooklyn wharves were just a stone's throw from the Clark Street station. The especially colorful mosaic depicts two steamships, a church spire, several trees, and what appears to be the outline of the massive St. George Hotel.

11. Canal Street, BMT Broadway line: Mosaic, Aaron Burr's Old Homestead (no longer visible). The mosaic reveals a little waterway flowing beneath a bridge adjacent to Burr's house. The waterway is the canal after which Canal Street was named.

12. South Ferry, IRT Broadway-Seventh Avenue line: Bas-relief of a sloop. In pre-steamship times, the vessels were dubbed Hudson River sloops and were the workhorses of the New York City port, carrying both freight and passengers. The sloops were about seventy feet long with a large mainsail well forward, a small jib and sometimes a topsail. They were fast and seaworthy and one captained by Stewart Dean of Albany sailed all the way to Canton, China, in 1785.

13. Court Street, Brooklyn, IRT Lexington Avenue line: Mosaic, Kings County Courthouse. Built in 1865, the Brooklyn courthouse was directly across the street from Borough Hall. It was the scene of a famous trial pitting Theodore Tilton, editor of the *New York Independent*, against Dr. Henry Ward Beecher, the abolitionist brother of Harriet Beecher Stowe and pastor of Plymouth Church on Orange Street. The courthouse was vacated in 1958 and razed three years later.

14. Whitehall Street, BMT Broadway local: Mosaic, Peter Stuyvesant's House, White Hall. In colonial Dutch times, the area around what is now Whitehall Street was called Schreijer's Hook. Stuyvesant built his house at the beginning of a street called Het Marckvelt. Originally, the residence was known as the Great House. However, the building was whitewashed and became known as the White Hall. Boasting an unobstructed view of the harbor, the house stood until 1776, when it burned down along with a quarter of the city in a mighty fire.

15. Broadway-137th Street, IRT Broadway-Seventh Avenue line: Mosaic, Seal of City College of New York. The first site of City College was a building at Fourth Avenue and 23rd Street. At the turn of the twentieth century CCNY moved to 137th Street and Convent Avenue. The seal is a variation on the Janus theme: three female heads facing different directions, with the Latin inscription Respice, Adspice, Prospice (Past, Present, Future). It has been said that some of the rock excavated in construction of the Broadway subway was transferred to the CCNY site and used for buildings on the north campus.

16. City Hall, IRT Lexington Avenue line: Mosaic, City Hall (station not visible to the public because original station is no longer used but plans are afoot to re-open it.) Fully utilized to this day, New York's City Hall was opened in 1812. At the time the city had a competition for the design of its new municipal building, offering $350 to the winners. The team of John McComb, Jr., and Joseph Mangin won the award. McComb, Jr., a Scot, and Mangin, a Frenchman, designed the structure, which went up on the site of the old almshouse. It was covered with white marble on the south, west, and east sides, with cheaper sandstone used on the north side. At that time no one expected the city to expand northward enough for people to have occasion to see the north side of the building.

A restoration job in 1956 included a covering of Alabama gray-veined limestone and Missouri red granite on all sides.

The use of mosaics was abandoned when the third and last major subway, the Independent system (IND), was constructed in the thirties. "Instead," said Irving Finkel, "on the IND they worked out a system of using colored tiles to acquaint passengers who couldn't read with their whereabouts. The system is fully keyed." However, hardly anyone on the Transit Authority staff has been able to decipher the key! Senior architect Walter Cozzolino simply called the idea "a noble experiment." Finkel wouldn't even go that far. He admitted that he didn't know the color of the tile at his home station. "But," he added, "I'm sure I'd sense something wrong if I got off at a station with different tile!"

Some original stations, such as 50th Street on the Broadway (Number One) Local, have enjoyed major renovations. The 50th Street Station features an <u>Alice</u> <u>In</u> <u>Wonderland</u> motif. And if it remains graffiti-free it will truly be a wonderland!

Smelly Kelly, Kass the Con Man, and Other Subway Characters

While the subway alternately is a menace, an annoyance and a general pain in the ears to many riders, it nevertheless has remained a love object to a small but ardent segment of the population. To them, the ultimate joy is the simple act of standing at the front window of an IRT Seventh Avenue express as it careens along the rails at 40 mph (it seems like 140 mph) through the tunnel between 14th Street and Chambers Street stations. The distillation of magnified speed, doubled decibels, and a sensation of the train about to jump track is not unlike the thrill of riding a Coney Island roller coaster.

Most subway buffs are paying customers, who have to ante up their tokens before

Tile and mosaic decorations from the first subway line get a washdown as part of routine maintenance.

savoring the many nuances of tunnel and track. But there always have been a select few who have had the pleasure of being paid while enjoying their transit hobby. These, of course, are the assorted employees of the subway system.

There are absolutely no bounds to their ardor, no limits to their pursuit of the ultimate train ride. Nobody carried this passion further than Harold Wright, a public relations official in the Transit Authority's Brooklyn offices during the early sixties. The extremely bald and often whimsical Wright had a lifelong passion to take the world's longest subway ride.

"Childe" Harold's dream was realized when the TA bought a fleet of new subway cars from the St. Louis Car Company in St. Louis, Missouri. "This," said Wright, "is the chance I've waited for."

Wright had some vacation time coming to him so he bought a one-way plane ticket to St. Louis. Then, using his TA credentials, Wright arranged to shepherd the train over the 961 miles from St. Louis to New York City. "I knew," Wright boasted, "that nobody had ever ridden a subway car 961 consecutive miles and I knew that I was well-equipped to do so."

His "equipment" included an overwhelming desire to have his name inscribed in the *Guinness Book of Records*, as well as several cardboard boxes filled with egg salad sandwiches and Thermos bottles of coffee, milk, and tea. The trip took three days.

"It wasn't exactly what you'd call a Pullman car," said Wright. "I had to sleep on the hard, plastic, longitudinal benches that pass for seats in a subway car."

The subway car was part of a fleet that was pulled by a standard diesel freight engine over the Pennsylvania Railroad tracks to New York. "On the whole," Wright concluded, "it was a rather bumpy ride but, then again, comfort was not my object."

Wright received the ultimate accolade upon his return when the *New York Journal-American* carried a six-column banner headline: RAILROADS TO A RECORD.

No less passionate than Wright was one George Horn, who began his professional career in 1947 as a trolley car motorman in Brooklyn. Horn was twenty-nine-years-old at the time but he had already put in more than twenty years of unofficial rapid transit study. When George was only seven he knew the number of every trolley on the Gates Avenue line in Brooklyn. He could tell by the *clank*, as it passed his door, which trolley it was.

This was quite natural for Horn. His grandfather had been a motorman on the Third Avenue Line and died in a powerhouse accident. His grandmother was a ticket agent for the Brooklyn Rapid Transit until she died, and his mother was in the transfer department. She couldn't look after George, but Aunt Lucy could. At the time, Aunt Lucy was a ticket agent on the Fifth Avenue and Fulton Street lines.

When little George got tired, he crept underneath the money board in the change booth and was rocked to sleep by the passing cars. Even then it was quite obvious to family and friends that George loved the enchanting world of banging wheels, trolley bells, hissing subway brakes, and percussive switches.

Horn became both a transit employee and a record-seeker. He paid the last fare on the old Sixth Avenue El. He piloted the last of the Vanderbilt Avenue trolley cars over Brooklyn Bridge and presided at the controls of the last Smith Street (Brooklyn) trolley car, the last 86th Street car, and the last Bay Ridge Avenue car. George paid the first nickel to ride the IND train that opened the Jamaica line. He also was a firster at the openings of the 23rd Street-Ely Avenue subway station, the Sixth Avenue Line at 34th Street, and the Euclid Avenue station of the Fulton Street Line.

George waited forty hours to be the first to drive through the Brooklyn-Battery Tunnel, but he dismisses the feat as *ersatz* record-breaking. "You've got to have rails under you to get the real feel of the thing," he claimed.

In 1951 Horn switched from trolley motorman to rapid transit as a motorman on the BMT and later the IND. "The TA people only let him work an eight-hour shift," said Joe Harrington, "but they didn't mind if he poked around an additional seven hours. He had a movie camera by then and recorded the operations of every elevated line and thirty-five streetcar lines. Then, he moved on to the subways."

George's heart really wasn't in his work once the New York City TA decided to eliminate all trolley car operations. After he retired as a yardmaster in 1970, he grabbed the first jet to San Francisco where he took a job as a motorman on the Market Street trolley! "George," said his pal Don Harold of the New York TA, "simply returned to his transit roots."

Equally passionate about trolleys and trains was Gilbert Reiter, a smallish Brooklynite who once had dreams of being a frozen-custard king and wound up becoming one of the most distinguished motormen in the TA. After graduating from high school, Reiter began selling frozen desserts at Coney Island. He became manager, then owner, of a stand that proved so popular that Reiter established a second frozen-custard place at Rockaway. Having acquired the beginning of a chain, Reiter saw his hopes dashed by the Depression. Too few people were buying the frosty fluff so he got a job in 1941 as a trolley operator. He enjoyed streetcars but not as much as subways. Finally, four years later he graduated to the BMT underground, piloting the Brighton local between Coney Island and Manhattan.

About this time Reiter was also developing into an avid artist. "I would get terribly absorbed in my work," said Reiter. "Once I spent three months in an art class that had a nude in front of the room. Not once did I look at the nude. I kept concentrating on a painting of a subway scene that I had in mind."

That's where Reiter's subway passion temporarily rolled out of control. He was obsessed with doing a painting of the inside of a tunnel as seen from his motorman's cab. Gil was particularly enthusiastic about the view on the Brighton local's run from Prospect Park Station in Brooklyn to Seventh Avenue.

There was only one problem: Reiter realized that it would be necessary to do a series of pencil sketches before beginning the actual painting. But he couldn't very well sketch with his left hand on the controller and his right hand on the brake handle. Eureka! Reiter had the solution. He would take the Brighton local out of Prospect Park Station, bring it to a point equidistant between Prospect Park and Seventh Avenue, stop his train for a minute, and knock off a quick sketch on his pad. And that is precisely what he did.

For about one week, riders on the Brighton local were perplexed by the unexpected screeching of the brakes inside the tunnel after leaving Prospect Park Station and the mysterious stop. Little did they know that motorman Reiter was busily drafting what would become a prize-winning painting.

The finished product, titled *Brighton Local*, was the Brighton tunnel seen in brave reds and yellows. Reiter sold the painting for $250, proving that the murky, forbidding subway tunnel could be attractive and profitable.

Another subway fan was Kassel "Kass" Pollock, one of the TA's legendary and lovable public relations officers. Among Pollock's jobs was trying to explain to newsmen and the public precisely why trains such as Gil Reiter's Brighton local were late. Built like a fire hydrant, Kass was a delightful character whose popularity was at its height in the late fifties.

The longer Pollock worked for the TA, the fonder he became of its rolling stock and its employees. And the fonder he became, the less able he was to recognize its blemishes. Pollock's loyalty eventually reached absurd proportions. He began denying that the subway system suffered, (a) derailments, (b) fires, and (c) crashes.

"Kass," said former colleague Joe Spaulding, "had his own particular vocabulary. Instead of admitting that there was a derailment, he could call it 'a misaligned wheel.' When there was a fire, he wouldn't call it a fire but rather 'rapid oxidation.' And small crashes were defined by Kass as 'hard couplings.' "

Pollock was at his PR peak the day a collision took place. When a reporter phoned Pollock's office and demanded details of the crash, Kass insisted, "They didn't crash. One train sort of *kissed* the other!"

Kass Pollock's devotion to duty was matched only by Irish-born James Patrick "Smelly" Kelly, who, in his sniffing heyday during the forties and fifties, was officially known as the superintendent of subway structures. Actually, Kelly's job was to patrol the 300 miles of IND-line tracks, sniffing for strange odors (potential gas leaks), eyeing leaky tunnels (he also was known as "Leaky" Kelly), and testing rock or soil on which the tracks rested.

On a good day, Kelly would find at least one malevolent odor and a couple of leaks, and nobody was prouder of his ability to detect them than James Patrick himself. "Quick ears, good nose, better feet— those are the requirements of my job." Kelly patrolled the TA's tracks for more than thirty years and established several subway records. His biggest accomplishment, in more ways than one, occurred at the IND's 42nd Street Station at Sixth Avenue. Kelly was summoned there because of bizarre reports that an elephantine odor was permeating the entire length of the underground station.

"I had heard elephant jokes in my time," said Kelly, "but this story was on the level."

Well, not quite on the level. Several feet under ground level Kelly discovered that there was, in fact, a distinctly zoological aroma covering both the express and local tracks. "In a word," said Kelly, "it smelled like elephants. But how could elephants get into the subway?"

With Sherlock Holmesian fervor, Kelly launched his investigations. He walked back and forth through the tunnel several times. Next he covered the same footage above ground, carefully eyeing the surface structures. Then he recalled a bit of history— and solved the mystery.

"I remembered that the old Hippodrome arena was at the corner of 43rd Street and Sixth Avenue. They had circuses there and used to bury the elephant dung somewhere in the sub-basement garbage bins. That was fine until one day years later a water main busted and we had a whole new ball game."

When the water main burst it soaked the long-buried elephant dung and the fumes permeated the IND station. Smelly was right!

Kelly was only one of several TA employees who have patrolled the tracks in search of sagging pavement, stained walls, and dangerous odors, but none ever has approached his record for accuracy and reliability. "In thirty years in the railroad business," said TA chairman Charles Patterson, "I have never encountered a man with the peculiar talents of Mr. Kelly."

Describing his job, Smelly once put it this way: "Mostly you walk. You make regular inspection trips beneath gasoline storage tanks of service stations, beneath raw chemical factories, beneath storage areas for manufactured gas. You check areas known to form pockets of sewer gas and areas beneath new construction jobs where a steam shovel might scrape gas mains.

"Sometimes a guy calls in and says he smelled something on a certain train which made him dizzy. You intercept the train and find some guy sitting in the corner with a ten-gallon jug of gasoline. You get characters like that up into the street fast. You'd be surprised how many people think nothing of riding the subways with explosive liquids."

In his book *The World beneath the City*, Robert Daley wrote, "If Smelly Kelly did not exist he would have to be invented....Only a Smelly Kelly, following his nose along the track, can find, identify and obviate fumes before they attain lethal concentrations."

171

Before his retirement Kelly broke in more than sixty qualified sniffers, saved at least two workers' lives in the tunnels, caught a two and-a-half-foot eel, a ten-inch trout, forty killifish ("always dead when caught"), and a pack of rats.

Less well known than Smelly but no less ardent was another TA employee, Frank Turdik, who worked for the IRT Division, supplying motor cars for maintenance trains. Turdik had a special affection for the IRT's passenger cars known in the transit trade as the "Low Vs," (for low voltage). By the mid-sixties the TA had decided that the ancient Low Vs were ready for the scrapheap. Turdik strongly objected and was determined to save as many of the Low Vs as possible. The question was how to hide a full-sized subway car, let alone a dozen of them coupled together.

Turdik had the answer. A veteran of the system, he knew every mile of track and remembered that there were unused storage tracks in the tunnel under the Esplanade on the IRT Dyre Avenue Line in a distant area of the Bronx. "What made these tracks even more useful," said Don Harold of the TA public relations department, "was the fact that they were in a tunnel, with a wall separating the storage tracks from the platform."

Turdik maneuvered several Low-V cars up to the Pelham Parkway tunnel where they were safe for the moment. But there was one catch. The missing cars remained on the TA's master inventory list.

A TA supervisor in charge of chasing down potential scrap noticed the cars on the inventory one day and wondered why they hadn't been scrapped. "You can't scrap what you can't find," he was told.

At this point the supervisor decided to check out every single track on the system. A week later he had not found the missing rolling stock. Then it dawned on him that he had forgotten to search out one piece of track on the IRT division.

"I'm off to the Dyre Avenue Line tunnel," he told an aide.

That was a crucial mistake. The aide was a close friend and ally of Turdik in the surreptitious "Save the Low Vs" campaign. The minute the supervisor left his office at Jay Street in Brooklyn, the aide phoned Turdik. "You'd better move the Low Vs," he warned, "because You Know Who is on the way to the Dyre Avenue tunnel."

Turdik sped to the rescue of his hidden train and deftly arranged to move the Low Vs to the IRT's 180th Street storage yard where they were placed, unnoticed, in a remote location.

In the meantime, the supervisor arrived at the Dyre Avenue line tunnel only to find it empty. He then returned to Brooklyn thoroughly perplexed about the disappearance of the Low Vs. Turdik persevered with his juggling act. Then one day in the mid-sixties the Transit Authority sent out a memorandum to employees to find a few cars that would be useful as a "Museum Train."

To the amazement of TA officials, Turdik moved a five-car train comprised of "Museum" Low-V cars to the 207th Street yard. "That wasn't all," Don Harold recalled. "Turdik managed to save all his Low Vs in one way or another. He realized that the TA didn't have much money for the repair of work cars so he made sure that whenever an old work car broke down, one of his beloved, functioning Low Vs would turn up as its replacement."

One of the most unusual railroaders was the Reverend Francis J. Cosgrove, probably the only priest who also was a qualified motorman.

Cosgrove, Jesuit associate pastor of St. Ignatius Loyola Church, 84th Street and Park Avenue, was also chaplain for many Catholic groups in the Transit Authority. He became interested in the subways in the late 1940s when he lived in the Bronx and used the old Third Avenue El to commute to Fordham University.

"A classmate's father was in charge of training motormen on the el," explained Cosgrove, "and one day he invited me down for the grand tour."

One thing led to another and soon Cosgrove was getting private instruction and practicing on empty trains. "It was the greatest training," he said. "The old el cars had primitive air brakes, nothing like today's equipment. It was like learning to drive on a car with manual shift. We had to use extreme caution. Except in certain areas, like around curves, there were no signals. You just had to eyeball the train in front of you."

Later, transit employees on their own time ran Cosgrove through the official motorman's course. He passed with flying colors. Several times a year he sharpened his skills by operating a work train or an empty train on its way to the yards.

He remembered an incident at the 86th Street Station near his church.

Cosgrove was there to pick up a work train and take it to the yard. He was not wearing his clerical clothing and the token-seller, who knew him, asked him to watch the booth for a while.

"I was in there pushing tokens and a fellow came down who worked in a store in the neighborhood. He stared at me without saying anything but I could see a big question mark on his face."

A few minutes later Cosgrove took out his train and operated it to the 125th Street Station, where he had to lean out a window to press a button alerting a dispatcher to his destination. "The same fellow was waiting on the platform there. Instead of a question mark this time I saw a giant exclamation point. It was like the legend in the Koran of Mohammed looking in all directions and seeing the face of the angel Gabriel. If he had a guilty conscience about anything he probably thought he was being haunted by this face of a priest."

Another time, Father Cosgrove piloted a work train into a station in the early morning hours, brought the cars to a stop, and called out to a passenger on the platform: "Come aboard, rabbi, this is The Clergy Special!" With the rabbi aboard, the train pulled out, leaving an astonished group of passengers on the platform.

Cosgrove, a native New Yorkers spent most of his life in the city. Once, however, he was assigned to a mission in the Caroline Islands in the South Pacific.

"Some friends of mine sent me a few subway kerosene marker lanterns. At night, when I was out on the water, I'd have them hung on the fish trap off shore. The IRT signal took me straight to my house."

For all we know, the old IRT lights are still guiding the islanders to port. "During typhoons, when every other lamp blew out, they always stayed lit," the priest recalled.

Cosgrove considered the entire subway system his parish and was well liked up and down the line. "He was the kind of friend who was always there when you needed him and religion didn't matter," said one long time TA employee.

Cosgrove held special masses in the TA building during a strike, when employees were on twenty-four-hour duty and could not go to church. He often went to the side of transit policemen shot while on duty. But it was the lighter moments he liked to recall. Like the time he was with a crew taking a string of derelict cars to the yard for scrapping and the yardmaster had not been told of their arrival.

"He saw this thing coming down the track—a train of old wrecks pulled by a diesel—and he knew one thing: he didn't want it cluttering up his yard. He started swearing a blue streak. One of the men told him there was a priest on board, but he didn't believe it and swore even louder."

When cars are transferred from one place to another, the process requires a pink form. "The crew prevailed on me to put on my clerical clothing and take the pink slip to the yardmaster," Cosgrove said.

Upon seeing Father Cosgrove, the yardmaster politely turned his blue streak to cautious amber and, finally, a healthy full-speed-ahead green. Father Cosgrove continued on his merry way, enjoying, like all subway buffs, his favorite set of electric trains, the New York City subway system.

Among the most interesting characters on the subway system in the 1970s were the Special Inspectors, otherwise known as "Beakeys." Their function was to observe and report the on-site behaviors of transit employees to insure compliance with departmental rules and regulations. It should be noted here that the overwhelming majority of transit employees are hard-working and diligent but at the time the TA believed that Beakeys were necessary.

Oh, yes, why are they called Beakeys? According to one transit source, the term is rooted in the early days of the 20th Century when the IRT was still an infant subway. August Belmont's line employed one H.F. Beakey as its Chief of Secret Service. Which really says it all.

Modern Beakeys served the Transit Authority through the early 1980s and in the course of their work encountered some curious episodes. The following was related by John Landers, himself a former Beakey. Working an 11 PM-7 AM shift, he was teamed with a retired transit policeman who vowed to teach him the business of Beakeying.

They eventually reached the Grant Avenue Station on the A Line at about 2:30 AM. Between Grant and its previous underground stop, Euclid Avenue, there were five layup tracks used for train storage.

The two Beakeys approached the stored cars for an inspection. They climbed one which had its lights out. "My partner instructed me to take out my identification, follow his lead and go to the head of the car," Landers recalled. "He slid open the door and announced, 'Gentlemen, we are Special Inspection. Would everyone please rise and have his employees' pass ready for inspection.'

"The novice Beakey went to the front of the car to check IDs. As he moved into position one employee with a battery-operated alarm clock set next to his head was in a deep sleep. "I attempted to wake the man by shaking his shoulder," said Landers. "Slowly he came to and rubbed his eyes."

Suddenly, the malingerer realized he was confronted by Beakeys. He bolted for the door, hopped to the tracks and dashed through the darkened tunnel to Euclid Avenue Station as the Beakey shouted at him to return.

"To my astonishment," Landers continued, "he came to a dead stop about 200 feet into the tunnel and calmly returned. I was amazed that he listened but upon his return the reason became obvious.

"He was barefoot. His feet were covered with dirt. In his haste to get away he had left his workboots and socks on the train next to where he had been sleeping!"

The Biggest Bust and Bargain of All

It would cost more than a billion dollars to build just one mile of subway in contemporary New York. But in 1940 New York City paid only $1,783,577 for a four-and-a-quarter-mile stretch of existing four track right-of-way. Even today it ranks as one of the most magnificent rapid transit runs in the world, boasting station buildings constructed of concrete in renaissance, mission, and classic style.

To thousands of New Yorkers it is known as the Dyre Avenue (Bronx) line, but old-timers still refer to the IRT route as "the old Westchester run" because in its youth the tracks belonged to the New York, Westchester & Boston Railway Company, an offshoot of the New York, New Haven & Hartford. Needless to say, the N.Y., W. & B. never was intended to be part of the city's subway system.

Soon after the beginning of the twentieth century, directors of the successful New York, New Haven & Hartford Railroad were on the lookout for more and better ways of turning a profit. New York City comprised five boroughs, each of which had growing numbers of potential customers for their railway. The New Haven's directors were most interested in the Bronx, because of its proximity to the New Haven line as well as prospects for growth in that borough.

"They were looking for a plushier trade than the nickel business of the subway," said one observer of the rail scene. And they set about building one of America's finest electric railways.

When it was opened in May 1912, the N.Y., W.&B. was the best railway of its kind in America. Trains sped on a four-track right-of way, along comfortable, deeply-ballasted roadbeds over rails that gave the effect of a smooth, endless carpet. The railroad incorporated the most modern devices at a time when tremendous strides were being made in train technology. The directors refused to be overly thrifty and opted for a four-track line when a two-track right-of-way would have been adequate. They planned on a sensible long-range basis rather than for short-term benefits. And, finally, their area of operations encompassed one of the wealthiest and fastest-growing urban-suburban corridors in North America.

Few projects that seemed so certain of success have failed as egregiously as the Westchester and the roots of the problem go back to just past the middle of the nineteenth century. The railway boom was approaching its peak then and investors began casting their eyes on the lucrative metropolitan New York market in hopes of building additional steel links between Manhattan and the outside world.

Among the more attractive possibilities were the Southern Westchester and the New York, Housatonic & Northern railroad companies. The Southern Westchester, when plans were fully realized, would operate from the edge of Manhattan—and the juncture of the Harlem and East Rivers—to White Plains in Westchester. At that point it would meet the New York, Housatonic & Northern. Joined together, the two railroads would then allow New Yorkers to ride all the way to Danbury, Connecticut, and, linking with other lines along the way, eventually to Boston.

The two companies merged in 1872 and construction of a modest one-track right-of-way was launched in Westchester County. Two years later the merged railroads folded. However, the disaster of the Southern Westchester and the New York, Housatonic & Northern merely inspired others to work on developing a new line from Manhattan to Westchester.

In the mid-1870s another group incorporated the New York, Westchester & Boston Railroad. Their plan was to run a line from the Harlem River through the Bronx, which then still was a part of Westchester County, with assorted branch lines to Long Island Sound and Elmsford.

"Together with the lines then operating— the New York Central & Hudson River, the New York & Harlem, and the New York, New Haven & Hartford—the New York, Westchester & Boston would form part of a rail network which virtually would guarantee the development of Westchester County as a major suburban residential area," wrote railway historian Roger Arcara in a book about the line.

But again the timing was wrong. Those who hoped to capitalize on the growth of New York City, which had consolidated in 1898 into five boroughs, had to wait for better financial times after the turn of the twentieth century.

Even then another venture, the New York & Port Chester Railroad Company, failed to reach its goal. The roadbed was actually graded in 1906 and a bridge constructed over a creek dividing the towns of Harrison and

Mamaroneck in Westchester. The bridge still stands, and the line itself didn't really die but, rather, was incorporated into the suddenly rejuvenated New York, Westchester & Boston which re-emerged in 1906, after quietly acquiring property for years before.

This time the N.Y.,W.&B. was being guided by Charles S. Mellen, president of the New York, New Haven & Hartford Railroad. Mellen's cronies, among the richest men in the country at the time, included J. P. Morgan and William Rockefeller, brother of John D. Rockefeller, Sr. In fact Morgan and Rockefeller helped put the Westchester back on the tracks in 1906 when they headed a committee that bought controlling interest in the New York, Westchester & Boston stock for $11 million.

Following a bit of litigation in which the Westchester swallowed up the New York & Port Chester, Mellen and pals were ready to really roll—with elaborate prime plans, alternates and lots of money with which to implement them. They could have utilized the facilities of the Grand Central Terminal then under construction at 42nd Street and Park Avenue in Manhattan as their terminus or they could develop a new one. Unwisely, although it didn't appear so at the time, they decided to build a new one.

Few could have challenged the logic in 1909. Even then the Grand Central Terminal was overtaxed with rail traffic. Commuters from other lines who used the Manhattan station were screaming over the high cost of riding the railroads into the city when five-cent subway rides were available in many parts of the city.

Mellen and his colleagues were aware of these complaints and believed that they had the answer. Instead of running the New York, Westchester & Boston Railway all the way to Grand Central, they would terminate the line in the Bronx. Their rationale was that they could lure commuters by lower prices, since riders would be able to connect with the city's five-cent subways in the Bronx and ride the rest of the way to midtown Manhattan on the

new underground. Knowing that much of the line would operate in what then was virtually uninhabited land, they nevertheless agreed to build a high-capacity railroad with four tracks, hoping that business and development would soon come.

Although the line was being built during the golden age of steam, Mellen decided to make the Westchester the only standard railroad in the area designed exclusively for electric power. Speed, efficiency, and beauty were the passwords. The Westchester scored on two out of three. It never really got a chance to prove how efficient it was.

"Though it was conceded that no really heavy volume of traffic was expected at first," wrote Roger Arcara, "the New Haven Railroad management at that time commanded sufficient resources to be able to sustain such an expensive undertaking while awaiting development of the much greater patronage the foreseeable future might bring."

Now came the key question for Mellen: "Where do we start and where do we terminate?" Since Grand Central Station had already been ruled out, the planners decided on the Bronx. They wanted the Westchester's terminus to link directly with the Interborough Rapid Transit (IRT) for the cheap connection to the city's subway. They searched for a prime location and finally found one at East 132nd Street and Willis Avenue.

The site was chosen for several reasons, not merely for the link with the IRT. It was deep in the South Bronx adjacent to the New Haven's Harlem River freight yards and passenger station. This enabled the Westchester to share the trackage of the New Haven's Harlem River Branch until West Farms junction, where the Westchester turned off to its own route.

At the Willis Avenue-East 132nd Street terminal, the Westchester connected directly to the IRT's shuttle elevated trains that ran to 129th Street, Manhattan (the Third Avenue El). Given a choice between Grand Central and a higher fare or the Bronx terminal and a lower fare, passengers by the thousands were expected to switch to the Westchester.

From Willis Avenue-East 132nd Street, the Westchester snaked up the Bronx. The second stop would be Port Morris (East 135th Street), followed by Casanova (Leggett Avenue), Hunt's Point (Hunt's Point Avenue), Westchester Avenue, 180th Street, Morris Park, Pelham Parkway, Gun Hill Road, Baychester Avenue, and Dyre Avenue. From there the route drifted over the city line north into Westchester County.

So ambitious was the project that the Westchester didn't need a press agent; its blueprints spoke volumes. For example, newsmen did not have to be coaxed into believing that the line would load and unload a great volume of passengers. All they had to do was glance at plans for the huge waiting rooms and the fact that freight facilities were virtually ignored. As for the speed potential of the line, Mellen merely had to take an inquisitive journalist for a tour of the construction sites to show that speed was guaranteed because designers had eliminated all sharp curves, steep grades, and grade crossings. They had learned their lessons well from the past.

Not to be overlooked was the cosmetic touch. Stations would get the grand architectural treatment. They would be, as one observer put it, "monuments, constructed of concrete in renaissance, mission or classic style." Or, as Roger Arcara put it, "The Westchester would have mansions where other lines were satisfied with sheds."

Structures built within the New York City limits—and now part of the A Division—were of the modified Mission type. Wherever possible, trees, shrubs, and hedges were planted around the stations. Terrazzo facing was used in all station interiors, including the ticket booths. The respected *Electric Railway Journal* commented in June 1912:

"The passenger stations and signal towers may be said to constitute the most attractive group of way structures possessed by any electric or steam railroad in the United States. The result was made possible by the progressive attitude of the company, which was ambitious to erect buildings which would add to rather than detract from the expected high-class suburban development of this territory . . . Many of the stations have cafes, haberdasheries and other stores in addition to the usual magazine and candy stands. Some stations have a room for baggage handling. At certain places the station building is being utilized as a natural headquarters for the local real estate development."

Since Mellen's New Haven Railroad had just electrified its own line with 11,000-volt, 25-cycle current, it immediately had a surplus of power and sold it to the Westchester. All that was needed now was to make the line operational. The first drills were put in motion in 1909, and construction proceeded rapidly. Instead of circling obstacles such as boulders and hills, engineers on the Westchester chose to bore right through them. Every item, from signal towers to viaducts, seemed to be built a little stronger, a bit more beautiful and somewhat bigger than the best seen until then.

On May 29, 1912 the elephantine project made its official debut. It ran from East 180th Street and Morris Park Avenue, near West Farms Square in the Bronx, to North Avenue, New Rochelle, Westchester. Much station and track work still remained to be done but nobody noticed that. What caught the eye were the majestic stations, the broad, smooth right-of-way and the splendidly speedy trains. The Boston & Westchester had purchased thirty steel cars, seventy feet long, which were equipped to draw current through the overhead pantographs.

The big green rolling stock, each of which could seat seventy-eight passengers, was equipped with powerful Westinghouse motors that could move the trains at speeds of sixty mph. Everything else about the cars' appointments was first-rate, from the electric lamps to white enameled ceilings, shaded windows, and roomy seats. From every aspect, the Westchester's cars were a 1912 commuter's dream-come true.

Why, then, did the Westchester dream turn out to be the New Haven's nightmare?

One mistake was enough to convert the most perfect railroad of its day into a money-sapping failure. "Passengers," wrote rail analyst Bernard Linder, "given a choice between Grand Central and a higher fare, or the Bronx terminal and a lower fare, chose the former. They hollered louder when fares went up, but that's all—they paid rather than change in the Bronx. The building boom came to Westchester all right; apartment buildings sprouted on pastures and in woods, but not many of them elected to locate along the swift, low-priced line which made a change in the Bronx necessary."

At first, the officials who converged daily at the company's magnificent office building (now used by the New York City Transit Authority for field offices and police district offices) adjacent to the huge East 180th Street station were sanguine about the receipts. In its first full year of operation (1913) the Westchester carried 2,874,484 passengers. By 1920 the figure had more than doubled, and in 1928 over 14 million paying customers rode the line. But while the numbers were impressive on paper they failed to reassure bankers, who had been led to believe 140 million rather than 14 million would be a reasonable passenger total for a year such as 1928. The bottom line, year in and year out, failed to produce what Westchester's supporters needed most—a profit. Rush-hour traffic was brisk but not substantial enough to offset the virtually nonexistent business at other times of the day.

In placing the Westchester's terminal in the Bronx, miles from mid-Manhattan, Mellen and his colleagues were operating on the Commodore Vanderbilt theory of city growth anticipation. In the middle of the nineteenth century when Cornelius Vanderbilt, boss of the New York & Harlem (later the New York Central) Railroad, considered a site for a new

Manhattan terminal for his line as well as the New York, New Haven & Hartford and the Hudson River Railroad, New York City's center was near the southern tip of Manhattan Island. At that time the area around 42nd Street (where Grand Central Terminal is located) was regarded by New Yorkers as far distant as the North Pole. Yet Commodore Vanderbilt insisted on building his main depot in the suburbs of 42nd Street on the theory that New York City inevitably must expand northward. "Some day in the not too-distant-future," Commodore Vanderbilt predicted, "Grand Central Station will be in the center of the city."

Vanderbilt's "folly" soon turned into Vanderbilt's gold mine. By the turn of the twentieth century it had become apparent that the commodore was correct in his assessment of the city's growth pattern. Mellen took that theory one step further. If Grand Central Terminal was the center of the business district in 1920 and expansion continued in the direction of Westchester, it was reasonable to assume that by 1930 the business and commercial district would extend to the South Bronx.

Mellen's theory was doomed by the city's first zoning law, written into the books in 1916 at a time when the Westchester was still hoping to have the Harlem River freight yards someday surrounded by tall office buildings. The new law limited Manhattan's commercial area to the precincts south of Central Park's southerly (59th Street) boundary. "Westchester's planners," wrote Roger Arcara, "could not reasonably be expected to foresee this development; to them it seemed, and rightly so at the time, that New York's business district was destined to go on expanding northward on Manhattan Island until, perhaps by the middle of the 20th Century, it would cover most of the Island, with its northern portion somewhere around 125th Street, right across the river from the New York, Westchester & Boston Railway."

Once the zoning law was approved, the

Westchester's directors realized that Mellen's plan was obsolete and new thinking was necessary. The natural solution was to extend the line from its Harlem River freight yard depot into Manhattan and south down to the midtown commercial district. All the Westchester needed to accomplish this was money. Therefore, the solution at once was no longer simple.

Ideally, the Manhattan extension could be built from the line's profits and thereby build still more profits. But no matter how the Westchester's accountants juggled the books, there simply was never a profit with which to work; therefore, no extension could or would be built. Thus the Westchester's depot remained in the Bronx, and the line continued to operate only by the grace of its parent, the New York, New Haven & Hartford.

Patience and money simultaneously ran out on the New Haven in 1935 when the line reorganized and began to liquidate its unprofitable holdings. New Haven officials claimed they spent $50 million on the Westchester in a futile effort to put it in the black. Hence the N.Y., W. & B. was the first to go.

In a last, desperate attempt to revive the line, the Westchester was put by court order under the trusteeship of Clinton L. Bardo, an efficient railroad man who had been general manager of the New Haven. Bardo had some sound ideas for saving the Westchester, but his reorganization plans required money. There was no cash available, and on April 15, 1937 the line was declared irrevocably insolvent. Less than four months later Bardo died. The railroad itself enjoyed its last *clickety-clack* at about midnight, December 31, 1937 when some fifty passengers, most of whom were railfans, rode the final run.

The big bust that was Mellen's idea turned out to be the biggest bargain in subway history, considering that the New Haven invested $50 million in the Westchester and New York City paid less than $2 million for a major portion of the line. However, the transfer of the N.Y., W. & B. to the Board of Transportation did not come easy. When the Westchester ceased to operate after nearly twenty-five years, the 26,000 passengers who had been riding the railroad each day protested vehemently.

"Bring back the Westchester!" the commuters pleaded but in vain. Several ideas for resuscitating the railroad failed to crystallize. Ironically, the plan that eventually was implemented originated with New York City legislators and was to sever Westchester County completely from use of the Westchester's tracks. In the late thirties residents of the Bronx demanded that the line's right-of-way be annexed by the New York City Board of Transportation and linked with the then burgeoning city subway system.

Unlike other moves to save the Westchester, the plan to buy it for New York City gained momentum. Still more impetus was provided in June 1940 when New York City bought the Brooklyn-Manhattan Transit Company (BMT) and the Interborough Rapid Transit Company (IRT).

Having united the BMT, IND, and IRT, New York City now owned the greatest rapid transit system of any municipality in the world. Mayor Fiorello LaGuardia and his constituents were appropriately proud of their subways and looked to further expansion. One such possibility was an extension of the IND Bronx Division past its 205th Street terminal farther eastward in the borough. This could be done for an estimated $2,500,000 and would probably have been done had it not been learned that the existing N.Y., W. & B. tracks within the Bronx from East 174th Street to the Mount Vernon (Westchester) border could be obtained for only $1,783,577. LaGuardia was persuaded that it would be more practical to buy the Westchester than plunge ahead with an extension of the IND.

The 205th Street extension was shelved and New York City instead took over the Bronx portion of the N.Y., W. & B., installed a third rail, and assigned twenty Third Avenue elevated cars to the run. To make the adjustment, several mechanical alterations had to be applied to the Westchester's right-of-way. Unused BMT signals were hooked up on the Westchester route; clearances were adjusted for the wooden, open-platform elevated cars and finally, the name of the line itself was changed to "The Dyre Avenue Line."

The new monicker was given because the city's latest rapid transit addition ran between East 180th Street and the Dyre Avenue Station, the last stop in the Bronx. The first IRT train rolled out of the terminal on May 15, 1941 and the shuttle remained in business with the antiquated rolling stock until 1954. Veterans of the Westchester had hoped that somehow the bankrupt line's passenger cars could be used but the equipage was not meant for city subway service. Some fifty of the cars were returned to the New Haven and rebuilt for local service in Boston. Most of the remaining forty-five were sold to the United States government for wartime use, as emergency transport for workers in war-related industries.

Meanwhile, the Dyre Avenue Line remained a curio to all but the few passengers who rode the shuttle during wartime and the immediate postwar years. "Even people who work for the city transit system are unfamiliar with it," was a comment in *Transit Magazine*, the journal of New York's subway workers. The Dyre Avenue shuttle was unique among all of the city's lines: it didn't always run. Every night it would close down at 1 AM and wake up again at 5:30 in the morning. What's more, its railway clerks worked only one shift, after which the conductors collected fares and made change right on the train in the finest *Toonerville* manner.

Slowly but surely, the Dyre Avenue Line did what its predecessor could never do: it got better and better; healthier by the year, so that by 1955 *Transit Magazine* observed: "The white elephant's skin is darkening already. And, barring the unforeseen, the Dyre Avenue Line will soon be more than paying its way." It

would, too, especially after track connections were made in 1957 with the IRT's White Plains Road line north of the East 180th Street station. Now trains from the IRT Seventh Avenue (Broadway) Line could run through, over the old Westchester route to Dyre Avenue.

In time the Transit Authority, successor to the old Board of Transportation, switched the Dyre Avenue line to the Lexington Avenue IRT tracks on Manhattan's East Side. Now designated the "No. 5 Lexington Avenue Express," it runs between Dyre Avenue in the Bronx and Flatbush Avenue in Brooklyn. "The orphan has grown up," a Transit Authority official boasted, "and all New York City subway riders can be proud."

Westchester commuters were less fortunate. Their pleas for restoration of the N.Y., W. & B. continued until 1939 when the first pieces of equipment were removed. With each month, another chunk of what was once America's finest railway was hacked away by the voracious scrap workers until all that remained were a few vestiges of the line, most of them on the IRT's Dyre Avenue run. The 180th Street Station, for one, stands handsomely, as it did in the early part of the century; likewise the enormous Morris Park Station, built in 1912, which appears more suited to a European branch line than the No. 5 Lexington Express.

To this day the Dyre Avenue Line in its own way remains the most attractive and charming run on the city's transit network, although it is not likely that you will see the occasional rabbit scuttling away at the approach of a train or the arboreal splendor that characterized the Westchester route when it wended its way through the last undeveloped area in the Bronx.

But as long as the Dyre Avenue Line remains in business it will stand as a monument to the biggest bust—and greatest revival—in the annals of municipal transit.

A two-car set of gate cars rounds the East 180th Street curve heading South on the opening day of subway service on the Dyre Avenue Line (May 15, 1941). The crews came from the IND Division and the conductors collected fares. The outside tracks were converted to third rail and soon the center tracks, complete with N.Y.W.&B. overhead catenary, would be removed.

The interior of a newly spruced up gate car on opening day of the Dyre Avenue Line.

The south face of the Gun Hill Rd. Station in 1947. By now the center tracks and catenary of the N.Y.W.&B. had been removed.

This Dyre Avenue Line train is crossing the widened and repaved Boston Post Road on a newly rebuilt trestle three days after the commencement of service.

The Freight Line, the Farm Line and the Line That Went to Sea

Only one branch of the New York City subway system has enjoyed the triple distinction of (a) being asked to carry a fully grown whale through its tunnels, (b) being the only railroad in the world where freight cars wore corsets, and (c) being the only New York rail line to turn a profit for more than fifty years. This remarkable line once was known affectionately to TA officials as the SoB. And for good reason, because the SoB was the South Brooklyn Railway Company (officially listed as SBK, however, to avoid confusion with the South Buffalo Railroad). It is the TA's very own freight railroad, whose total rolling stock consists of two diesel-electric locomotives.

Nearly eighty years old, the SoB operates over six and one-half miles of Brooklyn track—including a short stretch of tunnel which it shares with the BMT Fourth Avenue Subway. The SoB's run begins at portside along lower New York Bay. The waterfront yard at 39th Street and Second Avenue is adjacent to Bush Terminal, one of the large freight junctions in the country. From there the SoB heads west and then south, terminating at the TA's vast repair shop and yards in Coney Island.

The SoB's experience with the whale developed because of the line's proximity to the Coney Island amusement park. The whale had been killed in European waters, embalmed, and shipped to New York City for display at Coney Island. The SoB strapped the whale and its container atop a flatcar and directed the unique parcel toward the Fourth Avenue tunnel. It is an ancient tunnel built along extremely narrow lines—too narrow to accommodate the whale in its glass enclosure— and the SoB was unable to

complete the trip.

The whale episode is symptomatic of the SoB's congenital problem: insufficient hauling space. That's how the TA's freight cars came to wear corsets. Unlike subway cars, freight cars have a tendency to develop middle-age bulge. Sometimes the bulge reached such obese proportions that the freight cars simply could not negotiate the tunnel. Instead of throwing in the towel George F. Preiss, who was freight manager of the line, and his aides found a solution. Wire was wrapped around the pudgy cars and then the corset was tightened until the men of the SoB were sure that the freight car could negotiate the tunnel. "It cost us four or five hundred a year for wire," said Preiss.

In its time the SoB hauled some unusual pieces of freight. Once an Army plane crashed in Pennsylvania but the inquiry into the disaster was conducted at Floyd Bennett Field at the southern tip of Flatbush Avenue in Brooklyn. Since the airport was in the vicinity of the SoB's Coney Island terminal, the pieces of plane were shipped on the TA freight line.

Before Prohibition the SoB did a terrific business with breweries such as Trommer's and Piel's. The SoB also prospered during Prohibition, for then it hauled a huge tonnage of wine grapes for Brooklynites who made their own. Those were the days when the line also picked up mountains of ashes from factories, rubbish from all sorts of plants, and hauled these—for a fee—away from the premises. The ashes were carried to the Coney Island marshlands and dropped there, where they became valuable fill. Today thousands of homes in and around Coney Island rest securely upon those ashes and rubbish.

The SoB is credited with another freight first. In 1929 it instituted door-to-door delivery of carload freight lots by automobile trailer truck. "This," said former TA publicist Joe Harrington, "was some ten years before other railroads initiated such a service. The idea came because originally it operated freight trolleys, which, in the heyday of the trolley in Brooklyn, could snake through to almost any section of the city."

The flavor of a small railroad permeated the quarters of the SoB. "None of the flurry of a subway station existed in its offices," said Harrington. This was the case ever since the SoB emerged from its antecedent roads, including the Prospect Park and Coney Island Railroad, whose trackage ran along McDonald Avenue to Coney Island. "Thus the SoB was the only freight line in the world that used both former trolley tracks and subway tunnels," according to J. Porter Reilly, author of *Doughty, Dazzling Diesels.*

Although the road owned no freight cars, it hauled boxcars from all parts of the United States and Canada, making virtual doorstep delivery to industrial customers whose facilities abutted the right-of way. Normally freight was lightered or floated to Brooklyn on barges from Hoboken by the New York Dock Railroad Company, where SoB locomotives picked them up and brought them to their destination. Speed along SoB tracks was kept down to five miles per hour.

Sometimes the line's freight cars were pulled the "wrong way" against vehicular traffic along McDonald Avenue. Equally strange to see was the SoB's procedure of switching the locomotive from front to back en route from Bush Terminal to Coney Island. For the first half mile of surface track before it reached the subway tunnel, a diesel pulled the freight cars. Before entering the mile-long uphill tunnel, the diesel was detached, wrong-ended, and then pushed the boxcars over subway tracks.

"This was a safety measure," said onetime freight traffic manager Andrew DeLuca. "On the open right of-way, our engineer has visibility along his entire train; in the tunnel, he took precautions against a break-away rolling downhill behind him. With the diesel pushing, the possibility of any breakaway was averted."

The SoB's standard motive power for the first half-century was electric locomotives that resembled trolley cars with nothing more than a motorman's cab, a trolley pole in the middle, and a mini-caboose in the back. Since the SoB was regulated by the I.C.C., the trolley locomotives were put through monthly inspections. By the mid-fifties it had become harder and harder to pass these inspections and, finally, diesel locomotives were introduced. In March 1955 one of the SoB's oldest locomotives (dating back to 1904) was scrapped.

Although the SoB was a profit-maker for more years than most freight railroads, many of its profitable sources of revenue eventually vanished It no longer could go in for scavenging the way it did when it was hauling fill for Coney Island. And the wine-grape tonnage continually diminished as the art of wine-making died out in Brooklyn But one customer not likely to take its business elsewhere is the TA itself. All the heavy equipment and supplies for the Coney Island yards are freighted in by the SoB. Reilly noted that, "when the TA obtains new subway cars they are floated in from Hoboken on barges to Bush Terminal at 50th Street and First Avenue. Here, the New York Dock Railway Company unloads them and moves the equipment to 38th Street and Second Avenue. At this point the SoB diesels take over to shuttle them to the BMT station at Ninth Avenue where they are electrified to make the last leg of their journey over regular TA tracks to the Coney Island yards for preservice preparation and testing."

Just how long the SoB can remain in business is a moot question. But in its own curious way the line Brooklynites call their freight version of the *Toonerville Trolley* is as popular as it ever was. On September 20, 1975 the *Electric Railroaders Association* ran a "fan" special over the route that drew a capacity crowd. As one rail buff observed: "You don't often get a chance to ride a freight line within the city; and one that once tried to carry a whole whale and boxcars that wore corsets!"

It's hard to believe that this is a segment of the New York subway system. But it is! Note the trolley wire above.

SoB diesel #9 about to turn south under the McDonald Avenue El.

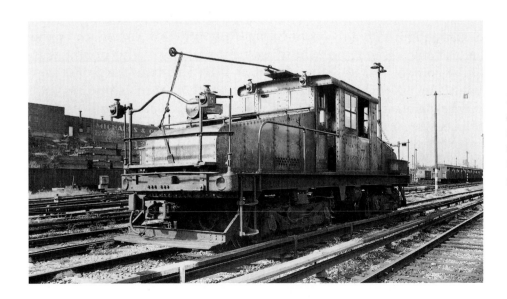

Electric motor #7, equipped to operate via third rail or overhead wire, awaits work at Coney Island Shops in October 1949.

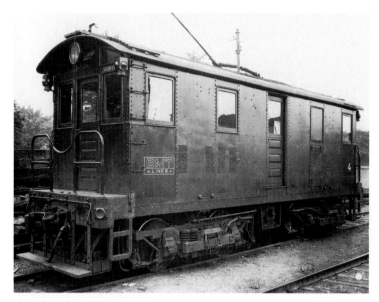

valuable piece of real estate. Ferry service was launched in 1713 but the first regular commuter service began in 1810 when Cornelius Vanderbilt, who was to gain fame as the boss of the New York Central Railroad, launched a ferry service. The sixteen year-old Vanderbilt, later to be known as "the Commodore," was on to a good thing. Staten Island (also known as Richmond, in honor of the Duke of Richmond) already had become a haven for transplanted New Yorkers, as well as others seeking a relaxed life within a relatively short ride of mad Manhattan. By the 1830s planners and investors realized that what the island needed to link its growing but far-flung communities was a railroad.

The first serious attempt at building one was organized in 1836 when Minthorne Tompkins, Harmon B. Cropsey, John Westervelt, John Thompson, and Richard Littell were granted a charter for the Staten Island Railroad. There was one catch; work had to begin on the new line within two years or the charter would be revoked. Work never did begin and the charter was revoked.

The second attempt at building a line, connecting Tottenville on the south of the island and Stapleton on the north, was developed in 1851. This time the project was promoted by both Staten Islanders and prominent citizens of nearby Perth Amboy, New Jersey. Like its predecessor, the second proposed Staten Island railway was almost immediately derailed by financial difficulties.

Searching for an "angel," the promoters approached Cornelius Vanderbilt, who had made a lot of money in the ferry business. In fact, at the time he was sought out by the Staten Island Railroad planners Vanderbilt had control of all the east shore ferries but he

In its own way the Staten Island Railway is the most offbeat passenger route in the five boroughs. Unlike the BMT, IRT, or IND lines, the SIR never rolled outside of Staten Island. In contrast with the other lines, the SIR always has suggested a farm land railroad, meandering from terminal to terminal at a slow pace. Its history tells you why.

From the very beginnings of New York City, Staten Island has been the stepchild borough across the bay. During the Revolutionary War, Staten Island remained loyal to King George. It has remained mostly rural while the rest of New York City is the epitome of urbanity. While much of Gotham traditionally votes Democrat, the good burghers of Staten Island go Republican.

In fact, Staten Islanders frequently even think of themselves more as New Jerseyites than New Yorkers. This, of course, can be explained by the fact that Staten Island sits right next to New Jersey while mainland New York looms far on the horizon. Were it not for an absurd boat race in 1687 Staten Island would be a part of New Jersey today. At the time both New York and New Jersey were vying for the island and it was decided that ownership would go to the colony that won a sailboat race from one end of the island to the other. New York's Captain Christopher Billop was the winner and New Jersey lost a very had never taken the plunge into railroading.

Vanderbilt came through with the money and in 1860 the line that eventually would become a part of the New York City transit system opened for business. It connected the towns of Vanderbilt's Landing (now Clifton) and Eltingville, seven-and-one-half miles south.

The railroad was a source of conversation even before its official opening. Its unique iron locomotive, the *Albert Journea*, named for the president of the railroad, caused quite a stir, as reported in the March 21, 1860 edition of the *Staten Island Gazette*:

"The locomotive has been indulging itself, since its arrival, by making pleasant little trips on the railroad as far as New Dorp, and has been quite useful in conveying materials where required for use. Each day it is the subject of renewed comment and admiration by those who reside along the line transversed.... One old man among the number had never seen a locomotive. He said he lived between 'Iron Spring' and 'Skunk's Misery,' and has walked five miles to take a look. As 'She' advanced with a shriek, he jumped about a foot, and exclaimed 'I swear,' but as he was dumb thereafter, we can not say what he thought of it."

A second locomotive was added in May 1860 and service extended to Annadale. A month later the line extended to Tottenville and the dream of a quarter century was realized. Staten Island had its railroad. But it wasn't a very pleasant dream right from the start. Revenue was slower in coming than the line's locomotives and, less than a year after it had opened, the railroad was threatened with foreclosure by the New Jersey Locomotive Works for failure to pay the bills for the two steam engines. An SOS was sent out to Commodore Vanderbilt, who responded by dispatching his son to Staten Island as the line's receiver and making some adjustments with ferry operators to synchronize their arrivals and departures with the railroad.

But good fortune never would smile on the Staten Island line and one of a long list of tragedies occurred on July 30, 1871 when the ferryboat *Westfield*, co-operated by the railroad, blew up at the Whitehall Street pier in lower Manhattan, killing sixty-six passengers. It also killed the railroad for a number of years.

The line made a comeback in 1883 when Robert Garrett, president of the Baltimore & Ohio Railroad, was approached as a backer of a revived Staten Island Railway. Garrett realized that the Baltimore & Ohio needed a railhead in New York City and immediately supported the plan. The new company was called the Staten Island Rapid Transit Railroad Company, becoming the first to apply the words "rapid transit" to a railroad. Thus the country's oldest railroad to become a rapid transit operation merged with the Baltimore & Ohio, America's oldest railroad.

On July 31, 1884, thirteen years and a day after the old line had ceased to operate, the SIRT began service between Clifton and Tompkinsville. New lines were added, and by the early 1890s it appeared that boom years were just ahead. But they never materialized. Trolley cars were introduced to the island before the turn of the century and they began cutting into the SIRT patronage. By 1899 the railroad was in big trouble again. It went bankrupt and, this time, was bought outright by the Baltimore & Ohio for the "upset price" of $2 million at an auction.

Although ridership was less than encouraging in the early years of the twentieth century, the Baltimore & Ohio bosses saw some hope in the possibility of a connection with Brooklyn across the bay. Engineers for the Brooklyn Rapid Transit Company (later the BMT) suggested that as part of the Fourth Avenue (Brooklyn) Subway project a connecting tunnel be bored under the Narrows (lower New York Bay) to St. George in Staten Island.

The idea was well received and likely would have been pushed to fruition were it not for a freakish turn of fate involving the BRT. In November 1918 a crash on the BRT's Brighton Line at Malbone Street in Brooklyn killed ninety-seven passengers and bankrupted the line. For the moment, at least, tunneling to Staten Island was out of the question.

Meanwhile revenues took an upward turn for the SIRT in the early twenties as the island's population grew. In 1921 more than 13 million people rode the Baltimore & Ohio's rapid transit route compared to only 2,460,000 in 1907. Tunnel talk was stirring again, and this time it appeared to be so much a certainty that realtors began speaking of a Staten Island land boom to follow the new subway tunnel. In 1925 headings for the tunnel were begun and an elaborate track connection in which the SIRT would link with the BMT Sea Beach line in the Fourth Avenue tunnel had been worked out. Unfortunately the planners never cleared it with the politicians.

New York's Mayor John Hylan had been an enemy of the BRT since 1907, when he had been working as a motorman on the line and his alleged carelessness had almost killed a towerman. He was fired and bore a grudge against the line, and its successor, the BMT, ever afterward. New York State's Governor Al Smith was, in 1925, owner of considerable Pennsylvania Railroad stock. A link between the Baltimore & Ohio's Staten Island line and the BMT could, conceivably, have hurt the Pennsylvania Railroad.

Cynical New York City political pundits believe that neither Hylan nor Smith wanted a Staten Island-Brooklyn rail tunnel to be realized. Work on the tunnel, which had begun in both boroughs, stopped abruptly soon after it had Started. Hylan has generally been targeted as the principal culprit and the project was never again resumed. Meanwhile, in anticipation of a coupling with the BMT, the SIRT had electrified the system and purchased a fleet of BMT-type cars for use on its own lines.

Despite the tunnel setback, the SIRT continued to move forward. Grade crossings were eliminated wherever possible, and by the early forties the line was as healthy as it ever would be. But soon after World War II had ended the city began consolidating transit facilities and, in 1948, the Board of Transportation annexed the Staten Island bus routes. It immediately reduced fares and, in so doing, sliced SIRT revenues by 60 percent.

The SIRT saw the handwriting on the wall and tried to unload the entire system on the city, but the answer for the moment was negative.

Once again there was hope of a rail link to Brooklyn—this time by bridge. The Triborough Bridge and Tunnel Authority was given approval to erect a huge bridge across the Narrows and in 1964 the span was completed. Unfortunately, its most vocal supporter was Robert Moses, who had vast political clout at the time. Moses, who consistently vetoed rapid transit in favor of the private automobile, insisted that the SIRT and the BMT be kept off the bridge and, as usual, Moses triumphed.

Still the SIRT limped along, serving those Staten Islanders who appreciated a pleasant train ride to the New York ferries. When the Metropolitan Transportation Authority (MTA) annexed the Transit Authority in 1968 new life was pumped into the SIRT. A fleet of shiny silver commuter trains was installed, replacing the old BMT-type cars that had been in use since 1925.

Cosmetically the SIRT was never in better shape but its financial state was less attractive. The failure of the line to link directly by rail with Brooklyn was its most significant drawback and ridership remained disheartingly low in the mid-seventies.

Still another blow was delivered to the SIRT late in 1975 when trainmen, angered over the MTA's refusal to grant them equal pay with their New York City subway counterparts, went on strike for four months. Charges rang back and forth, among them that the MTA was deliberately sabotaging the SIRT so that it could close the line and simply operate buses on Staten Island. The strike was settled in April 1976 and service resumed.

Renamed Staten Island Railway and

managed by New York City Transit, the onetime SIRT remains a throwback to another era. It maintains its same route but bounces less.

By the late 1990s newer, welded rail had replaced the lighter, traditional gapped tracks that for decades produced the sweet *click-clack* across the Island.

Air conditioned rolling stock, purchased in 1972, was overhauled in 1990 and 1991 for better riding quality. In addition, access for the handicapped was added to the system.

The 14.3-mile route is popular with Staten Island residents and can be expected to attract more than five million riders in a year while jealously holding its title as the most offbeat passenger route in the five boroughs!

(above) *A Tottenville Staten Island car is departing the wooden, now replaced, St. George terminal in 1948. These cars, similar in appearance to the BMT Standards, can be differentiated by their squared off celestory roofs and doors at the very ends of the cars. Some eventually were transferred to the BMT and were used on the Culver Shuttle and as yard offices.*

(below) *An Arlington Branch (North Shore Line) car meandering across the Port Richmond trestle in 1952. This Staten Island branch also became bereft of passenger service in 1952.*

By far the most scenic rapid transit unit of any of the divisions is the Rockaway Line, which extends from the mainland of Queens at Howard Beach to the long spit of land on the Atlantic Ocean known as Rockaway and Far Rockaway. To extend its IND line to the seaside area, the TA first had to build islands in Jamaica Bay, create bird sanctuaries, dig ship channels, and develop a few lakes here and there The result was the longest single extension of the rapid transit lines since the subway was built in 1904, adding 11.62 miles.

The Rockaway line extension was completed in June 1956, but the rail route itself dates back to 1892. It was then that the Long Island Rail Road (LIRR) drove 50,000 piles deep into the mud and sand of Jamaica Bay and built a new line across the slightly more than four miles of shallow water. The LIRR then began running trains across the short route to the Rockaways and simultaneously began wishing that it had never got involved with the idea of bridging Jamaica Bay.

Fire became the most common hazard. The trestle, only a few feet above water most of the way, was particularly vulnerable: The hot sun dried out ties; cigarettes popped out of open windows to land on dry, creosoted wood where they smoldered for five or six hours and then burst into flame, fanned by drafts through the open lattice of the ties.

But the Rockaways had many pleasures to offer the city dweller, and throngs continued to crowd the beaches despite the LIRR and its problems. The demand was so great in 1898 that the Brooklyn Elevated Railroad Company (BERC) made a deal with the LIRR to rent the track and run summer excursion trains over the trestle to the Rockaways. To do so the BERC had to build a special ramp at Chestnut Street and Atlantic Avenue in the East New York section of Brooklyn so that its trains could switch directly onto the LIRR tracks heading for the shore. As more and more Brooklynites took the trains to Rockaway, city planners began eyeing the Rockaway tracks for possible inclusion in the city transit system at some future time. But a succession of mayors managed to find a myriad of excuses for delaying the proposal.

It wasn't until 1950 that the project finally moved forward after someone flicked a burning cigarette out the window of an LIRR coach causing a fire that burned out 1,800 feet of trestle. The LIRR, financially shaky at the time, threw up its hands over the Rockaway Line and decided not to spend another fortune rebuilding its firetrap.

When the LIRR finally conceded defeat by petitioning for abandonment of Rockaway service, New York City moved in and acquired the line for $8,500,000, a bargain price. Of course the city had to spend an additional $47,500,000 to modernize the run and get it operative again but that, too, was considered a steal. It cost somewhat less than $5 million per route mile, the savings due primarily to large sections of road that were either salvageable or ready for use merely by modernizing the signals. Much of the money was invested in building a fireproof bridge across Jamaica Bay.

This was accomplished by creating two man-made islands, spanning most of the four-mile stretch across water. The ties were buried in ballast and sand, flush to their tops, so that no drafts could seep from underneath to fan into a destructive blaze started by a dying cigarette resting on a tie made flammable with creosote oil.

Among the more intense battles during reconstruction was a daily clash between transit men and squadrons of dive-bombing gulls that arrived from the nearby bird sanctuary which the TA also built as part of the new project. The gulls overflowed the sanctuary and began homesteading on the new railroad bed. When TA men approached the nests, the gulls attacked. "The damn things dive-bombed us," one of the field crew complained. "They knocked off hats and glasses in a wink."

The birds enjoyed the side benefits of the Rockaway trestle work. During the months when thousands of tons of sand were being pumped up to create the new islands, clams and fish also were retrieved, creating a cornucopia of gull goodies.

By construction standards, the Rockaway line was a topsy-turvy job. "It always had been a considerable problem disposing of fill," said Francis V. Hayes, division engineer of the project. "But in the Rockaway job we needed two million cubic yards to fill!"

To get it the contractors dug to the bottom of Jamaica Bay. Because the United States Defense Department wanted a ship channel, nearly one million yards of sand were pumped up and this formed what is now known as Sand Island. The birds almost immediately took possession of this island. The longer of the TA-created islands is known as the Embankment and runs for more than two miles across the bay.

To ensure that the new islands would not erode into the sea, the TA planted grass on a tremendous scale. At least 100 acres of the new land were planted practically foot by foot with beach grass, about the only vegetation that could thrive in the salty sand, to anchor the islands.

Before the new Rockaway Line was completed it had scored several "firsts" for rapid transit. One was the dispatching of a field engineer, Victor Lefkowitz, to the scene for the sole purpose of formulating a battle plan against mussels, creatures that destroy trestles as easily as lit cigarette butts do.

Camping in a pile crack, the mussels increase the size of the opening, permitting other marine life to get inside with them where they gorge themselves on tasty pile innards not protected by creosote. Piles used on the old LIRR trestle were found completely hollow inside the creosoted shell. Some 500 had to be replaced and these, together with the old ones, form the skeletons of the two man-made islands over which the line hops Jamaica Bay.

To outdo the destructive mussels, the TA engineers produced a concrete foundation. Another "first" was a floating concrete factory

that was towed along the line. The factory precast thirty-ton slabs of concrete, which were lifted by a fifty-ton crane. It then dropped them on the concrete trestle foundations, forming a virtually finished roadbed. "Shovels and wheelbarrows were practically unknown," said a TA engineer.

Building the new extension was a remarkable accomplishment in itself, but completing it on time was easily the most outstanding feat of the construction. Studies of the old trestle and the surrounding terrain had been conducted by TA engineers as far back as 1950. When the actual heavy work began in 1955 the target date for completion of the mammoth project was set at June 28, 1956. The reasoning was that the new Rockaway Line should open for business in time for the heavy July 4th crowds.

Construction moved along smoothly until the Westinghouse Electric Corporation went on strike on October 16, 1955. Westinghouse had the contract to provide the power equipment for the line, and as the strike dragged on, the deadline for completion seemed unlikely to be met.

The strike lasted for 156 days and when it was finally ended Westinghouse informed the TA that the equipment would not be ready until at least the second week of October, nearly four months after the deadline.

But the TA's bull-headed chairman, Charlie Patterson, would have none of that. He called a meeting on January 26, 1956 and asserted that the June 28 deadline would be met, come hell or high water.

Authority members were impressed with the chairman's determination but the workers at Jamaica Bay laughed when they heard what Patterson had said. "With this strike," one said, "how the hell does he expect us to open on time? What are we going to do for power equipment if Westinghouse can't deliver until the fall?"

Charlie Patterson had an answer to that one. He ordered his men to borrow some equipment from the IRT's Dyre Avenue Line and the Aqueduct substation was skeletonized. Arrangements were made to buy other power. By spring a few optimists at TA headquarters began thinking they just might pull off the impossible. During a meeting with trestle-builders at Jay Street headquarters in Brooklyn, one contractor told Patterson: "You know, I wouldn't be surprised if we are ready to run on June 28."

"Ready?" snapped Patterson. "We will be running then!"

In spite of strikes, dive-bombing gulls, and a horde of skeptics, the Transit Authority's trains rolled to Rockaway on June 28 just as Charlie Patterson had promised.

The Rockaway Line brightened the subway system through the 1990s, a glittering jewel because of its sweet run past Jamaica Bay.

The A train now serves both the Rockaway Park terminal on the South and the Far Rockaway depot on the North end of the peninsula. An S Shuttle also links Broad Channel Station with Rockaway Park.

Were he still around today, Charlie Patterson would be beaming over his favorite subway that followed the sea gulls.

A special moves on the Rockaway Line north-bound between the Aqueduct Race Track and Broad Channel Stations in June of 1962.

(above) *Southbound shuttle to Rockaway Park just north of the Broad Channel Station in June 1962. If you didn't know this was in New York City you would mistake the background for Nebraska.*

(below) *BMT-type "Q" cars on a Museum Special at Hammel's Wye in the Rockaways during November 1965. The TA's "Train That Goes Out To Sea" offers a unique ride.*

ANATOMY OF THE UNDERGROUND

Signaling and the Subway

One of the most perplexing problems confronting IRT subway planners early in the century was a very basic one: how to avoid crashes. One major underground collision could put the new subway line out of business. (That, by the way, did happen to the Brooklyn Rapid Transit in 1918.) So August Belmont, founder the IRT Subway, insisted that his engineers find an advanced, practical method of signaling.

A primary function of this signaling system would be to allow trains to operate regularly at headways of two and three minutes. This would not be a simple accomplishment since the IRT had no source of experience to turn to for practical advice. The London, Paris, Glasgow, Boston, and Budapest subways had not yet developed any sophisticated train regulatory equipment.

As so often was the case, New York City's first subway, the 1904 IRT, led the way in rapid transit innovation. When it came to signaling, the upstart IRT was the first completely electrically signaled railroad to operate in the United States. The IRT capped a series of signaling developments dating back to the early part of the nineteenth century when horses were being replaced by steam engines.

According to *Transit* magazine: "The locomotives brought tremendous speed but they also brought danger. Progressive-minded railroads maintained gangs of roustabouts at stations, who seized a train as it approached and dragged it to a stop by sheer strength at the station, or at least within walking distance of it. These monsters did not heed a cry of *Whoa*! And after the power was shut off, they rolled great distances. The human brakes and no signaling were all right until some prosperous railroads acquired two, even three, locomotives and operated several trains simultaneously on the single-track systems. The roustabouts weren't available between stations to stop the trains and accidents began to happen. Train schedules should have made it possible for trains to meet at predetermined points, where a second track was available for passing, but the schedules didn't mean much. Aside from the common breakdown, the farmers in many localities had the right, which they strongly defended, to use the railways to haul their produce to town in wagons fitted with flanged wheels. Thus, many an engineer, whose schedule called for a twelve-mile speed, crept slowly behind a wagonload of turnips drawn at two or three miles an hour by a pair of weary farm plugs."

The first signaling in America was on the New Castle and French Town Railroad, which ran seventeen miles through Delaware and Maryland from Chesapeake Bay to the Delaware River, an important rail link for steamship routes. Wooden masts, thirty feet high, were built three miles apart and from each was suspended an inverted peach basket. The baskets were covered with white or black cloth. When the train left the terminal, the white-covered peach basket was hoisted to the top of the mast. Three miles away, at the next tower, a man saw the signal through a marine spyglass, hoisted the white signal to the top of his mast, and so on. In a manner of minutes the other terminal was apprised that a train was coming through. The white basket, at half-mast at a station, told the engineer to stop for passengers or freight. The basket was raised to the top of the mast at each station as the train went through; after it passed the basket was lowered immediately to the bottom of the mast, in which position it meant *Stop!* If a train was disabled and could not proceed, a black basket was hoisted to the top of the mast to spread the word. In some form or another the ball-and-mast system of signaling, as it became known, still exists in various parts of the country.

It was the beginning of railroad signaling, but a slow beginning. Other railroads were in no hurry to develop signal techniques. Indeed, twenty-five years later, the Tallahassee, Pensacola & Georgia was dealing with the problems of trains confronting each other between stations by making a rule that,

in such case, "the dispute as to which shall retire shall be settled by the Conductors, without interference on the part of the engineers." The locomotive engineers were hotheaded prima donnas in those days, not to be trusted with diplomatic negotiations. Even so, the issue of which train was to back up to the nearest siding was not always settled by peaceable debate.

In America the saving of manpower by the use of signaling seldom entered the picture at all. In England, significantly ahead of America in safety advocates, it was pointed out that signaling could reduce the use of hired men. But here safety was the only issue. Railroads which could buy a gang of slaves to serve as brakes weren't at all concerned about conserving manpower. They were worried about passengers being injured in wrecks. Long lists of casualties discouraged people from riding new locomotive-hauled trains. Keeping people on the payroll simply to hoist a ball, or a flag, or show a colored light, or a disc was accepted casually. In retrospect this seems incredible, for the TA today has more than a million electric contacts doing the work of semaphoring, and 1,200 men who do nothing but serve the mechanical wants of these relays.

In 1863 the block system evolved in America. England already had a similar system, but in those days there was no free dissemination of information. Indeed, it is remarkable that railroad thinking in America developed so closely along British lines with virtually no interchange of thought.

In 1863 Ashbel Welch, chief engineer of the United New Jersey Canal and Railroad Companies, divided the track between Trenton, New Jersey and Philadelphia into sections, or blocks, about six miles apart. At each section border a building housed a crew and a simple telegraph apparatus. As a train passed, the telegrapher wired ahead that it was on its way, and an illuminated signal closed the track to all trains behind that one, until the telegrapher ahead flashed back word that the train had passed his point, at which time the track would be opened for another train. The system eliminated the danger that two trains could be on the same section of track at the same time, and even rear-end collisions could be avoided. The signal was manually operated, but otherwise "fool-proof."

To get around the problem of human failings, the signal man was replaced by an automated system. A train entering a block touched against an obstruction that immediately turned the signal behind it to "Danger!" It moved on and at the next block touched another obstruction that did the same, and, in addition, turned the signal at the previous block to "Proceed." The automated semaphores worked fine in the south. They worked fine in the north, in summer. But in winter, sleet drove into the works and the all-clear locked in ice.

Lighted semaphores were even worse. In 1841 an international committee of railway men met in Birmingham, England, and decided to settle the light question once and for all. They declared that a white light meant "Full speed ahead," red meant "Stop!" and green meant "Proceed cautiously." All over the world railroads changed to this design. All over the world trains crashed and a lot of people were killed.

The theory was sound. A white light had many times the carrying capacity of red or green or blue. But the crashes promptly pinpointed two things: if the red glass disc was smashed by any means, the "danger" bulb showed white and beckoned to disaster; if the signal wasn't working at all, the engineer would glimpse any white light and charge ahead to a crash.

Dr. William Robinson, horrified by a couple of accidents he had witnessed, set out to devise a system that would end railroad crashes once and for all. In 1869 he constructed, and showed in New York a year later, an open-circuit system of block control with signals that were not dependent on human control, but actuated by every pair of wheels entering a block, or section. This was accomplished by having electric current pass up from one rail, through the wheels on that side, through the car axle, through the other wheels, and, by that flow of current, actuate the signal behind the train to red. A polished and refined version of this passing of current from rail to wheel to axle to wheel to rail, or the breaking of that current, is what activates the signals of today.

But that was 1869 and the railroads didn't like Robinson's system at all. It was newfangled, complicated, too tricky, expensive, and experimental. Here and there it was tried out on small sections of track. It also was tried on the IRT thirty-five years later!

The electropneumatic interlocking signals of the IRT were considered the "marvel of the times" in 1904. At that time safety on the IRT was the primary issue. When the train passed a signal into a new block, the signal behind it turned red. As it did, the trip, a little metal arm beside the track, rose upright, to remain there as long as the signal remained red. A train that tried to pass before the signal changed struck this projection with its "trip cock," a lever which released compressed air from the braking system, causing the brakes to engage.

Normally, the motorman would have to "key by"—that is, come a full stop, and turn a key to release the trip lever. In the overlap system, there are always two red signals behind each train which means that the motorman would have to come to a full stop at least twice, turn the key, and proceed beyond two red lights before reaching the point where his own train could menace the train ahead. It was—and still is—possible for a motorman to crash into the car ahead, but it takes a lot of work to do it.

In time the actual turning of a key became outmoded. Now the train simply comes to a stop at a signal, activating the trip arm by moving the train forward just enough to get its front wheels on the track circuit ahead. The time element device is also used to retard trains going into stations and curves and such. This isn't what standard railroads call "speed control," although for all practical purposes it serves as such.

After 1904 the thought arose that signaling, used chiefly to stop or slow up trains, could also serve to increase track capacity and reduce delays As subways filled to overflowing, and construction costs for new lines soared skyward, the need for squeezing every ounce of carrying capacity from the old tunnels became a primary consideration.

Under the old system a train waited to enter a station at a complete stop if a train was already in that station. Until the first train got under way and cleared the end of the platform, the second train had to remain motionless. Now, of course, a "station time signal" along the station platform lets the second train get underway, slowly, while the train ahead is beginning to leave the station.

"Theoretically, the track space, between trains," said one signalman, "is wasted space. The less of it there is, the better, from an economic viewpoint. The ultimate in efficiency would be one continuous train running around and around on a conveyor belt principle. That idea isn't here yet. But the closer we can come to it the higher goes the efficiency in moving cargo. All right, we've got to stop at platforms for passengers, we've got to stop and go.

"But we can, and are, cutting down on the need for such wide spaces between trains. More signals means it is possible to run more trains safely over the same track. In a sense, it is like braking a train going forty miles an hour, as compared to braking it at twenty. At twenty you need only a quarter of the distance to stop. We don't have to slow up the whole railroad; it's just a matter of slipping extra trains in between."

The above statement was made in 1976. Since then the New York subway has not produced any major changes in its signalling system. Block control remains very much *de regueur*, for a very good reason; although it dates back to the 19th Century it is reliable. However, there has been a gradual modernization whereby the older IRT and BMT equipment dating back to the 1920s and earlier has been replaced by up-to-date models. Fewer changes have been made on the more modern IND sections.

In 1997 the Authority was spending more than $600,000,000 to repair and upgrade many of the system's low-tech signal lights. Target date for completion was just after the turn of the century, perhaps 2001.

To keep employees at speed in terms of the equipment the TA maintains a Manhattan switch and signal training center at Eighth Avenue and 14th Street near a passageway used by passengers connecting with Seventh and Eighth Avenues.

Instructors who work with the signalling people are fortified with mockups of model boards used to monitor subways, a set of genuine railroad tracks—including switches—and a model train set that explains how track signals work. Whenever new equipment is purchased switch and signal workers get to see the technology at the training center.

Although the signalling has been constantly tested and updated, glitches have appeared from time to time. What's more, accidents have occurred which have brought into question the efficiency of the signals in terms of the equipment being used.

An obvious example was the 1996 Williamsburg Bridge crash. The signals were working; the safety tripper functioned but the train could not be stopped in time because there was insufficient room between signals for the emergency brakes to stop the train in time.

Because the newer rolling stock boasted bigger, more powerful motors, the high command decided that it would alter the car's power train to limit speed. In addition a spate of new cautionary signals appeared throughout the system to lower speeds on curves and other potentially hazardous areas of track.

High-tech signalling now employed by systems in such cities as Vancouver, Canada, have been studied for possible use in New York. One such technique would be similar to the Vancouver *Sky Train* which functions without operators in a front car cab.

The Authority would not eschew the operator but in a 21st century system he or she would consult a computer screen in the cab to determine whether or not to proceed. Standard red, yellow and green signal lights would be eliminated. Computers would also eliminate the safety trippers. They would automatically activate the train's brakes if there was danger ahead. Rather than towermen pulling the switch levers, the switches would be automatically be activated by computers.

While some experts contend that the Authority has been "reluctant to be burned by new technology," a large segment of the train community remains hesitant to completely overhaul and dramatically change so vast and complex a railroad to the new technology.

Nevertheless, New York City Transit President Lawrence Reuter believes that the possibility of automated signalling for the system in the 21st century is a good one. But until everyone is convinced, the old, reliable block control will guide the trains in The Bronx, Brooklyn, Queens and Manhattan. And make no mistake, safety statistics prove that it is reliable.

(left and below) *The operator (towerman) here is responsible for the Essex Street Interlocking. This machine and the one below from Hammel's Wye, which controls the Rockaway lines, are NX-type (entrance-exit) machines. When a route is selected for a train the operator punches the button at the entrance and exit of the route and the machine automatically throws the switches and clears the signal for that route, blocking all possible conflicting and therefore interlocked routes.*

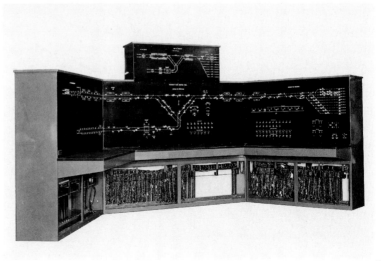

The subway system did use railroad style lower quadrant signals as seen here at the Westchester Avenue connection between the Third Avenue El and the subway. The photo was taken in 1904.

In Brooklyn before the lines to Coney Island were elevated, trains ran down the center of streets and obtained power a la trolley style from overhead wires. At junctions such as this one, lower quadrant semaphore signals are in use. Like the ones in the photo above, they bend down to indicate a clear track, rather than up as in the case of the regular railroads.

The subway and els started using target-type signals with the opening of the subways because the tunnel did not provide sufficient clearances for moving semaphore arms. There also was a need for greater illumination. The system the transit system uses at interlockings involves an upper aspect that indicates if the track ahead is occupied and a bottom aspect that indicates whether the train will be taking a straight (green) or diverging (yellow) route. A double red is an absolute stop signal whereas a single red (not at interlockings) is a stop and proceed with extreme caution. Interlockings are places where signals govern movement over switches.

Movie-making on the Line

Ever since Hollywood began making talking pictures, the New York City subway has been a favorite locale for MGM, 20th-Century Fox, and United Artists. One of the first—and best—was *Subway Express*, by Martha Madison and Eva Flint and directed by Chester Erskin.

Mystery film buffs still talk about the *dénouement* in which a dying victim's last words to the police were "See Beach Express!" At first detectives mistakenly believed the victim was referring to the BMT's Sea Beach Express and search in vain for the villain along the Brooklyn subway line. Only later is it learned that the victim was alluding to the Beach pneumatic subway tunnel which was sealed and allegedly still in existence adjacent to the BRT Broadway (Manhattan) Line. It developed that the murderer was living in the old, abandoned Beach tunnel. Hence "See Beach Express!"

Just a few years later, the Third Avenue El (then part of the IRT) figured prominently in one of the most widely-known films ever made, the original version of *King Kong*. In the movie's climax, the great ape lumbers down Third Avenue, smashing the landscape and, of course, the venerable el. The camera zeroes in on the interior of a train as unsuspecting straphangers read their newspapers and talk to one another. Unknown to them, Kong has ripped up the very tracks on which their local is rolling. Suddenly the motorman spies Kong up ahead and jams on the brakes. Passengers hurtle together. Kong's bloodshot eyes appear at the window of the car. Women shriek. Kong picks up the el car, flips it into the street, and ties knots in it. All this without a Metrocard!

Eventually Alfred Hitchcock, that indefatigable seeker of authenticity for movie sets, got into the act. He hired an IND train for *The Wrong Man*, a 1956 melodrama starring Henry Fonda. The master of suspense produced a scene with Fonda sitting in an R-1 car, reading a newspaper, as the train supposedly rattled through the tunnel. Actually, it was standing quite still in the IND's Fifth Avenue Station.

As the demand for more subway filmmaking sites increased, the TA obliged by renting to movie producers the abandoned Court Street Shuttle Line. Originally a tributary of the IND-Fulton Street Line in Brooklyn, the Court Street Shuttle (HH local) operated between the Hoyt-Schermerhorn Street Station, where it connected with the A express and GG local, and Court Street near Atlantic Avenue at the fringe of Brooklyn Heights. This was one of the system's bigger blunders and in June 1946 the line was permanently closed. "It turned out to be a blessing for movie-making purposes," said Dennis Wendling, a TA public affairs man. "The old Court Street Line has many of the features film directors look for in a subway—a curve, curtain wall, and switches."

Wendling, who had been the TA's liaison with filmmakers, television producers, and anyone else who wanted to use the subway for commercial purposes, had been called upon as the system's official safety adviser when actual filming took place. One of the most unusual problems occurred during the shooting of the TV movie *A Short Walk to Daylight*, in which the script called for a subway derailment. To accommodate the producers, the TA jacked a train off the tracks during the filming and then returned it to the rails once the movie was completed.

One of the busiest periods of subway filmmaking occurred from 1970 through 1975 when no less than thirty-six movies were made utilizing subway property in one form or another. In that period the most publicized film was United Artists' adaptation of John Godey's book *The Taking of Pelham One Two Three*. The TA was not at all anxious to rent a subway to United Artists for the film because the story concerned the hijacking of an IRT local. "It had," said a TA official, "the potential to spark irresponsible and dangerous

"We are going to kill one passenger a minute until New York City pays us 1 million dollars."

"THE TAKING OF PELHAM ONE TWO THREE"

Everyone read it. Now you can live it.

PALOMAR PICTURES and PALLADIUM PRODUCTIONS present
THE TAKING OF PELHAM ONE TWO THREE
starring
WALTER MATTHAU
ROBERT SHAW
MARTIN BALSAM
HECTOR ELIZONDO
Produced by GABRIEL KATZKA and EDGAR J. SCHERICK
Screenplay by PETER STONE
Based on the novel by JOHN GODEY • Music by DAVID SHIRE
Directed by JOSEPH SARGENT
R RESTRICTED   PANAVISION®   United Artists

behavior."

United Artists' associate producer Steve Kesten was adamant about shooting the movie on the IRT system. "There was no way to do it without a real subway," said Kesten. "There was some talk about using the Boston, Philadelphia, or Montreal system, but who're you going to fool? The Transit Authority got cold feet. They didn't want to be responsible for somebody stealing a subway. It took Mayor John Lindsay going to the wall to get it done. We wound up paying a terrific whopping insurance premium to take care of any such risk."

The TA was so fearful that a subway train would be hijacked as a result of *The Taking of Pelham One Two Three* that it compelled United Artists to pay $275,000 for the train and $75,000 for the anti-hijacking insurance. The film was eventually done in part on the IRT and on the IND at the Court Street Station. Starring Walter Matthau, Robert Shaw, Martin Balsam and Jerry Stiller, the film received generally good notices.

The subway also has done well on Tin Pan Alley. As far back as the nineteenth century the New York el inspired A. H. Rosewig to compose the "Rapid Transit Galop." By far the most popular tune of all was dedicated to the IND's speedy A express. Billy Strayhorn wrote the words and music for "Take the A Train" in 1941 and the immortal jazzman Duke Ellington recorded the tune, which has remained a pop classic to this day.

On Broadway, the New York underground made its greatest impact in David Merrick's production of *Subways Are for Sleeping*, which opened December 27, 1961 and ran for 205 performances.

The closest the New York transit system came to making an imprint on comic strips was Fontaine Fox's legendary *Toonerville Trolley*. The creation, interestingly, was modeled after a system within the greater New York area. Fox said he was inspired to draw the *Toonerville Trolley* by a friendly old bearded motorman who ran a rundown trolley in Pelham, New York.

"Fox had traveled on this line to visit cartoonist Charlie Voight's home," said Herb Galewitz, who compiled a collection of Toonerville cartoons "By the time Fox returned to his own home, he had recalled another rundown trolley line in Louisville, the Brook Street run. He merged the two lines into *The Toonerville Trolley That Meets All Trains* and its conductor-motorman, the Skipper. It was an immediate success."

The *Toonerville Folks* reached the end of the line when Fontaine Fox retired in 1955.

Through the 1970s, 1980s and into the 1990s, New York's ribbons of rails continued to draw filmmakers underground. The TA maintained its policy of cooperation although occasionally the subject matter—as in *The Money Train*—was found objectionable to the general staff at the Jay Street, Brooklyn headquarters.

In some films the subway only has a cameo role while in others such as *The Warriors*, it's an integral part of the entire script.

Who can forget the opening and closing scenes of *The Flamingo Kid*, a wonderfully poignant drama about Bensonhurst. At the

202

curtain-raiser we see the elevated line rumbling, barely visible—but still apparent—in the distance.

By contrast, films such as *The French Connection* and *Die Hard with a Vengeance*, starring Bruce Willis, place heavy emphasis on the subways as a vehicle for the melodrama.

In *Die Hard with a Vengeance*, Willis actually jumps on a subway car through the street grate above.

Among other films on the city tracks were *Ghost Busters II*—where the slime runs through the subway tunnels—as well as *Extreme Measures, Girl 6, Conspiracy Theory* and many, many others.

The variety of subway films proved a never-ending source of interest to critics and actors alike. Jerry Stiller, who had a key role in *The Taking of Pelham One Two Three* in the early 1970s, found himself starring more than two decades later in a made-for-television full-length feature, *Subway Stories*.

The HBO NYC Productions film was unique among the genre because the subway was the centerpiece for the entire movie rather than a mere backdrop. While the film obtained critical acclaim—especially Stiller—one reviewer took a very microscopic look at the details and mildly complained.

Writing in the *New York Times*, Clyde Haberman agreed that "the film did an admirable job of capturing the feel of the subways."

Nevertheless, he took issue with the fact that one detail was glaringly out of whack.

"The windows on the trains were all unscratched and perfectly clean," wrote Haberman. "In fact, that's worth repeating: unscratched and perfectly clean.

"That, as any subway rider knows, is as long a flight from reality as one can take without the aid of a controlled substance."

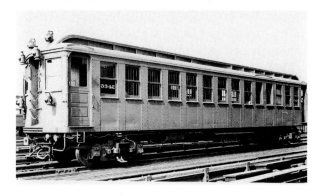

These two photos above show the conversion of an R-21 Type car for use as the money car in the movie "Money Train." Money cars are not used by the subway system today. However, at the left is a photo of an actual pay car used on the els and on the next page is a cash collecting car used by the IND.

(left) *Working on a scene from HBO's "Subway Stories:" The 5:24 with Bob Balaban, Steve Zahn and Jerry Stiller.*

The Most Dangerous Job

Steel-nerved workers who constantly examine the subway's energy source are a special breed reared only in the murky tunnels of New York's underground. Some 250 PD (power distribution) men drill, bolt, and weld the third rail while it is alive with enough current to kill a man in one blinding flash. This is considered the most dangerous transit job. Outside maintenance men can't take it. The IND division discovered that when it developed its special welding process. Outsiders accustomed to the sunlight on elevated tracks were lost in the subway darkness! A world that was alternately dazzling in the glare of welding arcs, or uncomfortably black in the presence of the deadly rail terrified them, while PD men leaned right on the rail with precisely three-sixteenths of an inch of rubber between them-selves and the current. One or two days of this and outsiders quit, their nerves frazzled.

The IND later recruited its men from among the track-walkers and other subway people who, over the years, developed a respectful familiarity with live third rails. They were goodnaturedly contemptuous of standard electric railroaders. Subway PDs viewed as sissified the custom of turning off the juice wherever possible, as practiced on some roads. Subway men always worked with "hot" equipment, raced tight headways that would have staggered outside power crews. They made no bones about considering themselves a sort of rail aristocracy.

One job they all dread is rescuing dogs and cats that continually stray into subway tunnels, become terrified, and crouch under the third rail. Invariably the dogs snap at the PDs, the cats maul them, and a goat once butted them. All in a day's work, caring for and repairing the subway's power supply.

The Rails They Ride On and How They're Replaced

To an uneducated eye the endless miles of rails lacing New York's subway system are permanently locked into place and will remain usable as long as the system is operating. Actually, the reverse is closer to the truth. There isn't a network of rails anywhere in the world subject to the incessant pounding and abuse absorbed by the New York system.

As a result subway maintenance men must constantly replenish the old rail with new steel, and do it without disturbing the normal flow of train traffic. Usually this happens at about midnight.

The lights are going off throughout the city. Out of the 207th Street yards rumbles the work train of the IND. For the twenty-four men who make up its crew, this is the dawn of a new workday. While the city sleeps, while trains interrupt at only twenty-minute intervals—that is the time when worn-out rails are replaced by new. The rusty new rails (in this particular field, it is the old, worn-out rails that glitter brightly) are laid out in rows on the flatcar.

On tangents—straight lines—rails live a long time. "Indefinitely" is the word. But on curves, the grind of steel wheels wears them out fast. Seventeen or eighteen months is a fairly long life for a curved rail; on sharper bends they may last as little as twelve or thirteen months And most of the rails on the flat car are for bends. Unlike standard railroads, where rails are fitted at the point of repair, every inch of new IND rail is fitted in advance for the particular few feet where it is to be placed—sawed to size, bent to fit the curve, drilled to take the plate.

As described in *Transit*, the work train rumbles out of the night and into the dark tunnel, just behind a southbound passenger train. In the passenger car the crewmen and the spare motorman drowse during the long trip down to the forties. This, like many work trains, is a double-ender. When the time comes to unload and load rails there will be a motorman fore and aft, for each full section of this rail weighs 1,100 pounds, and the movement of the train itself is used to load and unload.

They're up and alert, though, when the train comes to a halt in the forties. Now begins the operation that calls for footwork, as one observer put it, "as neat and dainty as the Rockettes—except that they don't have pretty legs." Twelve men, six on each side, each pair sharing a set of tongs, hoists the rails up to a chute, falling away as its tip finds the chuteway. The train twitches forward a little, and the rail goes down to the roadbed with a thundering clang. For perhaps seventeen minutes this work continues. Then the flagman whistles that a downtown local is coming. The work crew scrambles down, and the work train pulls away on its runaround.

This runaround is a fantastic jaunt. The train may go down to 34th Street (Pennsylvania) Station where it can be switched over to the northbound track. Now it may have to travel to 125th Street before it can be switched over to the southbound track on which the men are working. Before being switched over, it waits for a downtown train, so it can trail it. This is the only means by which the trackmen can be sure of having seventeen or eighteen minutes to unload, or, as the night progresses, to load the worn-out track. The runaround continues hour after hour until, just as the first sleepy work-bound passengers are appearing on the platform, it picks up its last used rails and heads back toward the 207th Street yards.

When rails were originally were put into place, the men who exerted the elbow grease required became known as *gandy dancers*. Railroads were built and rebuilt at the price of their sweat and aching backs. They swung six-pound spiking hammers for eight hours, plucked the great spikes out with claw bars, or tamped ballast. Now there was a test of whether a man would ever make a TA trackman. You stuck a tamper in his hands and set him to pounding away. If he lasted the first day through—a great many didn't—he had possibilities. If he showed up for work the next day and could still move his arms and legs, he was a likely prospect.

In 1956, Leo Casey, the TA's public relations boss, assigned one of his researchers to find the roots of the term *gandy dancer*. He went to three authorities.

"Gandy dancer," the first authority said. "derives from gander. Originally it was gander dancer. You'll find gander in the dictionary meaning 'simpleton' or 'fool.' Well, long ago railroads used to recruit their track crews from the flophouses of the Bowery and skid rows elsewhere. They were pretty low specimens—weak minds and strong backs. Hence the term gander dancers, changed later to gandy dancers."

Double-checking, the researcher went to another top authority. "It's an old term," the second etymologist said. "Once upon a time there was a slave-driving track foreman who worked his men so hard that they practically had to dance. The foreman's name was Gandy. Hence the term gandy dancer."

Triple-checking, the researcher tried a third authority.

"Sure, I know the origin," said he confidently. "Whereas now it is applied to all trackmen, originally it referred only to those tamping ballast. Ever notice the way a male goose will turn slowly and stamp when upset—well it's remarkably like the old walk of the man tamping ballast by hand."

So much for the origins of the term.

The gandy dancer is disappearing fast from the TA scene, and probably in time from the American railroad scene. Tireless little gasoline engines and compressed air have replaced the bulging biceps and mighty back.

Perhaps the surest sign of the change came in 1956 when the TA rebuilt the track and roadbed for approximately 1,000 feet between 25th Street and 36th Street, Brooklyn, on the northbound express track of the Fourth Avenue line.

By the standards of years ago, or even months before, this was a nine-week job, to be done in the late shift, and to produce in addition to the new roadbed, the usual crop of sprained ankles, cuts, and bruises, a hernia or two, countless backaches, and gallons of sweat. But this time it was different.

Into the tunnel, after rush hour Friday night, came new pieces of equipment—some never seen before in a subway. By rush hour Monday the job was finished—no cuts, bruises, hernias.

Not only were nine weeks of work compressed into a single weekend, but it was done more easily, at less cost, with fewer men. Toting up figures later, the engineers discovered they came to just 50 percent of the cost of doing it by the sweat-and-muscle method.

First the rails had to be taken up. The first of the new tools yanked 425 spikes in an hour and a half. It would have taken five times as long using manpowered claw bars.

The freed rails were pried out of their seats with crowbars and lifted to the toe bench—biceps and backs were still used here—and in the next operation, as the old ties were removed by hand.

Payloaders and bulldozers—then new to subway rebuilding— scooped up the old ballast. The roadbed was cleaned down to the concrete base. The flatcars hauled away fifteen carloads of the old ballast. In the old days this stuff had to be cleared by laborious hand shovel.

Now came the rebuilding process.

Tie plates had been laid on track ties in the yard at 38th Street and Tenth Avenue. These were brought to the work area, set on the concrete base, and the rails lifted back in place.

The power spike driver, the second new piece of equipment, drove spikes into holes previously drilled in the yard. Not a spike maul or muscle was called into play for all the spikes driven.

In came fifteen hopper carloads of stone ballast (broken trap-rock) which was distributed over the rails. Then, by track jacks, the track was raised and ballast tamped under it.

Again, not a muscle was raised for this—ordinarily the most tedious and back-breaking of the jobs. Instead, the third new piece of equipment came rolling through—a $45,000 mechanical ballast tamper, or mechanized gandy dancer. This machine was built by the Pullman Standard Manufacturing Company to TA specifications. It rolled, like the spike puller and spike driver, on wheels on the track. It had sixteen spade-shaped tamping heads of special steel, which bit into the ballast and jammed it under the ties to a firmness not possible with the strongest human muscles. Tamping with this machine cost one-sixth the price of hand-tamping.

Revolutionary as the Fourth Avenue operations were, they were just the beginning of a great new line of equipment that wrote doomsday for the gandy dancer. Among its work equipment arsenal, the TA now relies on two track geometry cars, two signal supply cars, three dump cars and three tank cars, among others.

Considering that the system includes 443 mainline track miles for passenger service underground and another 156 elevated and still another 57 at grade/open cut, the total of 656 mainline track miles require the utmost attention.

Add to that the 186 miles of track in the systems network of storage areas, shops and yards and you have no less than 842 track miles. As the TA likes to boast, "If laid end to end, this track would stretch from New York City to Chicago."

But it is now a distinctly different type of track than it had been during the BMT-IRT-IND era. Track improvements continued to be made in the last decades of the century and they have re-shaped the ride as well as the ambience of riding.

Easily the most significant change has been the switch from the traditional shorter rails, with connections every few yards, to welded rail which provides an infinitely smoother and quieter ride.

But the improvement has come at a cost to rail fans. The old time tracks had gaps of varying sizes at each connections and these gaps caused the entrancing *click-clack* sound that straphangers have heard for more than a century either on els or the subways.

Line by line, year by year, the gaps are departing and so are the sweet sounds of wheels thumping over the openings.

It is the price commuters pay for progress and comfort yet a stiff one for the many who spent their lives listening to *click-clack, thump-thump* and all the other neat sounds that went with old-time rails.

A BRT Southern Division tool car circa 1908.

(above) *A crane and boom car working in the East 180th Street yard in 1963. Assorted other work cars and equipment is visible in the background.*

(left) *A ballast tamping machine.*

(below) *This is an ex-Birney surface car converted to rail-grinder service. It is stored at Coney Island Yards in 1946 with hopper cars used for track and station maintenance.*

This the newest addition to the maintenance fleet of the transit system, ready to enter service in September 1997. It is a 5-car vacuum cleaner train built in France that cost 13.5 million dollars. It cleans steel dust as well as refuse from the tunnels, automatically sorting the refuse for recycling.

How to Love the Subways and Els

For the price of admissions New York's subways offer more than a mere ride. Fun and games are available with every trip— even some culture—if you play your MetroCards right and listen to the good vibes.

At once the Underground is an art museum, an architectural wonder, a symphony of sounds and a wondrous world of flora, fauna and diverse humanity.

Unfortunately the majority of straphangers, consumed with reaching their destinations, overlook the attractive means to those ends.

There is much to love about the Subway but to enjoy this romance of the rails one must take his or her mind off the rush and focus on the lush collection of offerings on the Metro menu. The following are some samples: ART: While waiting at your station, check out the art work. The IRT's (A Division) assortment of lines have mosaic-lined platforms, some with excellent examples of a bas relief. Ditto for the BMT (B Division I), particularly at Canal and Chambers Street stations. Multi-colored tile work on the relatively newer IND (B Division II) stations

also is attractive when viewed up close. Some of the IRT mosaics such as the Caravel Santa Maria at Columbus Circle station are almost a century old.

MUSIC: Subway sounds come in two basic styles—rhythm and screech. Rhythm has two sub-divisions of its own, switch-crossings and rail gap-crossings. The latter is responsible for the resonant *clickety-clack* heard when car wheels roll over gaps between the rails. On certain runs, such as the IRT Broadway elevated line between 122nd Street and 128th Street, the percussive beat is roughly equivalent to Gene Krupa's drumming behind Benny Goodman's band in "China Boy" or "After You've Gone."

It is more difficult than ever to find such rhythmic rides because noiseless, gap-less welded rail has been installed in many parts of the system, replacing the old gap kind. Yet some good ones still remain in the Subway. As late as 1997 the IRT Number One Local and Numbers Two and Three Broadway Expresses still offered a marvelous *Click-Clack* from Times Square Station North to 72nd Street depot.

Switches produce a different, cymbal-crash type of percussion. Sometimes the sound is downright loud as in a John Philip Sousa march and on other occasions it can be almost as delicate as a drummer playing his brushes over a high-hat. In either case the rider must train himself to listen carefully as the subway wheels cross the switches, otherwise the sound may not be acutely apparent. It could be either a heavier-sounding *Ba-doom-ba-doom-ba-froom*, or, if the switch-crossing is smoother, a softer *Tsa-soom, tsa-soom*,—the sound you would expect from a background drummer accompanying Nat Cole on "Tea For Two"—is produced.

On the other hand, "The Screech" is a Subway soprano chorus of a different coloratura. It is developed only on sharp turns such as the Q or D trains negotiating the ninety-degree curve into Brighton Beach Station and the Number One circling into South Ferry Terminal. As the steel wheel flange rubs hard against the rail, a C-above-high-C that would be the envy of any Metropolitan Opera diva echoes through the tunnel. With a full orchestra's backing the subway soprano could probably duplicate Bizet's "Carmen."

It must be clear by now that true subway love requires imagination and creativity. Aspects of the Underground that cause annoying reactions in some can converted into an absolute delight by following the Subway-Lovers Guide. Consider some of the following suggestions:

WINDOW GAZING: The objective of every genuine subway buff is establishing a beach head at either the front window of the lead car or the tail window of the last car. Once secured, the front window enables the viewer to imagine all sorts of wonderful things and imbibe all sorts of Subway sights. (SEE LISTING OF SIGNALS BELOW.)

To obtain the best view of the tunnel ahead—or behind you—cup your hands around your eyes, thereby shutting out light from the subway car which might distract you from the inner sanctum. That done, you're ready for the ride.

As the train accelerates, study the tunnel design (round, square, strutted) and the assortment of signs sprinkled along the tube. They offer clues about speed and signals.

The best window-gazing is available on the high-speed subway expresses, bridge-crossings and certain elevated lines. The worst are on boring, subway locals. Highly-rated are the IRT Numbers Two and Three Expresses between Chambers Street Station near City Hall and 96th Street on the Upper West Side. Also, the elevated portions of the Number One Local between 116th Street and 137th Street as well as any of the els that call Coney Island their final destination.

Well-schooled window-gazers learn to appreciate nuances in track work and how they affect the ride. A good example is the curve on the Number Two or Three Express in the middle of the Columbus Circle Station near Central Park. As the express heads north approaching the local station, it encounters a long curve that extends the length of the station. But within that curve—at the epicenter of the station—there's a still even sharper curve!

As the accelerating express hits the inner curve it is almost at top speed and jolts sharply to the left at the turn; but just sharply enough to cause a "Gee-I'm-Glad-It-Stayed-On-The-Track" kind of thought for the window-gazer.

The thrill is neutralized when viewing from the rear window but that is not to suggest that rear-viewing is a worthless pursuit. Actually it is underrated and lots of fun. For the best kicks, try either the F or G tail window as the train heads south from Carroll Street Station up the hill to the Smith-9th Street Depot.

Either back or front window is acceptable for the prize-winning IND A run to Rockaway from Grant Avenue or either the Sea Beach, West End or Brighton outdoor gallops to the Atlantic shore at Stillwell Avenue Terminal.

If you want to play motorman or motorwoman, just grab the door handle and tug on it when the train begins moving. Keep the handle in rhythm with the movements. Use your imagination and you're in business.

Should the front or rear windows be occupied there remain other games to be made of the subway ride. To wit:

KEEPING YOUR BALANCE WHILE STANDING: Since holding poles are not available to every rider on a crowded subway, some straphangers often find themselves at the mercy of the Law of Gravity, track curves and sudden braking. Despite these challenges, it is possible to remain vertical although the exercise requires some athleticism and concentration.

You can also make a game of it by imagining that your subway ride is like a run down a ski slope. The trick in both cases is to maintain your equilibrium. To do so, the commuter must ape the skier. Primary is keeping the knees bent. As the train swerves, brakes or otherwise disturbs your stance, you adjust your "knee-action" to accommodate the gravity pull. Remember: this subway move, like skiing, takes time to learn. By keeping the knees bent and flexible, you can adjust the bend to the turns or stops.

You also can make a game of it with or without a partner. The idea of the contest is to keep your balance longer than your pal or, if you are alone, keep a seconds-count from station to station. Either-way, the game is repeated until you reach your destination. Add up the seconds you remained upright without losing a step for the final score.

RATING THE OPERATOR: There are very good, average and below-average pilots of subway trains. The best are those who get you to your destination speedily and comfortably. In rating the motorman or motorwoman, two elements are to be considered: 1. How smoothly the operator brakes his train to a stop; 2. How swiftly he moves the consist from station to station within the constraints of safety signals.

Some operators are over-cautious or too slow for comfort. They brake too quickly for amber (caution) signals and accelerate too slowly for green (full-speed) lights. The result is a ride that unnecessarily delays the commuter. Operators can be judged by their reaction to the signals with an A, B or C rating usually sufficient.

Judging the braking to a stop is more fun and offers more variety. On a scale of one-to-ten a perfect braking performance is one in which the train enters the station at top speed, quickly decelerates and comes to a stop with such smoothness that a rider can remain vertical without any hint of losing balance.

Only a precious few operators can accomplish a ten—or A—rating. Some brake too soon and too slowly approach the "10" disk at platform's end before stopping. Others do the opposite, roaring into mid-station before actually braking. Thus, the stop tends to be harsh until the actual smooth conclusion is attained.

The worst, at the other end of the scale, are those whose braking hands are insensitive to their riders and their equipment. Their braking is harshest at the conclusion when it most counts. The result is like the culminating thrust of the Cyclone roller coaster at Coney Island.

Ultimately, you are the judge of the motorman. Rating his ride from station to station can take your trip from the banal to the sophisticate within just two stops on your favorite line.

THE BEST ELEVEN RULES OF SUBWAY ETIQUETTE:

1. After entering, move to the middle of the car.

2. Do not block the doorway.

3. Relinquish your seat for pregnant women, senior citizens or parents with small children.

4. Do not play radios—or Walkmen—loud enough to disturb fellow riders.

5. Put all food refuse in your own storage bags; beer cans and peanut shells included.

6. Refrain from screaming to your neighbor across the aisle.

7. Keep your bags, knapsacks or other types of luggage off empty seats.

8. Shoes should not be rested on poles—or seats, for that matter.

9. Holding on to two straps is a no-no.

10. Before entering the open doors, step back to allow exiting passengers to leave.

11. Remember that the words "Excuse me" and "Thank you" are not obsolete but rather pleasant on the ears.

SQUEEZING INTO A PACKED TRAIN: This is a daunting proposition but not nearly as difficult as it appears. The trick is to align yourself with the left or right corners of the door. Squeeze gently inward while always maintaining an air of decorum. Do not push or shove; let the door do it for you! As the door begins to close—listen for the tell-tale chimes—inch forward and allow the closing panels to nudge you over the goal line for a subway touchdown.

HOW TO AVOID SCREAMING WHEN YOUR TRAIN IS LATE: Delays are an inevitable aspect of mass transit, the Subway included. Make the most of them with the following techniques: A. Arm yourself with a daily newspaper or, B. A good book; C. Study the station from its tunnel architecture to the mosaics and tilework; D. Do deep-breathing exercises; E. Nap; F. Remind yourself that the Subway is still cheaper and less nerve-wracking than a cab ride; G. Walk to the end of the platform and examine the tracks inside the tunnel. You may see the alligator that for eight decades has been rumored to be roaming the rails!

HOW TO RELAX AND ENJOY A SARDINE-PACKED RUSH-HOUR SUBWAY CAR: 1. No matter how you shake it, life could be worse; 2. Casually study your fellow passengers. (Guess what each does for a living and where he or she lives;) 3. If you're near a subway map, examine the routes and understand what an amazing system we have; 4. Inhale and see how long you can hold your breath; 5. Visualize dinner at your favorite restaurant.

HOW TO READ A NEWSPAPER ON A PACKED SUBWAY: Before entering the train be sure to have the paper turned to the page you want to read. If it's a tabloid, (*Post, News, Newsday*), fold the paper in half. If it's full-sized (*Times*), fold it in half and then half again.

As you enter the car, hold the paper in front of your chest as if it were a shield. Once the doors close and you're packed in, gently lift the paper from chest level to eye level. The trick is to never, if at all possible, touch your fellow straphanger.

Once the train starts, lower your gaze to the paper. When it arrives at the next station, seize the opportunity and turn to the next page. Repeat as necessary.

READING AND KNOWING THE SUBWAY SIGNS: This too, requires front or rear-window viewings.

Approximately ninety-nine percent of New York's straphangers have no idea what the assortment of tunnel and el signage mean to operators and conductors and, to a certain extent, themselves.

Yet, each sign or symbol is enlightening in some way. Here are some of the most common:

** Blue Light: This signifies that a telephone, emergency alarm, and fire extinguisher are nearby in the tunnel.

** "S" On a Bank of Red, Amber, and Green Signals: This indicates that the signals are synchronized to the speed of the train. It is designed to limit the train's speed in a signal block. If the operator exceeds the required speed the train could be brought to an automatic stop by the safety tripper.

** Yellow Lantern Next to Tracks: This tells the motorman that he must proceed with caution.

** Single Buzz in the Operator's Cabin: This signals him to stop train.

** Double Buzz in the Operator's Cabin: This is the signal to proceed.

** Letter "T" on Disk in Tunnel: Again, this

shows the location of a telephone.

** Letter "R" on a Disk in Tunnel: This tells the motorman to resume travel along the track after a stop.

** Letter "C" on a Disk in Tunnel: This signal tells the motorman to let his train coast.

** String of Six Orange Light Bulbs alongside the Track: Signals caution that there is work in progress along the track ahead. It signifies a slow speed area.

** String of Six Green Light Bulbs alongside the Track: Signals the Motorman to resume speed out of the slow speed area.

** Blinking Amber Light: Same as a steady amber light. Entering a slow area, proceed with caution. Possible work ahead. Blow whistle. Await response.

** Trackman's Response to Operator's Whistle: A wave of a lantern in a horizontal fashion, using any color, signals the train to stop. A wave of the lantern in the vertical position, with any color except red, tells the Motorman to proceed with caution.

** Three Orange Lights strung Together above Station Platform: These lights are "hold lights" informing the conductor to keep the doors open and hold the train in the station until the lights go off.

A Guide to Knowing and Enjoying the Trains

New York City's subway system opened on October 27, 1904, and from that day until the present, New Yorkers have complained about it. While critics of the subway have valid arguments, it is high time someone came along and touted its virtues.

The IRT, BMT, IND divisions—now known as A, BI, BII—together have 842 track miles. The New York subway system is the largest 24-hour-a-day operation of its kind in the world.

For cleanliness, Toronto's underground is tops. Montreal's rubber-tired *Metro* is quieter and Moscow's subway is unquestionably more ornate and beautiful. But when the mechanisms are right, no subway is more exciting, more complex, more diverse, and more colorful than New York's. And it's still the best bargain in transit. What better proof than the fact that a rider can travel from 241st Street and White Plains Road in the Bronx to Coney Island for a lower price than a five-block cab ride?

The Smith-9th Street Station in Brooklyn, at 87.5 feet the highest in the city, offers a breathtaking panorama of lower New York Harbor and Staten Island. At the other extreme is the 191st Street (Broadway) Station in Manhattan, which burrows 180 feet below street level.

Curiosities abound on the subways for those willing to seek them out. For example, after midnight, the Transit Authority operates a rail-grinding machine, designed to smooth the ride by leveling the tracks. When in action, the rail-grinder creates a bizarre visual and audible scene as it shoots sparks and screeches from its Rube Goldberg-like grinding cars.

The rail-grinders first cousin, the vacuum-cleaner train, tours the system each night inhaling steel dust and other debris. If the results aren't obvious at your station it's because there is only one such contraption on the system although a new state-of-the-art vacuum train from France is now in service.

To the train buff, the most exciting aspect of any subway system is the ride itself. Tastes vary, to be sure. Speed fanciers prefer the breathtaking run in the Sixth Avenue tunnel from 34th Street to West Fourth Street; or the IRT's Broadway express dash from 72nd Street to Times Square. Those who prefer scenery combined with long and fast runs lean toward the Rockaway Line, especially the route between Howard Beach and Broad Channel stations—3.7 miles—the longest distance between stops on the system, past the Jamaica Bay Wildlife Refuge.

In general, a good subway or elevated trip must include at least some of the following ingredients: a speedy run, interesting scenery, rhythmical track music, and something to see and do at the end of the line. For example any one of the four lines (B, D, F, N) converging on Stillwell Avenue-Coney Island gets points because both the original Nathan's Famous and the Aquarium are only blocks away.

For children, the outdoor sprint of the Brighton express (Q) from Prospect Park to Sheepshead Bay, is one of the fastest and most exciting rambles on the system.

Similarly, Queens has a splendid elevated express on the Main Street Flushing Line that can match the old BMT's Jamaica run for speed and scenery. But unique is the Dyre Avenue Line in the Bronx. This route was once a section of the old New York, Westchester & Boston Railway, and the original handsome stations remain alongside the dirt embankment.

From the same era is the Rockaway Line, which travels a right-of-way that once belonged to the Long Island Rail Road. This delight has the special attraction of crossing Jamaica Bay at two points before swinging west to the Rockaway Park terminus or east to Far Rockaway.

The lines in the next section are rated as follows (based on scenery, speed, uniqueness, historical qualities, and rhythm):

★★★★★Highest rating
★★★★Among the best
★★★Good, but not great
★★Fair, with minimal fun
★Hardly worth the token

The Lines

★★★★★

Eighth Avenue Express (A):

During the rush hours, from 6:30 am to 9:30 am and from 3:30 pm to 8:00 pm, the train runs from 207th Street, Manhattan, to Lefferts Boulevard or Far Rockaway or Rockaway Park, Queens. These are all express runs. Running times as express during rush hour: 93 minutes.

From 9:30 am to 3:30 pm, the midday hours, the train runs from 207th Street to Lefferts Boulevard or Far Rockaway. Again, acting as an express.

For the evening hours, 8:00 pm to 12 midnight the line runs from 207th Street to Lefferts Boulevard or Far Rockaway. In the Manhattan area, 145th Street to Canal Street, the line acts as an express but after 9:00 pm in Brooklyn the line serves as a local.

On weekends the line again runs from 207th Street to Lefferts Boulevard or Far Rockaway. In Manhattan, the line is an express and in Brooklyn it is a local.

From 12 midnight to 6:30 am, late nights, the line goes from 207th Street to Far Rockaway only. During this time the whole line runs as a local.

There are several reasons why the A Train deserves to be near the top on any list of favorite lines.

1. It's the only route to have had the honor of an enduring jazz tune written—by Billy Strayhorn—about it and further to have the inimitable Duke Ellington Orchestra record a classic version of the song.

2. It's the only route to be included in a mambo—*Un Pequito De Tu Amor*—that eventually reached the top of the charts in Latin music during the early 1950s.

3. When the Independent System was built, the A Train was the first line opened. It ran from Washington Heights to Chambers Street near City Hall and premiered in 1932.

4. It boasts one of the best express runs in the world, between 59th Street-Columbus Circle and 125th St. in Harlem. No less than seven local stops are bypassed on the sprint.

Subway though it is, the quadri-borough (Bronx, Manhattan, Brooklyn, Queens) A comes up for air after crossing the Brooklyn-Queens border. It delivers a dazzling outdoor run from Aqueduct through Howard Beach-JFK and better still across Jamaica Bay—past the Wildlife Refuge—to Broad Channel and the Rockaways.

Sadly, the A never reached its full potential as an express. Originally, the Board of Transportation had planned to use the four tracks running under Fulton Street in Brooklyn as a high-speed run from Utica Avenue to Hoyt-Schermerhorn.

The parallel local track would carry the Fulton Street Local through to Court Street which was to have been the final depot for the local in Brooklyn.

Had this blueprint reached reality, The A would have been the most sensational of express runs. Nevertheless, it still manages to produce assets galore.

One of the best is its bargain ride. It has the longest run—31 miles—for one fare in town. The voyage starts at 207th Street near the top of Manhattan, zips down the island's spine before taking an East River tunnel to Brooklyn.

After leaving Grant Avenue Station in East New York, it crosses the Brooklyn-Queens line and soon turns right for a five-star passage past Ozone Park and into Aqueduct Race Track Station.

Next is Howard Beach-JFK Airport, the jumping off point for a remarkably beautiful setting. The train parallels Cross Bay Boulevard with the Jamaica Bay Wildlife Refuge side by side with the tracks which soon reach Broad Channel and thence the Rockaways.

For a single price of admission, that's quite a bargain.

Hey, this line which had a hit song named after it isn't called A for nothing!

Avenue of the Americas—West End Line (Sixth Avenue) (B) Express:

This line runs from 168th Street, Manhattan, to Coney Island, in Brooklyn. From 168th Street to 59th Street it works as a local and from 59th Street to 36th Street it runs as an express. This

operation schedule is followed during the rush hours and during midday hours.

During the evenings, the train runs from 21st Street/Queensbridge, Queens to Coney Island. Here it serves as an express in both Manhattan and Brooklyn.

Finally, the train runs from 36th Street to Coney Island as a local and connects with the (N) at 36th Street. Running time during rush hour: 76 minutes.

This is not the best BMT (now Division B Group-I) has to offer but it's right up there with *la creme de la creme* of the Brooklyn runs.

The West End boasts some of the richest history of any line in the city with its roots dating back to the mid-19th century.

The current elevated segment in Brooklyn began operation in 1916. It ran from 9th Avenue and 39th St. via New Utrecht Avenue and 86th Street (16.5 miles) to Coney Island.

Its ancestor, the Brooklyn, Bath and Coney Island Railroad was the first steam railroad to run tracks to the Atlantic Ocean at Coney Island. The BBCI opened in 1864 and reached the resort in 1885.

As Alan Paul Kahn and Jack May noted in *The Tracks of New York/Brooklyn Elevated Railroads,*—the BBCI was reorganized in 1885 as the Brooklyn, Bath, and West End Railroad. "It ran from 27th Street and Fifth Avenue, where it connected with Brooklyn horsecars, and from 39th Street and Second Avenue, where it connected with ferry boats to South Ferry, Manhattan, to Tivoli's Hotel in Coney Island. In later years it ran from 'Union Depot' at 36th Street and Fifth Avenue, where it connected with Fifth Avenue el trains. At different times it was known as the 'Dummy Road,' after the steam dummies used for motive power, 'Gunther's Road,' after one of its early developers, and finally, the now familiar 'West End Line.'"

The West End was electrified in 1893. As late as 1916 the West End was running at street level until it was elevated at the end of 1916.

Despite modernization, the West End

through the 20th century has been a sweet ride with many nuances.

At 36th Street Station in Brooklyn there's a marvelous junction where the sister Sea Beach Line continues south while the West End turns east toward 9th Avenue. Daylight, which follows on the West End, offers more novelty than I was accustomed to seeing on the Brighton Line, which surfaces from the tunnel at Prospect Park Station.

When the West End comes out out of the hole it rolls through the kind of delightful maze one expects to find on a model electric train layout but not on a subway system.

On either side tracks climb a concrete incline while others sneak out of curved tunnels. It is a junction worthy of Metro North's Croton-Harmon Station or New Jersey Transit's Port Jervis complex.

This wonderful pot-pourri of tracks and switches gives way to the Ninth Avenue Station followed by the elevated track to Coney Island.

The West End above-ground crisscrosses some of Brooklyn's sweetest neighborhoods, Park Slope, Borough Park, Bay Ridge, Bensonhurst and Dyker Beach before joining its D, F, and N cousins at Stillwell Avenue, Coney Island.

The last leg of the Coney run is special whether one enters Stillwell Station on the Sea Beach, Culver, Brighton Sea Beach or the West End Line.

Any native Brooklynite could sense that more than a half-century earlier steam locomotives pulled their wooden passenger cars to the same web of tracks and for the same purpose, Coney's fun.

As the track plates reverberate over the wheels, a front-window observer tries to guess which switch will take the West End to which terminal track. The delectable *thump-thump* of wheel over switch is the final percussive closing of a marvelous symphony of subway sound. The culminating final rush of air brakes when the B Train reaches the bumper is like a closing crash of the orchestra cymbal.

Eighth Avenue Local (C):

For the rush hours the train runs from Bedford Park Boulevard, the Bronx to Euclid Avenue, Brooklyn. During the midday hours the train runs from 145th Street, Manhattan, to Euclid Avenue. During the evenings, the train runs from 145th Street and Euclid Avenue.

On weekends, the train runs from 168th Street to the World Trade Center. There is no service offered on the (C) during the late night hours. The (A) must be used instead. Running time during rush hour: 107 minutes.

The C local has little to commend. The all underground run from the Bronx through Manhattan to Brooklyn is practical for the rider but boring to the rail fan. Original IND stations lack the variety of BMT and IRT counterparts.

A local run does not have to be tiresome, as proven by the IRT's #1 and #9, but the C is strictly from Snoresville. This is depressing to those who remember that the original C, which opened in 1933, was a rush-hour express, the Bronx's version of the A. At the time the local was called the CC.

When the C made its debut during The Great Depression, it was considered a state of the art design. Joseph Cunningham and Leonard DeHart took due note of it in *The Independent System and City Ownership*.

They noted that the C left its A cousin via a lower level at 145th Street. "It ran via 155th Street, a Harlem River tunnel and River Avenue to the Grand Concourse. It continued north as a three-track line until Bedford Park Boulevard, where a large inspection shed and storage yard were located. Two tracks extended to 205th Street, the new route's terminal. Service was provided by a rush hour C express and a CC local. Officials declared they were gratified with the traffic on the new line and would seek Federal aid (under Depression programs) on future lines."

The aid never came but the C prevailed although the CC disappeared when the C was reduced to local service only.

Avenue of the Americas (Sixth Avenue)—Brighton Express (D):

This line runs from 205th Street, the Bronx, to Coney Island, Brooklyn. During the rush hours the train runs as an express in the Bronx in the peak rush hour direction only and as an express in both directions in Manhattan.

For all other times of the day the line runs as an express in Manhattan between 145th Street and Grand Street and as a local in the Bronx and in Brooklyn. Running time during rush hour: 82 minutes.

It may seem difficult to believe at this turn of a century, but the Sixth Avenue subway, of which the D Train always has been an integral part, once was THE unquestioned jewel of Father Knickerbocker's underground railroad.

If it were possible, stations such as the 47 - 50th Street Rockefeller Center were constructed on a more grand scale than its Eighth Avenue cousins, which it met at Columbus Circle.

The D made its debut in 1940 when the Sixth Avenue Line opened amid pomp, circumstance, and celebrity. Legendary John D. Rockefeller attended the curtain-raiser; which was only appropriate since the financier also had been on board the first IRT in 1904.

Over the years its route has changed as has its attraction to subway buffs. In its current life the D's most attractive virtue is geography. It begins its run just north of the Bronx Botanical Garden, bores under the Harlem River into Manhattan at 145th Street and eventually dives under the East River for its long run through Bklyn. to Coney Island.

The express is at its zippiest best in Manhattan but turns local in Brooklyn for a lengthy, often plodding, ramble along the old Brighton route.

If you have the time, the trip can be scenic and fun, especially from Avenue H south through the arboreal magnificence of Flatbush.

By far the most fun is delivered in Coney Island where the D reaches Odessa-by-the-Sea and Brighton Beach, otherwise known as the largest Russian community in North America. A walk under the el along Brighton Beach Avenue is like being transplanted to the land of caviar and the Kremlin. Just around the corner from Little Russia is the Aquarium, which marks the edge of the amusement area.

That's worth the lengthy trip alone even if you boarded at 205th Street in the Bronx!

Eighth Avenue— Queens Express (E):

This line operates between between Jamaica Center, Queens, and The World Trade Center, Manhattan. In Queens, during the rush hours and midday, it serves as an express while it remains a local in Manhattan.

For the other hours of the day the line operates as an express in Queens between 71st Avenue and Queens Plaza and as a local in Manhattan. Running time during rush hour: 52 minutes.

The original IND Queens Express, The E, made its debut in 1933 in an abridged form to a temporary Roosevelt Avenue Terminal. It eventually was extended to Union Turnpike in 1936 and finally on to Jamaica a year later.

In some ways, the E is as good as an express as you'll find anywhere. The best runs are between Queens Boulevard-Roosevelt Avenue and Roosevelt Avenue-71st Street-Continental Avenue in Forest Hills. At its speediest, this well-planned express route ranks with the A for underground efficiency. The fun ends in Manhattan where the E turns local and laboriously limps downtown to its terminal at the World Trade Center.

Avenue of the Americas (Sixth Avenue)—Queens-Brooklyn—Culver Line Local-Express (F):

This line runs from 179th Street, Queens, to Coney Island, in Brooklyn. For all times of the day, except late nights, it serves as an express from 71st Avenue to Queens Plaza and a local in Manhattan and Brooklyn.

During the late night hours it runs from 21st Street/Queensbridge, Queens, to Coney Island. Running time during rush hour: 88 minutes.

Difficult as it might be to imagine, the part-express part-local F traces some of the most historic trackage in New York City, all of it in Brooklyn.

From Coney Island (Stillwell Avenue) to Ditmas Avenue in Flatbush, the F follows a route that once was known as The Culver Line. Its origins are found in 1878 when the Prospect Park and Coney Island Railroad was constructed by Andrew R. Culver, from 20th Street and Ninth Avenue to Cable's Hotel in the West Brighton section of Coney Island. The Culver Terminal—at Surf Avenue and West 5th Street—was adjacent to an amusement park featuring the world's first roller coaster.

Before the 19th Century had ended the Culver was sharing northern terminals with the nearby West End Line at 36th and Fifth Avenue and 39th Street and Second Avenue. In 1899 the Culver switched from steam to electrification.

The Culver Line remained at surface (street) level until 1919 when the cars were transferred to the new elevated structure which ran from Ditmas Avenue to Kings Highway in March and Avenue X in May.

Its present incarnation as part-subway part-el came about when the IND's Smith Street (subway) Line was linked to the Culver el by a ramp completed in 1950. Thus, the F now leaves its former terminus at Church Avenue and climbs to the surface and ultimately the el at Ditmas.

The F enjoys the same nifty-express run in Queens as its sister (Eighth Avenue) E train. What sets apart the F is its varied meander through Brooklyn. The most arresting feature is the climb out of the Carroll Street subway portal to the languorously sweet curve leading up to Smith - 9th Street Station.

A rider standing at the front window is in position to gaze off to the right at a panoply of docks, highways and, of course, the Statue of Liberty. At the crest the F pulls in to a massive concrete station 87 feet above the surface and Gowanus Canal. Apart from the "Suicide Curve" on the defunct Ninth Avenue Line at 110th Street, the Smith-9th viaduct over Gowanus Canal is the all-time champ for height.

The F also stops at the 4th Avenue Station, also above ground before returning to the subway as it burrows under Park Slope.

After a stop at Church Avenue, which once was the final depot for the IND in Brooklyn, the F climbs a ramp until it is on the original el structure at Ditmas Avenue. It then follows the old Culver route along McDonald Avenue until it reaches Coney Island. It then heads right after the Neptune Avenue Station to the double-decked West Eighth Street terminal across from the New York Aquarium. From there it is one stop to the last station—Stillwell Avenue Coney Island—and Nathan's hot dogs, the Cyclone rollercoaster and other goodies-by-the-sea.

Brooklyn-Queens Crosstown Local—(G):

This line runs from 71st Avenue/Continental Avenue, Queens, to Smith Street/9th Street, Brooklyn, during the rush hours, midday's and evenings.

On weekends, the line operates from

Court Square, Queens, to Smith Street/9th Street and during the late night hours the line operates from 179th Street, Queens, to Smith/9th Streets. Running time during rush hour: 49 minutes.

The most attractive feature of this otherwise drab two-borough local is its orbiting out of the tunnel south of Carroll Street Station in the Carroll Gardens neighborhood. Like the F-Train, which uses the same tracks, the G climbs to what once was the most modern elevated station in the city.

From the Smith-9th depot platform, a commuter can enjoy an unparalleled vista of Downtown Brooklyn, New York Bay and Red Hook's docks.

Otherwise, the G—originally christened the GG—offers little of interest other than an unusual middle (third) track at the Bedford-Nostrand Station. It was meant to link with a proposed Bedford Avenue Line which never was built.

One other distinction: the G is the only line to tunnel under Newtown Creek, which separates Brooklyn and Queens, while also bridging over Gowanus Canal!

Nassau Street Express—(J):

This line runs from the Jamaica Center, Queens, to Broad Street, Manhattan during the rush hours, midday hours, evenings, and late nights. On weekends service runs from Jamaica Center to Chambers Street, Manhattan. For rush hour and during the middays the J acts as an express from Myrtle Avenue to Marcy Avenue in the peak direction only and as an express throughout Manhattan.

For the evening hours the train becomes a local all along the line. On weekends it also acts as a local, terminating at Chambers Street with transfers to the 4, 5, and 6.

Late nights the train is a local, to Chambers Street only on weekend nights.

Running time during rush hour: 48 minutes.

In an earlier era this was known as the "Broadway-Brooklyn" Line although it crosses the Queens border at 75th Street-Elderts Lane Station near the once-famous Dexter Park baseball field, home of the Bushwicks.

The Broadway Line's lineage is rich, dating back to the late 19th Century when the Brooklyn Elevated Railroad began erecting els—starting with one that ran from Fulton Ferry to Van Siclen Avenue—in the most populated parts of The City of Brooklyn.

From its terminus at Broadway (Brooklyn) Ferry along the East River, the Broadway elevated line was built in 1888 and by 1910 it moved in a southeasterly direction linking with many other routes. Moving west, it crossed the newly-constructed Williamsburg Bridge to an underground subway-trolley terminal at Delancey Street, in Manhattan.

The Myrtle Avenue Line met it at Broadway and several blocks later the Lexington Avenue Local joined it for a run to Manhattan Junction in the East New York section of Brooklyn. From there the Broadway Line rolled east to what then was its final depot at Cypress Hills.

Like other parts of Brooklyn's vast elevated web, the Broadway Line underwent major changes starting with the Dual Contracts of 1913. A third (express) track was added to the Broadway Line between Marcy Avenue Station and Manhattan Junction (later Eastern Parkway) Station.

Where once the Broadway Line terminated at 168th Street it now concludes its run at Jamaica Center (Parsons-Archer) but for the most part the elevated section remains the same as it did 80 years ago.

For movie and television buffs, it's worth noting that the J passes the early homes of Mae West and Jackie Gleason. The express run from Myrtle Avenue to Marcy Avenue down the center track is always a kick.

Avenue of the Americas (Sixth Avenue) Express—(Q):

This line runs as an express from 21st Street/Queensbridge, Queens, to Brighton Beach, Brooklyn, during the rush hours and midday hours. During the evenings there is no service offered after 9 P.M. and the B must be used for Queens and the D for Brooklyn.

On weekends there is no service offered at all as is the case during the late nights. On weekends the B can be used for Queens and the D for Brooklyn while during the late night hours the F can be used for Queens and the D for Brooklyn. Rush hour running time: 52 minutes.

At its best, the Brighton Line was the belle of the BMT. In the 1930's and early 1940's it featured BMT Standard cars with a front window that opened. This afforded train buffs a thrill unmatched on most lines.

The Standards are gone but the Brighton Line remains one of the most pleasurable on the system especially when it heads south from Grand Street in Manhattan, crosses the Manhattan Bridge and then spins toward the ocean.

When top speed is attained under Prospect Park, from Seventh Avenue to Prospect Park Station, the Q is just getting its second wind.

By far the best of the Brighton is evident once it snakes out of the tunnel under Flatbush Avenue and Empire Boulevard. From that point on south the Q traces the route of its original Brighton Line which opened in 1878.

At that time it linked Atlantic Avenue in Brooklyn—connecting with the Long Island Railroad and the Hotel Brighton in Coney Island. It later was reorganized as the Brooklyn and Brighton Beach Railroad and in 1896 was extended north from Atlantic Avenue to Fulton Street.

The present Brighton configuration between Prospect Park and the ocean came about as a result of the 1913 Dual Contract agreement. It provided for re-building the two-track open cut between Prospect Park and Church Avenue to a two-mile four-track open cut. The four tracks would climb a hill to an embankment south of Newkirk Avenue.

To this day that stretch offers myriad rail-fan opportunities. From Prospect Park to Church Avenue, the express lumbers over a bouncy switch arrangement before picking up speed at the Parkside Avenue curve. A couple of small tunnels allow the Q a now-you-see-me-now-you-don't thrill before bombing into the Church Avenue Express stop.

From Church Avenue to Newkirk Station the Q remains in the open cut. Special sounds abound but none are more pleasant than the rhythm of wheels over rails as the express negotiates the sweet left-hand curve at Beverly Road station then straightens out at Cortelyou Road for a final sprint to Newkirk.

Then the fun really starts. Up, up, and away. The Q departs Newkirk climbing the hill to the embankment where a panorama of Flatbush greets the eye. On the left is Avenue H station with the towers of Brooklyn College in the background. On the right are tree-lined streets and beyond the grand boulevard Ocean Parkway.

Riding speedily above Flatbush, the Q bypasses Avenue H, Avenue J and Avenue M on its gallop to the express stop at Kings Highway. The dance continues with more passes at Avenue U and Neck Road before arriving at Sheepshead Bay, the prelude to Coney Island joy.

14th Street —Canarsie Local—(L):

This line runs from 8th Avenue, Manhattan, to Rockaway Parkway, Brooklyn, as a local at all times of the day and all days of the week. Running time during rush hour: 41 minutes.

Among the more eclectic parts of town, distant Canarsie has over more than a century alternately been a romantic resort and—in later years—an outpost of some derision.

In the late 1930's the mere mention of Canarsie by Brooklynites in areas such as Williamsburg and Crown Heights moved people to gales of laughter, if not tears.

Through it all, Canarsie has been both a place to go and a place to live. The current Canarsie Line follows a route dating back to the last year of the Civil War (1865), when the Brooklyn and Rockaway Beach Railroad was built, linking East New York and Canarsie Landing. At that point a connecting ferry floated over Jamaica Bay to Rockaway Beach.

In time, the portion of tracks between Canarsie and Pitkin Avenue became part of the Brooklyn Rapid Transit, predecessor to the BMT.

However, the present 14th Street-Canarsie Line did not come about until a 14.82 mile construction segment was approved in 1913. It would become a two-track subway linking Sixth Avenue and 14th Street in Manhattan to Brooklyn via an East River Tunnel. The subway would continue underground before turning el, connecting with the Eastern Parkway Junction and moving out to Canarsie. However, the final route was not determined until 1923. The massive Eastern Parkway Station was completed in 1919.

The "new" Canarsie Line itself didn't open until 1928. Opening ceremonies featured an auto parade on Bushwick Avenue in Brooklyn, and a rally at Irving Square Park in Manhattan.

While the current 14th Street-Canarsie Line is hardly the system's best, the line offers some scenic wonders not the least of which is the breathtaking Broadway Junction at Eastern Parkway and the fun ride to Canarsie and its ground level terminal at Rockaway Parkway.

Broadway Local (N)— Sea Beach Line:

For the rush hours and midday, this line runs from Ditmars Boulevard, Queens, to Coney Island, Brooklyn. In Queens and in Manhattan the line runs as a local and in Brooklyn the line runs as an express.

On weekends and during the evenings and late nights the line runs from Ditmars Boulevard to Coney Island as a local throughout.

What could be more romantic than a subway named "The Sea Beach Line?"

What could be more grand than a train that chugged and puffed its way to the Sea Beach Palace Hotel in Coney Island?

The seemingly prosaic N-Broadway Local of the late 1990's actually is the Sea Beach Line whose 100th birthday was celebrated in 1979!

A century earlier it all began with the New York and Sea Beach Railroad which ran from 65th Street in Bay Ridge, where it connected with steamboats to South Ferry and to Coney Island (Sea Palace Hotel). Serious construction on the Sea Beach Line took place in the late 1870s with steam trains plying a regular route to Coney Island's shores. The locomotives remained in vogue until 1897. In that year trolleys made their appearance along the same run, replaced by elevated trains in 1907.

All beach-bound rolling stock terminated at the Sea Beach depot—between the Culver and West End terminals—in Coney Island and did so until 1909. In 1910 it moved to the nearby West End terminal.

The major breakthrough for Sea Beach modernization came as part of the Dual Contracts of 1913 which provided for a 16.05 mile replacement of the surface lines with a four track open cut line from the Fourth Avenue subway (now used by the B, M and R Lines as well as the N) to Coney Island.

At 59th Street (Brooklyn) Station, The Sea Beach turns left (East) taking its own route to the shore.

While construction was underway on the Sea Beach cut in 1914, the Fourth Avenue subway was being completed. Both attracted keen attention because the grade-separated Sea Beach speedway would result in the fastest rapid transit run to Manhattan over a four-track subway-express line.

Better still, opening of the Sea Beach also promised the debut of the Brooklyn Rapid Transit's fleet of new 67-foot long steel subway cars. With amenities never seen before on any line in New York, the BRT "Standards" would represent the acme in subway car construction for years.

At noon on June 22, 1915 service began on the new Sea Beach Line. It not only featured state of the art rolling stock but long, handsome concrete open cut stations, a magnificent right-of-way and a trans-East River connection via the Manhattan Bridge.

On May 30, 1919 the Stillwell Avenue elevated terminal was completed enabling the Sea Beach Line to have a new, permanent depot on the Atlantic Ocean.

Since then the Sea Beach Line has undergone many metamorphoses. Where once it operated from Coney Island to Times Square under the BMT flag, the contemporary Sea Beach is a tri-borough route of excellent variety.

At its Northern depot in Astoria, The N departs Ditmars Avenue elevated station which opened as part of the IRT Dual Contracts expansion to Queens. The above-ground trip over 31st Street takes passengers through one of the city's most diverse neighborhoods before dipping under the East River through the 60th Street Tunnel which was completed in 1920 and its first stop in Manhattan at Fifth Avenue and Central Park South.

The N then heads South on the original Broadway BMT subway route before entering the Montague Street Tunnel—connecting Whitehall Street Station in Manhattan to Lawrence Street (MetroTech) Station in Brooklyn—which was completed in 1920 as well.

In Downtown Brooklyn The N also stops at the DeKalb Avenue junction which has been altered over the years to accommodate the many converging BMT Lines. The underground run through Brooklyn hits

daylight along its original routing and follows the the same open cut right-of-way that welcomed the Standards in 1915.

The beauty part is the homestretch over the ancient, rickety el from 86th Street to the Stillwell Avenue terminal.

Make no mistake, The N is not for speed merchants but it offers a cavalcade of subway and el vistas matched by few lines.

Nassau Street Local (M)— Myrtle Avenue Line:

During the rush hours this line runs from Metropolitan Avenue, Queens, to Bay Parkway, Brooklyn. For the midday hours the line runs from Metropolitan Avenue to Chambers Street, Manhattan.

On weekends, and during the late nights and evenings, the line runs from Metropolitan Avenue to Myrtle Avenue, Brooklyn.

One of the oldest elevated lines in the city, The Myrtle Avenue run is a far cry from its original trail linking Downtown Brooklyn with Ridgewood.

The Union Elevated Railroad—a subsidiary of the Brooklyn Elevated Railroad —built the first Myrtle El in 1888. Its western terminal was at Sands Street. From there it moved over Myrtle until Grand Avenue where it connected with the Lexington Avenue elevated line which carried the trains to Broadway (Brooklyn).

Its popularity was instant and soon the Myrtle Avenue Line was extended along Myrtle and beyond Grand Avenue to a junction with the Broadway Line on the Williamsburg-Bushwick-Bedford-Stuyvesant border. Where once the Myrtle route dipped to street level beyond Wyckoff Avenue station, it was moved up to a new elevated structure in 1915. The el carried the trains until a downhill alongside the Fresh Pond yards before the lope to Metropolitan Avenue depot.

Eventually, the Myrtle Line went beyond Sands Street and rolled over the Brooklyn Bridge to a huge terminal at Park Row across from New York's City Hall.

A looping el connection was constructed at Myrtle-Broadway to enable the heavy, steel BMT Standard cars to operate along the double-track route from Metropolitan Avenue to Broadway and then switch to the three-track run from Broadway to the Williamsburg Bridge and on to Manhattan. The elevated loop rubbed shoulders with private dwellings as it curved south from Myrtle and then west on to Broadway for its journey to Manhattan.

The original Myrtle Avenue El remained intact through the World War II years using such vintage open-platformed rolling stock as 1907 Jewetts as well as cars made by Laconia and Osgood Bradley. Ancient stations including Grand, Tompkins, Nostrand, Franklin and Sumner Avenues featured pot-bellied stoves and carried the same aura as the Third Avenue el cousins in Manhattan.

Conductors stationed between the cars pulled iron levers to open the twin gates which constantly had to be oiled for leverage. This throwback to an earlier era remained a part of the Myrtle Line's existence until April 11, 1958 when the Transit Authority replaced all the antique cars with rebuilt Q-type cars which required only one conductor. They remained in use until service on the Myrtle Avenue el was terminated from Sands Street to Myrtle-Broadway on October 4, 1969 and that section of the elevated was then razed.

Without the original el, the M Myrtle Avenue Line—like the old, gray mare—ain't what she used to be. It still operates from Metropolitan Avenue in Middle Village and that's the fun, outdoor part.

The romp above Ridgewood, Bushwick and Williamsburg still is as pleasant as ever including the climb over the Williamsburg Bridge to Delancey Street and the subway stroll to Chambers Street in the Wall Street area.

En route to Brooklyn again, The M makes a final Manhattan stop at Broad Street before burrowing into the Montague Street tunnel through Downtown Brooklyn and the Fourth Avenue Subway. South of 36th Street it follows the West End tracks to its terminus at Bay Parkway in a Bensonhurst community that has remained virtually the same as was a half-century ago when the original Myrtle Avenue El was in its prime.

Franklin Avenue Shuttle (S):

This line runs from Franklin Avenue to Prospect Park, Brooklyn.

Once a key, early-century link between Park Row in Manhattan and Coney Island in Brooklyn, the Franklin Avenue Line has lost most of its luster of yesteryear but, like The Little Engine That Could, it has surmounted a few obstacles.

During its halcyon decades just after the turn of the century and through the World War II years, the Franklin route was an offshoot of the Fulton Street El which was built by the Kings County Elevated in 1888.

A connection at Franklin and Fulton Streets enabled Brighton Beach-bound trains to switch right (South) and proceed first along elevated tracks and then to a downhill where the tracks eventually were depressed into an open cut near Prospect Park. At that point the line continued South to the shore.

Changes would be made along the route including reconstruction of the Prospect Park Station in 1918. It would result in the present four-track, two-platform local-express station at Prospect Park. However, the transformation included construction of a 90-degree S-curve under Malbone Street (now Empire Boulevard) which was the site that same year of the calamitous Brooklyn Rapid Transit disaster killing 97 riders.

Through service from Fulton Street on to the Franklin Line was discontinued in 1920. At that point the Franklin Line took on a completely different character, now limited only to Brooklyn and with Fulton Street as its new terminus.

The Franklin Line hereafter would offer two types of service. The best was an express from Prospect Park to Brighton Beach. Riders always could tell it was "The Franklin Avenue Express" because of the big, white disk affixed to the front car. The FAE was a six-car unit—ancient station platforms along the start of the run did not permit longer trains—and one of the most delightful excursions on the system.

The other service was a shuttle connecting Fulton Street with Prospect Park. It covered only three other stations—Dean Street, Park Place and Consumers Park—but was a convenient as a testing ground for experimental equipment such as the stainless steel Budd Zephyr which operated on the route for several years during World War II and thereafter.

Once the express was removed, the Franklin Avenue Line became no more than a forgotten spur—and still is. It has fallen on hard times and became so little used that the Transit Authority threatened to close the line altogether.

Neighborhood civic groups protested loud enough and long enough to keep the line alive although just barely. Except for historians and rail buffs who want to re-visit the site of the Malbone Street wreck or study tiny, backyard, *Toonerville*-type operation, the Franklin Avenue Shuttle is not highly recommended for its ride.

42nd Street Shuttle (S):

This line runs from Times Square to Grand Central in Manhattan. There is no service during the late nights. During those hours the Number Seven is the replacement.

This not only is the most famous rail shuttle in North America but also a line—short though it is—rich in historic significance.

New York's original subway crawled up the East Side of the island and swung sharply to the left (West) at 42nd Street under Grand Central Station. It continued West on what presently is the Shuttle route up to Times Square where it turned sharply to the right (North) and continued up Broadway.

In the IRT's original 1904 form, there was no such spur as the Shuttle. But when the Dual Contracts were approved and executed, a new branch of the IRT—the Lexington Avenue Line—extended North of the original route at Grand Central. This "H" System of two separate lines—East Side IRT and West Side IRT—would be linked in the middle by a shuttle.

On August 1, 1918 the "H" System was set in motion. No longer would the IRT line proceed from the East side to the West side. Instead, it would run all the way up the East and West sides, respectively.

However, the "H" would be crossed by the Shuttle which would run from Grand Central to Times Square and back over the existing track from the original IRT subway.

From opening day the Shuttle was an instant hit. On August 2, 1918 it proved so popular that it had to be closed because there were too many people using it.

While planners sought ways and means to relieve the overcrowding the Shuttle remained closed. Finally, on September 28, 1918 it re-opened utilizing colored bands to lead passengers from the East or West Side trains to the Shuttle. In later years colored lights would be added as guidelines.

Although the Shuttle has been manually operated for most of its existence an assortment of suggestions have been made over the years to improve its service. One attempt to install an automated Shuttle was aborted following a suspicious fire that—some cynics suspect—allegedly was ignited by workers who opposed it because they were threatened with job loss.

Observant Shuttle riders will find many remnants of the original subway including a special door with KNICKERBOCKER lettering above it. The door once led to the Hotel Knickerbocker. Other vestiges of the original subway line abound at both the Times Square and Grand Central ends of the Shuttle.

It's worth a ride even though the trip from station to station only takes a minute.

★★★

The Rockaway Park Shuttle(S):

This shuttle runs from Broad Channel to Rockaway Park in Queens. It is a local that connects with the (A) at the Broad Channel Station.

While it only travels from Broad Channel to Rockaway Park, this version of the S is the most scenic shuttle in the city. It skirts Jamaica Bay before taking a right turn (south) to the Beach 90th Street Station, the Beach 98th Street Station, and the Beach 105th Street Station before finishing its sweet little journey in Rockaway Park. As shuttles go, this one can truly be called a scenic railway sprinkled with salt air!

★★

(R)—Broadway Local, BMT Fourth Avenue (Brooklyn) Line:

The line runs from 71st-Continental Avenue in Forest Hills, Queens to 95th Street in Bay Ridge, Brooklyn.

Rail transit service to the Bay Ridge section of Brooklyn began late in the 19th Century when the steam-powered New York and Sea Beach Railroad connected the 61st Landing—near The Narrows section of New York Bay—with Coney Island.

The Fifth Avenue Elevated, which originated in Downtown Brooklyn, was extended to 38th Street and Fifth Avenue by 1890. It reached 65th Street in Bay Ridge by 1900 and was the sole rapid transit service to Bay Ridge and the developing Brooklyn dock area.

It wasn't until the Dual Contracts were approved in 1913 that Bay Ridge would be the depot of a major league rapid transit system. Blueprints called for a four-track subway from the Manhattan Bridge through a junction at DeKalb Avenue and then to proceed to Fourth Avenue.

The new subway would run under Fourth Avenue from Pacific Street near the Downtown Area to 89th Street in Bay Ridge. South of 62nd Street in Brooklyn the line would become two-tracked although provisions were made for eventual four-track operation. The run would encompass about 24 miles.

By January 1916 sufficient progress had been made to inspire city officials to ride a six-car train from Chambers Street in Manhattan to the 86th Street depot in Bay Ridge. The event was significant enough for Bay Ridge High School to host a dinner commemorating the opening of service.

The R Train rolls over much the same route today although it now terminates at 95th Street in Bay Ridge. Had BRT-BMT plans ever been realized the line would have continued under The Narrows and linked with the Staten Island Rapid Transit. Unfortunately, the Brooklyn-Staten Island subway tunnel was never built.

A three-borough subway, The R Line begins its run in the north at 71st-Continental Avenue in Forest Hills following the G Line tracks. It branches off in Manhattan and slothfully heads South along the original BMT Broadway Line before heading to Brooklyn through the Montague Street Tunnel.

The first two-thirds of the trip have little to commend but the run through Bay Ridge offers some nice touches, station-wise and otherwise.

Number One-Number Nine
Broadway IRT Local:

This line runs from 242nd Street, the Bronx, to South Ferry, Manhattan, the (1) as a local and the (9) as a local with skip stop service between 242nd Street and 137th Street.

During the rush hours the (9) is in service while during all other hours only the (1) is in service. The rush hour running time for the (1) is 53 minutes with the rush hour running time for the (9) being slightly shorter.

Very few locals have as much to commend, both historically and visually, as The Number One. Nor can many claim that they also are pseudo-expresses.

The IRT's original local, The Number 1 confines its run to the boroughs of Manhattan and The Bronx, running from South Ferry near the Staten Island Ferry to 242nd Street and Van Cortlandt Park in The Bronx.

Because it was the first, the Number One boasts many architectural wonders, not the least of which is the magnificent steel arch supporting the 125th Street Station at Broadway in Harlem.

Nearby the local glides through a giant concrete arch tunnel under Broadway between 116th and 122nd Streets before the train reaches daylight at the portal and proceeds along the trestle which overlooks the Hudson River and New Jersey.

Built for the most part by the open trench method, the tunnel housing The Number One was built with the finest material available using the best designs and after intensive testing.

Its subtle beauty is apparent in station after station where mosaics such as the caravel Santa Maria (at 59th Street-Columbus Circle) adorn the walls.

Some of the very deep stations—168th Street and 181st Street —required elevators and still do.

But the Number One Line—including Times Square Station and the southern portion thereafter—does not fully follow the original route. After the Dual Contracts were signed, the newer portion of the local was extended to the Southern tip of Manhattan and now follows that run to South Ferry.

Working with its sister Number Nine in rush-hours, Number One employs a *skip-stop* system enabling it to bypass every other station for a spell up north and thereby give an express feel to an otherwise slower pace.

Nevertheless, as locals go, Number One is speedy for its genre with nifty long runs, especially those through the deep arch tunnels of Upper Manhattan—145th Street to 157th Street is one of the better sprints—and across the Broadway Bridge at Spuyten Duyvil. If you stop at 125th Street from the platform you can observe marvelous Morningside Heights vistas. On a clear day you may even catch a glimpse of offbeat messages on Fairway's electronic billboard while riding the el past West 133rd Street.

South of Times Square, The Number One turns boring although it passes innumerable sites such as the World Trade Center, Bowling Green, Madison Square Garden and Battery Park.

Its most riveting aspects can be found north of the 116th Street (Columbia University) Station where The One meets daylight only to return to the tunnel beyond the 125th Street Station. At 168th Street one can still view vestiges of the lavish appointments, including hanging light fixtures, which were part of the original station.

When the train climbs out again in upper Manhattan, views are priceless, especially in the Inwood area north of the Dyckman St.reet Staion

As locals go, The Number One is fully deserving of its title!

Number Two, The IRT Flatbush Avenue Express— White Plains Road Line:

This line runs from 241st Street, the Bronx, to Flatbush Avenue, Brooklyn, during all hours of the day. In the Bronx and in Brooklyn the line serves as a local while in Manhattan it runs as an express.

While the Bronx was not exactly a frontier town at the turn of the century (19th Century, that is) it still was filled with farm land and waiting to be exploited by real estate interests.

It was a fertile place for development, made more so by construction of new subway-elevated lines including the White Plains Road Line which was a major element in the 1913 Dual Contracts plan.

A 13.7 mile route was laid out which, among other things, straddled Bronx Park and more particularly The Bronx Zoo. El planners had to describe something of a detour around The Zoo because zoological experts were concerned that reverberations from the elevated line would upset the animals.

The terminal at 241st Street (Wakefield) would be the northernmost stop of either subway or el. On its southern route, The Number Two would follow new (Dual Contract) construction from Atlantic Avenue in Downtown Brooklyn continue under Flatbush Avenue to Eastern Parkway and then swing East to Buffalo Avenue. At that juncture, a two-track branch would head South on Nostrand Avenue, terminating at Nostrand and Flatbush Avenues.

By the end of World War I considerable progress had been made in constructing the White Plains Road Line and it was completed in 1920 with much the same trackage available today on The Number Two.

One of the best New York expresses, the Number Two has much to commend, especially its steel pathway through the South Bronx and then the last leg over White Plains Road north of The Bronx Zoo.

Riders will get a glimpse of a part of the city that in many ways looks the way it did a half-century ago. The run along Bronx Park's perimeter offers an arboreal delight to the eyes followed by the inevitable slide into the tunnel for a cruise through Spanish Harlem (*El Barrio*) and thence a right turn (west) under the Northern portion of Central Park to an eventual climb up a hill into the 96th Street and Broadway subway station.

From 96th Street to Chambers Street, The Number Two delivers some of the finest express runs in the world, including 96th to 72nd; then 72nd to Times Square; 34th to 14th and 14th to Chambers.

At that point The Number Two slows for curves that eventually lead to the IRT's second (Clark Street) tunnel to Brooklyn which was opened on April 15, 1919.

The trip to Flatbush Avenue is rather prosaic by comparison and somewhat annoying to those who envisioned that someday the line would follow a natural extension south along Nostrand Avenue to Avenue U and Sheepshead Bay. That plan never was realized but The Number Two nevertheless is first-rate.

Number Three, The IRT Lenox— New Lots Avenue Express:

The number (3) line operates between 148th Street, Manhattan, and New Lots Avenue, Brooklyn, during most of the day. In Manhattan it serves as an express while in Brooklyn it acts as a local.

On Sundays the (3) only runs between 148th Street and 135th Street until 10:00 A.M.. During the late night hours there is no service whatsoever on the (3) and the (2) must be taken instead.

The Number Three Express does not venture as far north as its sister line, The Number Two, but it is a beauty nonetheless and compensates with other assets.

To begin with, The Number Three—like The Number One IRT Local—is an original. It began its run at City Hall, ventured along August Belmont's primary route up to Grand Central, then swung to Times Square and rolled up Broadway.

Whereas The Number One continued straight ahead to Upper Manhattan, The Number Three swung under Number One's tracks, headed east under Central Park and emerged at the 110th Street and Lenox Avenue subway stop. It then proceeded north up Lenox to the terminal at 145th Street, adjoining the Harlem River.

When the Dual Contracts of 1913 provided for an extension of the IRT's subway-elevated lines in Brooklyn, tunnels were extended under Eastern Parkway beyond Utica Avenue. The subway portion ended at the Buffalo Avenue portal from where the trains climbed to the el that continued to New Lots Avenue in East New York. This segment was completed in 1922 and remains in use although extensions beyond New Lots Avenue never were realized.

Since The Number Three meets The Number Two at 96th Street in Manhattan, the pair of expresses zoom along the same tracks from The Upper West Side through Franklin Avenue in Brooklyn where they diverge; Number Two heading to Flatbush Avenue and Number Three to New Lots.

If, therefore, Number Two is a winner, the same holds for Number Three. In fact, Number Three holds an edge when one takes into account its more scenic outdoor Brooklyn homestretch compared with Number Two's dreary waltz to Flatbush.

By contrast, Number Two wins on the Northern section since Number Three terminates underground while Number Two offers first-rate sightseeing from Bronx Park

and beyond. Conclusion: Both are excellent rides.

Number Four, IRT Lexington Avenue—Jerome Avenue—Woodlawn Express:

This line runs from Woodlawn, the Bronx, to Utica Avenue, Brooklyn. In the Bronx it runs as a local while it is an express in both Brooklyn and Manhattan. The 138th Street Station is skipped during the rush hours in the peak rush hour direction only.

On Sundays, the (4) operates to New Lots Avenue until 10:00 AM. For late night travel, the number 4 goes from Woodlawn, the Bronx, to New Lots Avenue, Brooklyn, as a local.

When subways planners decided to extend the IRT North of Grand Central Station, the plan was to operate four tracks to 125th Street and Lexington Avenue. A tunnel then would be burrowed to the Bronx at 135th Street under The East River.

In The Bronx, the line would carry three tracks from 135th Street to Jerome Avenue and which point it would become an elevated line over Jerome Avenue to a depot adjoining Van Cortlandt Park at Woodlawn.

The line was completed to Woodlawn Road in 1918, giving the IRT an exemplary express in Manhattan and an efficient local in the Bronx as well as a local to Brooklyn.

The result is another splendid bit of railroadiana. The Number Four ride south is wonderful—so are the names such as Mosholu Parkway, Kingsbridge Road—and even includes a stop at Yankee Stadium, 161st Street.

More modern than its West Side counterpart, the Number Four express to Grand Central hustles from 125th Street to 86th Street and then from 86th to 59th Street. Following Grand Central, Number Four plies the original 1904 express tracks to City Hall.

But that's not the end of the historic trail. After curving past Bowling Green and South Ferry, Number Four enters the first subway tunnel ever built under the East River.

The ribbon-cutting took place on January 10, 1908 when the first train rolled into Borough Hall station in Brooklyn. This was a momentous occasion, hailed by a capacity crowd on the train as well as thousands of New Yorkers who understood the significance of the accomplishment.

Still in use, that same Borough Hall station services The Number Four which continues into Crown Heights, terminating at Utica Avenue Station.

That's not exactly as scenic as the ride on to New Lots but Number Four has nothing about which to be ashamed. It provides many pleasures and much speed; precisely what a three-borough express is expected to do.

★★★★★

Number Five, IRT Express, Dyre Avenue—Lexington Avenue— Flatbush Avenue Line:

During the rush hours this line runs from 238th Street or Dyre Avenue, the Bronx, to Flatbush Avenue, Brooklyn. It is an express in Manhattan and express in the Bronx in the peak direction only.

For the midday hours the line runs from Dyre Avenue, the Bronx, to Bowling Green, Manhattan. During these times it runs as a local in the Bronx and an express in Manhattan. During the late night hours the line runs from Dyre Avenue to East 180th Street, the Bronx. Here it is a local that connects with the (2) train at East 180th Street.

The newest—and most suburban-looking— of the IRT Lines came about by default. In 1938, the four-track New York, Westchester and Boston Railroad folded after being in operation for 26 years.

When opened the N.Y.W.&B. RR offered a state of the art right-of-way that still was effective and efficient when operations ceased just prior to the start of World War II.

Seizing the opportunity, New York City annexed the line and gradually turned it into an IRT operation to a northern depot at Dyre Avenue, Eastchester.

The Number Five is the latest in a series of trains which have utilized the N.Y.W.&B. RR route and it is a beaut.

Though running local in the Bronx, Number Five passes through an urban countryside before returning to the more harsh backdrop of the South Bronx.

Once it meets the main Lexington Avenue Line in Manhattan, The Number Five turns express and enjoys the same Mercury-like run as The Number Four all the way down the island.

It stays on the same route with Number Four in Brooklyn until they part at the switch following Franklin Avenue. Heading right (South), Number Five concludes its lengthy, diverse trek at Flatbush-Nostrand terminal adjoining Brooklyn College.

The bucolic Bronx segment and the madcap Manhattan express run give Number Five a five-star rating.

★★★

Number Six, IRT Pelham Bay, Brooklyn Bridge Local— Part-Time Express:

This Lexington Avenue Local runs from Pelham Bay Park or Parkchester, the Bronx, to the Brooklyn Bridge, Manhattan. The number six to Parkchester runs as a local while the number six to Pelham Bay Park runs as an express in the Bronx in the peak rush hour direction only. It is also a local in Manhattan.

During the midday hours, evenings, and weekends the line runs from Pelham Bay Park to the Brooklyn Bridge as a local. For the late night hours the line runs from Pelham Bay Park to

----

While the Bronx does not feature any amusement area nor beach remotely close to matching the festive Coney Island, it does have Orchard Beach and Pelham Bay Park.

Neither sits on the Atlantic Ocean but Orchard Beach is a pleasant swimming area and Pelham Bay Park is one of New York's many underrated chunks of parkland, ranking in beauty with Central and Prospect Parks, among others.

When the 1913 Dual Contracts provided for a subway-elevated Pelham Line, this undeveloped area of the city was opened to the public.

It began with three tracks from 135th Street in The Bronx east via 138th Street, Southern Boulevard to Hunts Point Avenue. The route then hiked above Westchester Avenue on the elevated to Pelham Bay Park.

The 21.4 mile stretch was completed over the 1918-1920 period, reaching Pelham Bay Park Station on December 20, 1920.

Number Six follows this path South, linking with the main Lexington Avenue Line at 125th Street in Manhattan. A plodding local journey continues all the way to City Hall, offering little of substance until original subway stations are reached in Lower Manhattan.

The Astor Place stop, for example, displays the beaver mosaics in tribute to merchant prince John Jacob Astor whose fortune was built on beaver pelts.

But by far the best part of The Number Six Line can be found in the communities of Parkchester on north to Pelham Bay.

Its other claim to fame is in Hollywood. The film—and book—*The Taking of Pelham, One, Two, Three* remains one of the best subway-based melodramas every written or filmed.

Number Seven IRT
Flushing Line:

This line runs from Main Street, Queens, to Times Square, Manhattan. During the rush hours only the number seven runs as an express in the peak rush-hour direction only and as a local in the other direction.

For all other times of the day the number seven runs as a local, again from Main Street to Times Square.

Talk about history, The Flushing Line still click-clacks through an East River tube originally conceived in 1888 by the East River Tunnel Company. Actual work on the project began more than a decade before the first IRT was launched.

However, a series of physical and fiscal mishaps produced delays well into the 20th Century when it was to open as a trolley line. The Manhattan terminal was at Third Avenue and 42nd Street while the Queens depot occupied a small station at Jackson Avenue in Long Island City.

The trolley project was aborted whereupon the city stepped in and purchased the still-unused tunnel for $3 million. Conversion to subway operation required installation of a third rail and the Steinway Tunnel was ready for use.

Eventually the line was opened between Manhattan and Queens beyond Jackson Avenue, coordinating with a number of arresting subway-el projects on both the East and West sides of the East River.

In Manhattan the terminal was extended westward after stations were added at Fifth Avenue and then 42nd Street-Times Square, its final stop.

By far the most impressive elevated line built in the city was erected for The Flushing Line along Queens Boulevard from Rawson Street to Roosevelt Avenue. Its *nouveau* concrete viaduct was resplendent with mosaics and other ornaments that set it apart from the traditional skeletal steel designs. What then was called the Corona Line made its debut on April 21, 1917 amid pomp and circumstance, not to mention fireworks at the Corona depot, Alburtis Avenue and 103-104th

Streets.

However, not until January 21, 1928 was the line extended to its present terminus at Main Street, Flushing. Interestingly, the train dipped from its el structure after bridging across Flushing Creek and entered a tunnel that led to Main Street terminal.

This was a signal achievement greeted by big-time celebrations at Fifth Avenue in Manhattan in the morning only to be repeated later at Flushing.

Since then the IRT's Flushing Line has enjoyed both prosperity and hard times. Its once-efficient middle track express service was cancelled in the 1980s and 1990s because of interminable construction difficulties which reduced the line to local-only operation.

But even as a local, The Number Seven delivers a most captivating ride, starting with those ancient tunnels in Manhattan. When the Seven reaches the Queens side it climbs above the vast Long Island-Amtrak railroad yards past a maze of el structures before taking on the art deco elevated road along Queens Boulevard.

After 111th Street Station in Corona it passes alongside Flushing Meadow Park and stops at Willets Point, adjoining Shea Stadium, home of the Mets baseball team.

All in all, The Number Seven does its job well.

The Best, The Worst And The Most Unusual

THE BEST VIEW FROM A STATION: Smith-Ninth Street Station in the Carroll Gardens section of Brooklyn is a marvel for many reasons. For starters, it is the highest station on the system, 88 feet above the Gowanus Canal which the massive concrete-and-steel superstructure straddles. From the platform one can obtain a panoramic view of New York Harbor not to mention the Downtown Manhattan skyline as well as some precious vignettes of Brooklyn

including the Gowanus Expressway and the Red Hook piers. (G and F Lines)

THE WORST ELEVATORS: Buried deep below Broadway, the 168th Street Station of the IRT Local can only be reached by elevators. Until September 1997, the Transit Authority operated four of the slowest lifts known to mankind. During warm weather, they also were among the hottest spots away from The Equator. A trip—which could have been negotiated quicker on foot—seemed to take a lifetime. A new set of elevators was installed late in 1997 and not a moment too soon.

THE MOST UNUSUAL TURNABOUT: After decades of proclaiming that air conditioning the subway was both impractical and too difficult to accomplish— even though the PATH Hudson Tubes successfully solved the problem—the TA finally rolled out its first fleet of air-cooled cars on July 19, 1967. Running on the F (Sixth Avenue) Line, the refrigerated rolling stock was an instant hit.

THE WORST CLOSING: When The Third Avenue El was shuttered on May 12, 1955 many a New Yorker lamented the move. The El was to Manhattan what cable cars are to San Francisco. At the very least, it should have been retained as a tourist attraction. Promises that Manhattan's last elevated line would be replaced by a new Second Avenue Subway never were realized.

THE BEST RIDE BETWEEN STATIONS: The Howard Beach/JFK Airport stop in Queens is in an area that could pass for Peoria, Council Bluffs or some other part of Middle America. From there, The A Train highballs to Broad Channel station. Apart from being nautically scenic, that 3.5 mile stretch happens to be the longest run between stations on the entire system.

THE MOST UNUSUAL STATION: Featured in subway photos galore, including one depicting the opening of the original IRT in

1904, the City Hall Station was closed in 1945. It was then deemed irrelevant to the locals which stopped at the Chambers Station just North of the City Hall stop. But because of its innate beauty, City Hall Station has been restored to its original glory in preparation for a return to service.

THE BEST BUY ON THE SYSTEM: If one were to take a taxi from Far Rockaway in Queens through Brooklyn and up to 207th Street in upper Manhattan, the cost would top $50 not counting the tip. That same 31-mile run—longest of all subway rides in the city—costs only $1.50 on The A Train. .

THE MOST UNUSUAL VERTICAL TREK: Digging deep for a subway is one thing but the sandhogs seemed to overdo it when they built the 191st Street IRT Broadway Line Station in northern Manhattan. It is 180-feet below the sidewalks of Inwood which automatically qualifies it as the deepest platform on any of the three systems. It's on the Number One route.

THE WORST AUDIO SYSTEM: Although there are no official statistics to prove the point, it has been estimated that the loudspeaker systems in the TA stations can be understood for—at most—three out of ten words in any sentence. Precious information invariably is lost amid the static and general inaudibility of the public address messages.

THE BEST SUBWAY ART: The Bas-relief of the beaver at Astor Place local station on the original (1904) IRT Line not only symbolizes builder August Belmont's accent on platform esthetics but also honors John Jacob Astor, who originally made his fame in the beaver trade. The mosaic of a steam locomotive at Grand Central Station has a neat railroad touch.

THE MOST UNUSUAL SHOP UNDER AN EL CURVE: As the trains enter and exit Brighton Beach Station, their wheels screech around the 90-degree curve over Coney Island and Brighton Beach Avenues.

Oblivious to the sounds, pedestrians endlessly stream into Mrs. Stahl's knish store nestled directly under the middle of the curve. Her knishes—especially potato—are the city's best.

THE BEST HUNK OF OUTDOOR ARCHITECTURE: The Manhattan Valley Viaduct at 125th Street on the IRT West Side (Number Nine and Number One) Local has a total length of 2,174 feet. Its most important feature is a two-hinged arch of 168.5 feet span. Opened in 1904, the handsome trestle ranks among the finest examples of railroad architecture in the East.

THE MOST UNUSUAL LIGHTING: When the original IRT was built designers arranged for a number of areas along Broadway where open grates would allow sunlight to pour into the tunnels below. This system of natural lighting still can be found on the Upper West Side, among other places. It should be noted that the openings not only allow light to reach the darkness but snow and rain as well.

THE WORST SUBWAY RAZING: Among the handsomest aspects of the first subway were the entrances to stations. Called kiosks—an Americanization of the Turkish word *kushks*, or summer houses—the IRT subway entrances were elaborate coverings whose style was borrowed from an earlier Budapest subway. The kiosks were not only attractive but functional. Unfortunately, they were deemed impractical long after the IRT was annexed by the City and the Board of Transportation by the Transit Authority. All kiosks were razed and replaced with pedestrian entrances. Only later did someone in command realize the mistake and more recently a copy of an original kiosk was erected at City Hall.

THE BEST ACTING IN A MOVIE ABOUT SUBWAYS: Walter Matthau in "The Taking of Pelham One, Two Three." No one could possibly have captured the spirit of a New Yorker better than Matthau as the beleaguered subway dispatcher. Matthau was ably assisted by Jerry Stiller—his aide in the flick—whose part was smaller but whose acting job was just as excellent. Stiller also starred in the 1997 made-for-tv Home Box Office movie, *Subway Stories*, the best non-Hollywood full-length film about life in the underground.

THE MOST UNUSUAL EXPRESS: By definition, an express is a train which bypasses local stops as in The A Express bypassing the Spring Street Station. However, the Transit Authority also runs locals posing as expresses. These locals—numbers One and Nine, for example—perform a "Skip-Stop" service. Between 137th Street and 242nd Street Stations, the locals alternately skip certain local stops during rush-hours. By doing so, POOF! The locals become expresses. The same routine holds for the J and Z Trains on the Jamaica Line.

THE WORST PIECE OF PLANNING: When the 1939-40 World's Fair in Queens was in its blueprint stage, city officials laid out special trackage on the GG (Brooklyn-Queens Crosstown Line) to the fairgrounds. Instead of extending the line to nearby LaGuardia Field at the close of the fair in 1940 the tracks were ripped up and the valuable extension to Flushing Meadow disappeared. It was an egregious oversight. To this day there is neither a direct subway connection to heavily-used LaGuardia nor Kennedy Airports.

THE BEST ARENA LOCATION FOR SUBWAYS: Madison Square Garden sits next to more subways—the PATH Hudson Tubes are only a block away—than any other arena or ball park in the world. Both the Seventh and Eighth Avenue Lines burrow under MSG and the Sixth Avenue Subway is only a block away. Amtrak, Jersey Transit and the Long Island Rail Road also service Penn Station under the Garden.

THE MOST UNUSUAL NUMBERS: Although the common perception is that el lines are obsolete and mostly history this is far from the case. There remain four route miles of els in Manhattan, 28 route miles of elevated lines in Brooklyn, 20 in Queens and 18 in the Bronx. The grand total of el route miles is 70. Apart from that, the TA has 23 more route miles of outdoor track which embraces open cut—as in the Brighton and Sea Beach Lines—embankment and surface trackage.

THE WORST LOSS FOR FRONT WINDOW-LOVERS: Ever since the old, open-platformed els allowed riders to enjoy a breeze in transit, rolling stock permitted ways and means for enjoying fresh air. The BMT Standard—and later, the Triplex—cars featured front windows which opened. Some equipment built after World War II did likewise. Any subway buff will tell you that nothing could beat the thrill of sticking one's head near an open front window. Alas, they are no more. The advent of air conditioned cars meant the end of the open window. All are sealed leaving the breeze to the straphanger's imagination.

THE BEST FOLLOW-THROUGH ON A PRESIDENTIAL PROMISE: When David L. Gunn succeeded Daniel T. Scannell as Transit Authority president, Gunn vowed to rid the subway system of graffiti that defaced most of the rolling stock. Although skeptics doubted that such a feat could be accomplished, Gunn orchestrated a clean-up system that did, in fact, achieve his goal.

THE MOST UNUSUAL MAP: In April 1993 New York City Transit created a subway-el map for the visually-impaired. Produced in braille, the map not only covered the entire system but provided extra maps for heavily-used lines.

THE WORST DESIGN: When the TA introduced a new fleet of cars in the 1980s they included sculpted seats which, hypothetically, were form-fitting for normal body-sizes. But, as any rider would have attested, the sizes were better suited for pygmies. As a result, passengers inevitably overlapped each seat, or were compelled to severely tighten their bodies in order not to disturb the adjoining passenger. In plain English, the planning was unrealistic and the cause of rampant discomfort—except for the anorexic and The Thin Man, or Woman!

THE BEST RIDE: The installation of welded rail through most of the system produced some of the most pleasant runs in the history of the subways. None is smoother than the downhill from 122nd Street (over Broadway) south to the 116th Street Station on the IRT West Side Local. The train comes off the steel-based elevated structure on to concrete-embedded ties installed in 1993. The combination produces a hitherto unattainable glide punctuated by a soft yet lyrical curve just inside the tunnel portal.

THE WORST OVERCROWDING: Because the Third Avenue Elevated Line never was replaced by the promised—and partially-begun-but-never-completed—Second Avenue Subway the East Side of Manhattan is serviced by only one North-South route, the Lexington Avenue Line. The West Side roster includes the Eighth Avenue, Seventh Avenue, Sixth Avenue as well as PATH under Sixth Avenue. As a result the worst overcrowding takes place on the Lexington Avenue Line.

THE BEST MAP: After years of complaints about hard-to-read maps, the TA produced a "modern" bit of geography created by chief map-designer John Tauranac and introduced on June 23, 1979. Tauranac later improved upon his original concept and in the 1990s produced and marketed his ultra-modern edition which became available in bookstores and other outlets. Many critics regard Tauranac's updated version as the best New York subway map ever designed. It is!

THE MOST UNUSUAL LINE: Covering 14.3 miles—all of it out-of-doors except for the St. George Terminal in Richmond—the New York City Transit-managed Staten Island Railway is as un-Big Apple-like as possible. Its run through the arboreal outer-borough is more reminiscent of an interurban trolley ride of the 1920s than a contemporary rapid transit run. Still, it carries more than five million passengers a year.

THE WORST FEELING: Your express has just come into the station and the local is awaiting you. Quickly, you rush out the opening doors and across the platform. Just as you reach mid-platform the conductor on the local closes the doors and you are left standing in your tracks. Just reverse the sequence from local to express and you have the same, sinking feeling.

THE MOST UNUSUAL MISSING SMELL: For decades riders on the Culver (F) El would have their nostrils pierced by a rare odor emanating from McDonald Avenue. It was horseradish being made by Gold's Foods below. Alas, the horseradish memories remain but Gold's factory has since moved to Hempstead, Long Island.

BEST HANDS-ON PERFORMANCE BY A SUBWAY LEADER: When he was TA Chairman, Charles Patterson enjoyed touring the various lines to get a first-hand view of operations. One day when he was in the IRT Union Square Station, Patterson discovered that a train was stuck at the platform. He approached the motorman and asked him about the problem. Not realizing who had approached him the motorman demanded to know who he was. Patterson explained and then produced his I.D. for good measure. The motorman explained that one of the car motors had broken down and the train had to be uncoupled before removal to the yard. "Tell me where," said the chairman rolling up his sleeves. The motorman pointed out where the cars had to be uncoupled. Patterson, a veteran railroader headed down the platform and then down to the tracks. He uncoupled the cars and waved the motorman on his way.

WORST CASE OF HANDS-ON REPORTING: During the 113-day newspaper strike of 1962-63, the TA hired several reporters as "consultants." Their function was to write a tenth anniversary report for the TA. The reporters included Leonard Ingalls of the *New York Times* and Ed Silberfarb of the *Herald-Tribune*, among others. On one occasion the "consultants" were taken to the IRT yards to learn how trains were repaired. During the visit, Silberfarb strolled away from his guide and walked over to a car that appeared unconnected to the third rail. He innocently was about to kick the third rail "shoe" when his guide rushed over and pulled him away. "That thing is 'live.'" he shouted. "Kick that and you're dead." As it happened the car's third rail shoes on the other side WERE connected. Silberfarb escaped by an inch!

THE MOST UNUSUAL CAR DISPARITY: Although the New York subway system is unified its cars are not. The IRT cars, originally designed for owner August Belmont, were deliberately ordered thinner by him so that wider cars could not use his tunnels. The BMT and IND rolling stock, which followed, were longer and wider. Consequently, neither BMT nor IND cars can fit in IRT tunnels. However, IRT cars do use BMT/IND tracks when in need of repairs at the Coney Island Shops. There are four connections between the A and B Division tracks: 1. The 207th Street Yard links with A Division Number One Line and the B Division Eighth Avenue Line; 2. The A Division Number Seven connects on the upper level of Queensborough Plaza with the B Division N at a diamond crossover. Interestingly, this is the only place where the Flushing Line mixes with any other route; 3. New Lots meets with the Canarsie Line. The A Division Number Three connects (one-track) with the B Division L near Junius Street

Station. This provides access for the Linden Yard which employs diesel-powered work trains; 4. In the Bronx, the B Division Concourse Subway connects with the Number Four Line at the yard near Kingsbridge Road Station and 205th Street.

THE BEST CARS: Most of all, you have to like the veterans; known to buffs as "Redbirds." For longevity alone, they are winners. These oldtimers date as far back as 1958 but have been rebuilt and rejuvenated with air conditioning. Their deep red color is neat. In the trade they're numbered R-26, R-28, R-29, R-33, R-36. The latest of this group are the World's Fair Cars with larger windows which run on the Number (7) Line. Other senior citizens are the Brightliners of IND-BMT descent. When these stainless steel cars arrived in 1964 they sported blue side and front end doors and were known as R-32 and R-32A. Two years later the stainless steel trains with corrugations arrived and are still running on the A and C Lines. These R-38s carried a thin blue stripe beneath the window level.

THE MOST UNUSUAL CARS: For sheer, drawing board creativity the Raymond Loewy-designed R-40s were the best looking. They were the only cars with a distinctly slanted nose that gave the trains a truly futuristic look. The problem was that they created some safety flaws that eventually were addressed. But as good as they looked, the R-40s were otherwise bad. Their MDBF rates were inferior and the safety additions marred the otherwise beautiful lines. The R-42 followed as an R-40 without the slanted nose and marked the last of the 60-foot IND cars. They were introduced in 1969-70. Another unusual car was the R-44-46 which, when introduced in 1971-73, became the longest pieces of rolling stock on the system. Measuring 75 feet, these stainless steel cars became part of the Staten Island Railway as well. However they could not run on either the J, M, Z or L lines of the BMT Eastern Division.

POSTSCRIPT

A ride on the New York Subway still can be a lot of fun although many of the old-time amenities are gone.

If San Francisco can make a tourist attraction out of its cable cars, imagine what New York City could have done with its fleet of outdoor platform el cars which *clickity-clacked* on Brooklyn's Myrtle and Lexington Avenue Lines. Or imagine what could have been accomplished by marketing the wonderful, open window rides on the 67-foot Standards that plied the Brighton Line. The thrill of gazing out of an open front window while the breezes caressed you around the Beverley Road curve is gone, having been doomed with the advent of rail fan–unfriendly hermetically-sealed cars.

Comfortable rattan seats, a feature on all pre-1950 cars, have given way to hard, plastic planks seemingly designed for the *derrieres* of the Seven Dwarfs. Loudspeakers on the new cars are occasionally inaudible and air conditioning, when it works, is often too cold for comfort.

When I began riding the trains more than sixty years ago, the system was speedier, more efficient and more economical than it is now. The West End Express would almost fly off the tracks as it sprinted from DeKalb Avenue past innumerable local stops to 36th Street in Brooklyn. The Brighton Express ate up the straight-away between Kings Highway and Newkirk Avenue like a *20th Century Limited* and the E was a veritable blur between Roosevelt Avenue and Continental Avenue in Queens.

Alas, the speed is gone. In its sensitivity to a few rare accidents, the MTA imposed a system-wide set of restrictions that is tantamount to outfitting a Ferrari with flat wheels. Even more ironic is the fact that speed-inducing welded rails have been installed on many of the supposedly high-speed lines, including the Brighton.

Still, a ride can be a lot of fun. The IRT Broadway Express (2 or 3) somehow manages to race like a filly between Times Square and 72nd Street. The run is especially exciting as the train enters the left-handed curve at 59th Street running at top speed (about 40 mph) and at mid-station negotiates a surprisingly harsh track coupling that supplies a gasping jolt to the entire car.

And where else in the world could you ride from The Bronx to Rockaway Beach for only a buck-and- a-half?

Like Times Square, Yankee Stadium and most everything else in New York City, the subway simply ain't what it used to be but, when all is said and done, it's a damn sight better than those poor imitations in Chicago, Boston, Toronto and Montreal, just to name a few.

Now, if the MTA would only bring the speed back to the pre-war level, we'd *really* have a subway to brag about.

APPENDIXES

Trains to the Best Sites in Manhattan

Site	Line	Station
American Museum of Natural History Central Park West at 79th Street	B,C 1,9	81st St. Station 79th St. Station
Carnegie Hall 881 Seventh Avenue	N,R B,D,E 1,9	57th St. Station 7th Ave. Station 50th St. Station
Cathedral of St. John the Divine Amsterdam Avenue and 112th Street	1,9 B,C	110th St. Station 110th St. Station
Central Park Zoo Fifth Avenue and 64th Street	6 N,R	68th St. Station 5th Ave. Station
City Hall Broadway and murray Street	4,5,6 N,R J,M,Z A,C	Bklyn Br. Station City Hall Station Chambers St. Sta. Chambers St. Sta.
The Cloisters Fort Tryon Park	A	190th St. Station
Cooper-Hewitt Museum 2 East 91st Street	4,5,6	86th St. Station
Empire State Building 350 Fifth Avenue	6 N,R B,D,F,Q	33rd St. Station 34th St. Station 34th St. Station
Grant's Tomb National Memorial Riverside Drive and 122nd Street	1,9	116th St. Station
Gracie Mansion East End Avenue and 88th Street	4,5,6	86th St. Station
Hayden Planetarium Columbus Avenue and 81st Street	B,C 1,9	81st. St. Station 79th St. Station
Metropolitan Museum of Art Fifth Avenue and 82nd Street	4,5,6	86th St. Station
Metropolitan Opera Columbus Avenue and 65th Street	1,9 A,B,C,D,	66th St. Station 59th St. Station
Museum of Broadcasting 1 East 53rd Street	6	51st St. Station
Museum of Modern Art 11 West 53rd Street	6 E,F	51st St. Station 5th Ave. Station
Museum of the American Indian Broadway and 155th Street	1 A,B	157th St. Station 155th St. Station

Site	Line	Station
Museum of the City Of New York Fifth Avenue and 103rd Street	6	103rd St. Station
New York Historical Society 170 Central Park West	1,9 B,C	79th St. Station 81st St. Station
New York Public Library Fifth Avenue and 42nd Street	7 B,D,F,Q	5th Ave. Station 42nd St. Station
New York Stock Exchange 20 Broad Street	2,3,4,5 N,R A,C	Wall St. Station Rector St. Station Broadway-Nassau St. Station
Radio City Music Hall Sixth Avenue and 50th Street	B,D,F,Q	47-50th Sts.-Rockefeller Ctr. Sta.
Schomberg Center for Research in Black Culture 515 Lenox Avenue	2,3	125th St. Station
South Street Seaport Museum 16 Fulton Street	2,3,4,5 J,M,Z A,C	Fulton St. Station Fulton St. Station Broadway-Nassau St. Station
Statue of Liberty Liberty Island	1,9 4,5 N,R J,M,Z ***	South Ferry Station Bowling Green Sta. Whitehall St. Sta. Broad St. Station Then take ferry
Trinity Church Broadway and Wall Street	2,3,4,5 1,9 N,R J,M,Z	Wall St. Station Rector St. station Rector St. station Broad St. Station
United Nations First Avenue and 46th street	4,5,6,7 S	Grand Central Sta. Grand Central Sta.
Whitney Museum of American Art Madison Avenue and 75th Street	6	77th St. Station
World Trade Center 2 World Trade Center	1,9 C,E	Cortlandt St. Sta. World Trade Ctr. Sta.

Opening Dates

Explanatory Notes

Name of Line: The name by which the line may be most easily followed on the map (not necessarily the official name).

Section of Line: For quick location on the map, each new section is listed by the names of the nearest stations (not necessarily the exact section placed in public operation). (U) next to the station name indicates that the actual station is underground although the section of line is above ground. (A) indicates that the station is aboveground on an underground section of line. (G) indicates that the station is on an elevated structure although the sec
tion of line listed is on the surface.

Type of Line: C=Open cut; E=Raised full or embankment; L=Elevated structure (virtually all are over public streets); R=Private surface right of-way. S = Subway.

Tracks: The number shows how many tracks are constructed into the main body of the section indicated. It does not include sidings, storage tracks, etc., but does include express or middle tracks if in existence, whether or not in use by regular trains.

Opening Date: This is the date regular service began for the public. It is not the date of (a) the first test train or (b) "official" opening by the mayor, etc. Both events were sometimes held several days before the public opening. With less than a dozen exceptions, the dates came from two sources: The Rapid Transit Commission reports and the daily newspapers, which were checked against each other.

IRT DIVISION (Now A-Division)

Name of Line	From	To	Type of Line	Length in Miles	Tracks	Opening Date	Note Reference
		Section of line					
Original Route Opened	City Hall Loop	Brooklyn Bridge	S	.1	1	Oct. 27, 1904	1
	Brooklyn Bridge	Broadway & 96th St.	S	6.5	4	Oct. 27, 1904	
	Broadway & 96th St.	Broadway & 145th St.	S	2.5	3	Oct. 27, 1904	2
Broadway-Van Cortlandt Pk.	145th St.	157th St.	S	.6	2	Nov. 12, 1904	
	157th St.	Dyckman St. (A)	S	2.1	2	Mar. 12, 1906	
	Dyckman St.	215th St.	L	.8	3	Mar. 12, 1906	
	215th St.	225th St.	L	.4	3	Jan. 14, 1907	
	225th St.	242 nd St.	L	1.2	3	Aug. 1, 1908	
Lenox Ave.-White Plains Rd.	Lenox Ave. & 145th St.	148th St.	S	.3	2	May 13, 1968	
	Broadway & 96th St.	Lenox Ave. & 145th St.	S	3.0	2	Nov. 23, 1904	
	Lenox Ave. & 135th St.	Jackson Ave. (A)	S	1.1	2	July 10, 1905	3
	149th St. & 3rd Ave. (el station)	180th St.-Bronx Park	L	3.2	3	Nov. 26, 1904	3
	177th St.	219th St.	L	3.4	3	Mar. 3, 1917	
	219th St.	238th St.	L	1.1	3	Mar. 31, 1917	
	238th St.	241st St.	L	.4	3	Dec. 13, 1920	
Brooklyn	Bklyn. Br. [Manhattan)	Fulton St. (Manhattan)	S	.3	2	Jan. 16, 1905	
	Fulton St.	Wall St.	S	.2	2	June 12, 1905	
	Wall St.	South Ferry	S	.5	2	July 10, 1905	4
	Bowling Green	Borough Hall (Bklyn)	S	1.6	2	Jan. 9, 1908	
	Borough Hall	Atlantic Ave.	S	.9	4	May 1, 1908	
	Atlantic Ave.	Utica Ave.	S	2.8	4	Aug. 23, 1920	
	Utica Ave. (U)	Junius St.	L	1.9	2	Nov. 22, 1920	
	Junius St.	Pennsylvania Ave.	L	.4	2	Dec. 24, 1920	
	Pennsylvania Ave.	New Lots Ave.	L	.6	2	Oct. 16, 1922	
Nostrand Ave.	Franklin Ave.	Flatbush Ave.	S	3.0	2	Aug. 23, 1920	
7th Ave.	Times Square	Pennsylvania Station	S	.4	4	June 3, 1917	
	Pennsylvania Station	Chambers St.	S	2.6	4	July 1, 1918	
	Chambers St.	South Ferry	S	1.0	2	July 1, 1918	5
	Chambers St.	Wall & William Sts.	S	.8	2	July 1, 1918	
	Wall & William Sts.	Borough Hall	S	1.5	2	Apr. 15, 1919	
Lexington-Jerome Aves.	Grand Central	125th St.	S	4.2	4	July 17, 1918	
	125th St.	138th St.-Grand Con.	S	.7	2	July 17, 1918	
	138th St.-Grand Con.	149th St.-Grand Con.	S	.4	3	July 17, 1918	
	149th St.-Grand Con. (U)	Kingsbridge Rd.	L	3.8	3	June 2, 1917	6
	Kingsbridge Rd.	Woodlawn	L	1.7	3	Apr. 1 5, 1918	
Pelham Bay Pk.	125th St.-Lenox Ave.	138th St.-3rd Ave.	S	.9	2	Aug. 1, 1918	
	138th St.-3rd Ave.	Hunts Point Rd.	S	2.5	3	Jan. 8, 1919	
	Hunts Point Rd. (U)	177th St.	L	2.0	3	May 30, 1920	
	177th St.	Westchester Square	L	1.1	3	Oct. 24, 1920	
	Westchester Square	Pelham Bay Park	L	1.3	3	Dec. 20, 1920	

Name of Line	Section of line From	To	Type of Line	Length in Miles	Tracks	Opening Date	Note Reference
Queensborough	Times Square	5th Ave.-42nd St.	S	.4	2	Mar. 14, 1927	
	5th Ave.	Grand Central	S	.4	2	Mar. 22, 1926	
	Grand Central	Vernon-Jackson Aves.	S	1.3	2	June 22, 1915	
	Vernon-Jackson Aves.	Hunters Point Ave.	S	.3	2	Feb. 15, 1916	
	Hunters Point Ave. (U)	Queens Plaza	L	.9	2	Nov. 5, 1916	
	Queens Plaza	103rd St.	L	4.3	3	Apr. 21, 1917	
	103rd St.	111th St.	L	.4	3	Oct. 13, 1925	
	111th St.	Willets Point Blvd.	L	.6	3	May 14, 1927	
	Willets Point Blvd.	Main St., Flushing (U)	L	.9	3	Jan. 21, 1928	
Dyre Ave.	180 St.	Dyre Ave.		4.0	2	May 15, 1941	7

IRT Division Notes

1. From Brooklyn Bridge station to City Hall and back is a single track loop, and the City Hall station is the most ornate in New York. However, it is no longer open to the public, although Lexington Avenue locals operate around the loop without stopping in order to reverse their direction.

2. Due to a deep valley at that point, the 125th Street station on Broadway is on an elevated structure. The line emerges from underground at 122nd Street and returns underground at 135th Street.

3. Before subway train operation was extended under the Harlem River to the Bronx from 135th Street and Lenox Avenue, that portion of the new line between 149th Street and Third Avenue, and 180th Street, Bronx Park, was serviced by Third Avenue el trains reaching the new line via a connecting structure from the 149th Street el station. When through subway operation began, the trains emerged from underground beyond the subway's 149th Street and Third Avenue station, and climbed up to the previously used structure near the Jackson Avenue station. The stub end of the line at 180th Street was shut down after August 4, 1952 and the 0.2-mile structure demolished.

4. The South Ferry loop is double track and is accessible to both Lexington Avenue and Seventh Avenue trains. The original station is on the outer loop, and the inner loop was at first used for midday storage. The present station on the inner loop was added in 1918.

5. The South Ferry station on this section is the same one described in 4, above.

6. This section operated by shuttle service in advance of through Lexington Avenue train operation from Grand Central.

7. The Dyre Avenue line operates along the former right-of-way of the defunct New York, Westchester & Boston Railroad, an electrified suburban line which extended to points beyond the city via two routes. The City of New York purchased that portion existing within the city limits for rapid transit use. Connecting tracks for through operation off the White Plains Road branch at 180th Street are completed but not yet in use. Although it was originally four-track, only two exist today. The character of the line varies, with short adjacent portions of open cut, raised embankment, and tunnel. The Pelham Parkway station is underground.

New R-12's arrive at Coney Island Yard in 1948 while a set of "Standards" passes overhead. South Brooklyn Railway engine #9 is now at a trolley museum in Kingston, New York.

BMT DIVISION (Now B-Division, Group I)

Name of Line	Section of line From	To	Type of Line	Length in Miles	Tracks	Opening Date	Note Reference
Centre & Nassau Sts.	Essex St. (Delancey)	Canal St.	S	.8	4	Aug. 4, 1913	1
Loop (Manhattan)	Canal St.	Chambers St.	S	.4	2	Aug. 4, 1913	
	Chambers St.	Connection to Tunnel from Whitehall St. to Court St	S	1.0	2	May 30, 1931	2
Manhattan Bridge-							
So. Side -	Chambers St. (U)	Myrtle Ave. (Brooklyn) (U]	B	2.3	2	June 22, 1915	3
No. Side	Prince St. (U)	Myrtle Ave. [Brooklyn) (U]	B	2.4	2	Sept. 4, 1917	3
4th Ave. (Brooklyn)	Myrtle Ave.	59th St	S	4.4	4	June 22, 1915	4
	59th St	86th St.	S	1.4	2	Jan. 15, 1916	
	86th St.	95th St.	S	.4	2	Oct. 31, 1925	
Sea Beach	59th St. & 4th Ave. (U]	86th St.	C	4.4	4	June 22, 1915	
	86th St.	Stillwell Ave. (G)	R	1.1	2	June 22, 1915	5
West End	36th St. & 4th Ave. (U)	*9th Ave.		.9		June 24, 1916	6
	9th Ave.	*18th Ave.	L	2.7	3	June 24, 1916	
	18th Ave.	*25th Ave.	L	1.1	3	June 29, 1916	
	25th Ave.	*Bay 50th St.	L	.7	3	July 21, 1917	
	Bay 50th St. [G]	Stillwell Ave. (G)	R	.8	2	July 21, 1917	
Brighton Beach	DeKalb Ave.	Prospect Park (A)	S	2.3	2	Aug 1, 1920	
	Prospect Park	*Church Ave.	C	.8	4	Sept. 26, 1919	
	Church Ave.	Newkirk Ave.	C	1.0	4	1907	7
	Newkirk Ave.	Sheepshead Bay	E	3.4	4	1907	7
	Sheepshead Bay	*Ocean Parkway	L	1.1	4	Apr. 22, 1917	
	Ocean Parkway	*West 8th St.	L	.4	4	May 30, 1917	8
	West 8th St.	*Stillwell Ave.	L	.4	2	May 29, 1919	9
Culver Line	9th Ave. (U)	*Ditmas Ave.	L	1.1	3	Mar. 16, 1919	10
Myrtle Ave.	Broadway (Brooklyn)	Central Ave.	L	.6	2	July 29, 1914	
	Central Ave.	*Wyckoff Ave.	L	.7	2	July 1, 1918	
	Wyckoff Ave.	*Fresh Pond Rd.	L	1.0	2	Feb. 22, 1915	11
Jamaica	Essex St. (Manhattan)	Marcy Ave.-Broadway (Brooklyn)	B	1.7	2	Sept. 16, 1908	12
	Marcy Ave.	*Myrtle Ave.	L	1.4	3	Jan. 17, 1916	
	Myrtle Ave.	*Alabama Ave.	L	2.5	3	Dec. 21, 1916	
	Alabama Ave.	Cypress Hills	L	1.9	2		13
	Cypress Hills	111th St.	L	2.0	2	May 28, 1917	
	111th St.	168th St.	L	2.4	2	July 3, 1918	
Bklyn. to Manhattan via	DeKalb Ave. (Brooklyn)	Whitehall St. (Manhattan)	S	2.0	2	Aug. 1, 1920	
Tunnel & Broadway	Whitehall St.	Prince St.	S	1.8	2	Jan. 5, 1918	
	Prince St.	14th St.-Union Square	S	.8	4	Sept. 4, 1917	14
	14th St.-Union Square	Times Square	S	1.4	4	Jan. 5, 1918	
	Times Square	57th St. & 7th Ave.	S	.8	4	July 10, 1919	
	57th St. & 7th Ave.	Lexington Ave.-60th St.	S	1.7	2	Aug. 1, 1920	
	Lexington Ave.-60th St.	Queens Plaza (A)					
Astoria	Queens Plaza	Ditmars Blvd.	L	2.5	3	Feb. 1, 1917	15
14th St.-Canarsie	8th Ave. & 14th St.	6th Ave. & 14th St.	S	.3	2	May 30, 1931	
	6th Ave. & 14th St.	Montrose Ave.	S	3.9	2	June 10, 1924	
	Montrose Ave.	Broadway Junction (A)	S	3.6	2	July 14, 1928	16
	Broadway Junction	*Sutter Ave.	L	.6			17

* Dates for these portions refer to new construction replacing older route either on surface or older structure.

BMT Division Notes

1. There are three tracks through Essex Street station.

2. Last portion of the Dual Contracts completed.

3. Manhattan Bridge, spanning the East River, has two separated pairs of tracks, one on each side of the bridge. The pair used by trains between Brooklyn and Times Square is on the north side; the pair on the south side is used by trains between Brooklyn and the Centre-Nassau streets loop.

4. This section includes a six-track portion through the DeKalb Avenue station due to the two Brighton Beach line tracks merging with the Fourth Avenue line at that point.

5. Before the completion of the eight-track Stillwell Avenue terminus, trains used a temporary Surf Avenue terminal.

6. This section has both a short two-track tunnel and a six-track open-cut approach to the double-decked Ninth Avenue station with three tracks on each level.

7. The section Church Avenue to Sheepshead Bay was converted from two to four tracks in 1907 by the Brooklyn Rapid Transit Company for Fulton Street-Brighton Beach el train operation. The open cut ends south of Newkirk Avenue.

8. West 8th Street station has two 2-track levels.

9. This portion is a double-deck structure with two tracks on each level. The data on this line refer only to the upper deck.

10. This is part of an original through route to Stillwell Avenue. On October 30, 1954, the IND division assumed Culver operation to Coney Island, and thereafter the BMT terminated at Ditmas Avenue.

11. The line from Fresh Pond Road to Metropolitan Avenue is an original unimproved el train surface right-of-way.

12. Original el train route.

13. Original unimproved el structure.

14. This portion opened in connection with the northside tracks of the Manhattan Bridge.

15. Opening date refers to original IRT operation. Although originally built for and part of the IRT's Queensborough lines, this section transferred to complete BMT operation on October 17, 1949.

16. The Wilson Avenue station on this section is double-decked with one track on each level. The upper, or outbound, track is on a raised embankment; the lower, or inbound track is underground.

17. This section (Broadway Junction-Eastern Parkway to Atlantic Avenue) is a very complex network of intertwined tracks providing connections from the Broadway line to the Jamaica, Fulton Street, and Canarsie lines, and from the 14th Street line to the Fulton Street and Canarsie lines. It is an improved former el. Atlantic Avenue station has six tracks. Various connections were placed in service between October 17 and December 18, 1918.

A new R-1 at the Stillwell Avenue Terminal after testing on the Sea Beach Line in 1932.